THE CITIZEN

THE CITIZEN
PAST AND PRESENT

**Edited by Andrew Brown
and John Griffiths**

MASSEY UNIVERSITY PRESS

First published in 2017 by Massey University Press
Private Bag 102904, North Shore Mail Centre, Auckland 0745, New Zealand
www.masseypress.ac.nz

Text copyright © authors as credited, 2017
Images copyright © as credited, 2017

Text design copyright © Massey University Press
Typesetting by Sarah Elworthy
Cover design by Gideon Keith

The moral right of the authors has been asserted

All rights reserved. Except as provided by the Copyright Act 1994, no part of this book may be reproduced, stored in or introduced into a retrieval system or transmitted in any form or by any means (electronic, mechanical, photocopying, recording or otherwise) without the prior written permission of both the copyright owner(s) and the publisher.

A catalogue record for this book is available from the National Library of New Zealand

Printed and bound in China by Everbest

ISBN: 978-0-9941363-2-9

CONTENTS

INTRODUCTION THE CITIZEN: FROM ANCIENT TO POST-MODERN **9**

Andrew Brown

1. **TWENTY-FIRST-CENTURY CITIZENSHIP:** CRITICAL, GLOBAL, ACTIVE **23**

   Emily Beausoleil

2. **CITIZENS & SERPENTS IN CLASSICAL ATHENS** **37**

   Daniel Ogden

3. **THE PEOPLE & THE STATE IN EARLY ROME** **61**

   James H. Richardson

4. **MEDIEVAL CITIZENSHIP:** BRUGES IN THE LATER MIDDLE AGES **93**

   Andrew Brown

5. **JEWS & CHRISTIANS AS SECOND-CLASS CITIZENS IN ISLAMIC EGYPT** **119**

   Christopher J. van der Krogt

6. **CITIZENSHIP, COMMUNITY & DISEASE IN AN EARLY MODERN CITY** **147**

   Karen Jillings

7. PERSONAL, LOCAL & ENDURING: MASCULINE CITIZENSHIP IN FIRST WORLD WAR BRITAIN **171**
David Littlewood

8. SPORT & CITIZENSHIP IN NEW ZEALAND **197**
Geoff Watson

9. THE FORMATION OF THE 'GOOD CITIZEN': USING HISTORY TO BUILD A FUTURE IN MID-TWENTIETH-CENTURY NEW ZEALAND **223**
Rachael Bell

10. ALL THE RIGHTS & PRIVILEGES OF BRITISH SUBJECTS: MĀORI & CITIZENSHIP, TAKING THE LONG VIEW **249**
Michael Belgrave

11. FROM 'CITIZENS' TO 'DILETTANTES' & BACK AGAIN? THE WORKERS' EDUCATIONAL ASSOCIATION & ITS STUDENTS SINCE 1945 **275**
John Griffiths

ABOUT THE CONTRIBUTORS **301**

INRODUCTION THE CITIZEN: FROM ANCIENT TO POST-MODERN
Andrew Brown

'Who is the citizen?' asked Aristotle; 'Whom should we call one?'[1] These questions are as pertinent today, and as difficult to answer, as they were when Aristotle posed them. We might define citizenship simply as a legal relationship between the individual and the state; as a balance between the duties owed to the state and rights expected from it; as a sense of belonging to the state, and the degree of participation within it. But a concept that relates in some way to rights and duties, as well as to status, identity and values, is a concept that will utterly defy consensus. What Aristotle also said over two millennia ago is just as true now: '. . . there is no unanimity, no agreement as to what constitutes a citizen.'

Aristotle's questions related to the Greek city-state, and are answered very differently within the modern democracy: 'citizenship' has constantly evolved within the Western European tradition.[2] We can identify several key shifts in definition as being particularly significant for the modern world, and roughly date their appearance to the eighteenth century. The most obvious is the shift from small to large scale, from an urban-based notion of citizenship to one focused on the nation-state. The novelty of this change can be overstated. The idea of a citizen as the subject of a state, and as a legal entity, had emerged within the Roman empire; 'states' and 'nations' arguably existed in the medieval West; and early modern theorists (such as Jean Bodin) had discussed citizens as subjects. But revolutionary Europe and America in the late eighteenth century did usher in a sense of citizenship as a more inclusive and potentially more democratic category.

A consequence of this shift was to turn the citizen, or at least the definition of one, from an active into a more passive being. Aristotle had considered citizenship — meaning membership of a city-state (*polis*) — to be natural, and that participation in political life would encourage virtue, but that active participation would be impossible in a city-state that was 'excessively large'.[3] Most members of a modern nation-state cannot be full citizens in Aristotle's sense. Not that urban-based citizenships ever involved the whole population: being a citizen in classical Athens or a medieval city was a privileged status, often restricted to elites. But large nation-states that submerge the individual into a general will, and demand loyalty to the state, weaken the correlation between citizenship and direct political participation.

A third trend has been the shift in emphasis towards citizenship as a matter of 'rights' more than of 'duties'. Benjamin Constant in 1819 was already distinguishing the 'liberties of the ancients' from the 'liberties of the moderns': whereas the former had drawn their freedoms from collective participation in the common good, the latter were to expect liberties free from excessive state interference.[4] A 'liberal' conception of citizenship, emphasising civil liberties, is said to have superseded an older 'civic-republican' tradition. A strong emphasis, inherited from the ancient world, on the obligations required of active citizens, and on the virtue of fulfilling them, was replaced by an emphasis on the civil rights that passive citizens could demand of their nation-state.

Again, the degree of change can be overemphasised: in the ancient or medieval world, rebels against ruling regimes frequently demanded liberties of various kinds; states in the nineteenth century hardly granted democratic freedoms to lower classes, minorities or women. Inequalities also gradually generated ideas that the rights expected from the state should be more than political and civil. T. H. Marshall's (1949) emphasis on the need to reconcile the inequity between social classes and the equality implied by 'citizenship' added the notion of 'social' rights to the lexicon of modern citizenship.[5]

These broad shifts in ideas of citizenship, from 'urban' to 'national', 'active' to 'passive', and 'duties' to 'rights', have never gone unchallenged, however. Some of the continuities between modern societies and earlier ones are worth highlighting. Urban-based citizenship, for all its ideals of community, was fundamentally an exclusive category; and during the transition to state-based

INTRODUCTION

citizenship, some of its exclusionary character was smuggled in with the name. The elitist values of medieval patrician classes morphed imperceptibly into the 'bourgeois' standards expected of the early modern citizen.[6] A tension between duties and rights has been constantly felt. Even the most liberal views of citizenship retain a sense that it entails obligations necessary for the proper functioning of society; that these obligations require an educated citizenry, and therefore an engaged and active one.[7]

Some of these challenges and problems have become the focus of present-day debates on citizenship in the face of rapid social change, especially since the 1990s. Globalisation has further destabilised simple association between citizenship and the nation-state.[8] This association was never total, not least because political arrangements, below or above the level of the state, have existed in many forms in the past; and because the idea of the nation as a natural focus for loyalty has often been denounced as specious. The ideal of the 'world citizen' in fact has ancient roots.[9] But present-day acceleration of contacts and migrations between countries, and environmental concerns that affect the whole planet, have strengthened the need to develop a global kind of citizenship, and weakened a sense of belonging simply to a state.

Even so, effective legislation to deal with global issues seems achievable only if enacted at the level of the state: the nation-state remains a primary locus of citizenship, especially in the legal sense. More challenging to this primacy has been the rise of new forms of cultural politics, loosely labelled 'postmodern'.[10] These give as much attention to questions of identity as to rights and duties. The concept and value of national identity as mono-cultural, especially if assumed to be based on a common ethnic identity, has been seriously tested: multicultural and plural identities within a state, and the agendas resulting from them, may have to be addressed for any sense of common citizenship to be entertained. But addressing them therefore seems to point in contradictory directions: away from community and towards antagonism or confrontation; but also, somewhat idealistically, towards a more meaningful consensus on rights and duties of citizens. These problems have made the question of citizenship arguably more urgent to us than ever before: the exponential increase in 'citizenship studies' that began in the late twentieth century shows no sign of slackening today.

Present-day concerns form the starting point for this volume. Emily Beausoleil (Chapter 1) begins with the 'rights' and 'liberties' expected by twenty-first-century citizens in liberal democracies, but emphasises the tensions that lie at the heart of the relationship between the individual and the democratic state. How does the citizen, largely excluded from decision-making processes, participate in the political arena? A new, active kind of citizen may be demanded in the modern democratic world, one who confronts and is critical of accepted norms.

If citizenship studies are about taking on the political problems and injustices of the present, what account do we need to take of the past? Emphasising the 'global', 'active' and 'critical' places citizenship in a thoroughly modern context, as does defining citizenship as a 'social process' through which individuals or groups might engage in claiming rights.[11] The relevance of past forms of citizenship begins to seem tenuous. But there are important ways in which an historical perspective contributes to modern debates.

One approach is to trace the evolution of theories of citizenship: exploring how past ideas turned into present ones, how they evolved and why, generates a critical attitude to current norms and assumptions. This volume, however, does not deal with citizenship as an evolving set of ideas. Its contributors offer collectively a more comparative approach. Each discusses aspects of citizenship as they have appeared in past societies, and in particular ideas of citizenship as they have appeared in practice, as part of social processes. The historical sources examined are not limited to the political theorisings on citizenship in any one period: values and ideologies connected with citizenship must be accessed from a wider range of evidence, from the literary to the legal. Citizenship in practice is often a fluid and messy affair, and is not easily categorised as part of liberal or civic-republican 'traditions'. This becomes even more evident if we move away from 'Western European' concepts to other related ideas found elsewhere, for instance within the Islamic world or the

INTRODUCTION

Pacific. A comparative approach to citizenship disrupts the grand narratives that move us smoothly from past to present.

Even so, the similarities between different societies are also worth attention. The past may be a 'foreign country', but were things always done differently there? While 'global', 'active' and 'critical' citizens are current ideal types, they have manifested themselves in various guises before. Several contributors to this volume discuss issues and patterns of past citizenships that are familiar today, despite emerging in other, very different, societies and polities. The 'global' citizen is fundamentally about relating 'local loyalties to wider communities'; how individuals or groups become part of communities, and relate to them as they change, are central themes of this volume.

In none of the societies discussed here was citizenship ever static. As James Richardson argues, on the evolution of the early Roman republic (Chapter 3), the coalescence of individual companions, into a *gens* (people), then into tribes and a city-state, was long drawn out. Andrew Brown shows (Chapter 4) that the meaning of citizenship in medieval Bruges changed: integrating individuals into the city, and gradually into a wider state, was a troubled process. Chris van der Krogt points to the problematic integration of Jews and Christians into the new Islamic polity of medieval Egypt (Chapter 5). Rachael Bell explores the shifts in ideas of citizenship in New Zealand between the two world wars (Chapter 9): critical engagement with contemporary and global issues emerged then as a key component of the ideal citizen. Yet as Michael Belgrave shows (Chapter 10), modern New Zealand has inherited a long history of fraught negotiation over Māori rights and participation in the processes of citizenship, which continues to raise sharp constitutional questions about loyalty to the state.

Identifying with a community has often meant identifying with the land it occupies: being or becoming a citizen involves a sense of belonging to a particular space.[12] In past societies, active steps could be taken to promote this feeling of common identity. In medieval Bruges, the city council's investment in city walls and gates, and in processions that followed the city's perimeter, marked out the profile of the city and encouraged identification with it. As

Karen Jillings shows for early modern Aberdeen (Chapter 6), the patrolling of city walls was a means to preserve the integrity of the citizen body within. In classical Athens, as Daniel Ogden argues (Chapter 2), identification with territory was strongly made by connecting citizens with the soil itself, especially through the symbolic association of both citizen and soil with serpents — which were perceived as creatures quintessentially of the land. In modern New Zealand, the unique and indigenous kiwi was quickly adopted as a symbol of patriotism: as Geoff Watson demonstrates (Chapter 8), it became associated with sports teams.

Myths associated with a territory have often generated a feeling of attachment to place. Within modern states, promoting a sense of nationhood has often meant connecting nation and citizens with the land in semi-mythical ways — or as Ernest Renan suggested, by getting one's history wrong.[13] No wonder that 'citizenship' itself has been described as a myth.[14] On the other hand, the debunking of myth, as well as righting the perceived wrongs of the past, has also been viewed (in modern New Zealand) as clearing a path to a more genuine and inclusive identification with nationhood (Chapter 9). But as the history of New Zealand also reveals, the process of identifying with the land can be problematic in other ways. Preconceptions underlying the relationship between citizenship and the land proved divisive in the nineteenth century. Settler assumptions that full citizen rights were related to individual land ownership flew in the face of indigenous customs of tenure and status, and contributed seriously to the disenfranchisement of Māori (Chapter 10).

Identifying with place and community has invariably meant identifying with the values associated with them: this theme also appears in several chapters. Cities and modern nation-states have often expected a new citizen to make a formal declaration of commitment: in ancient Rome or medieval towns, this took the form of swearing sacred oaths to uphold the ideals of the community. But words have never seemed quite enough to bind citizens to the state (especially if the meaning of those words, as in the Treaty of Waitangi, is disputed). In ancient Greece, legislators were troubled by people who were 'citizens in word but not in fact'.

Building the walls of Troy. In the medieval period, the legend of ancient Troy became a powerful source of myth. For some citizens and cities, Troy was an idealised model of urbanity, but as a pagan city its destruction also served as a Christian parable.
BRITISH LIBRARY ROYAL 17 E II, FO. 250

Thus, conformity to the public good has often had to be proved by a degree of active commitment from the citizen, even one not directly involved in political life. In Catholic Bruges or Protestant Aberdeen, the spiritual values encouraged in these cities were intended to apply to all inhabitants, even if they were not fully enfranchised. A citizen's proof of commitment was demonstrated bodily through honest work, associated with virtue, particularly within a craft guild. The requirement to give somatic demonstrations of civic virtue persisted into the era of the nation-state. The muscular virtues of sport were encouraged in nineteenth-century New Zealand, and integration of new arrivals was helped by participation in sporting activity. The masculine virtues of fighting for one's country were keenly emphasised in the First World War, as David Littlewood shows from conscription trials (Chapter 7): proof of one's 'worth' as a citizen — and a man — could be demonstrated by enlisting in the army.

The promotion of values thought appropriate for the citizen meant defining those that were not. As several contributors point out, citizenship was both an inclusive and an exclusive process. In medieval Muslim Egypt, Christians and Jews were classified by their religion as *dhimmi*s, in effect as second-class citizens. In other places citizens were categorised according to standards of morality. The idea of the 'worthless' citizen appears in ancient Athens; and also in medieval Bruges and early modern Aberdeen where beggars were the unvirtuous opposites of hard-working craft-guild members. The somatic proof required of the ideal citizen created its own group of outsiders: in societies that associated illness with sin, the unhealthy could also be excluded for being among the worthless and immoral. The diseased had to be removed from the citizen body of Aberdeen; the sickly could be regarded as a burden on the nineteenth-century New Zealand state; the non-conformist during the First World War, according to some, had to be combed out of the social body like 'lice'.

In modern democratic states, such draconian conformity would seem intolerable and hard to enforce. Yet it has been difficult to escape a sense that citizenship involves some form of commitment to shared values, and also a suspicion that some values, however apparently benign, conceal elements

INTRODUCTION

of social control. The emphasis on communal and equal participation in New Zealand's sports may obscure social disparities or inequities in Māori representation at a political level. And as John Griffiths comments (Chapter 11), in relation to the Workers' Educational Association in Britain since 1945, the encouragement of 'active' citizens by the government may well be considered a form of soft-policing.

What also emerges in this volume, however, is that even in strongly conformist societies, communal values associated with citizenship are complex, malleable, and often beyond the control of governing agencies. The emphasis on the need to uphold the 'common good' has not always served the agenda of ruling groups, and instead has proved (as in ancient Rome and medieval Bruges) a useful tool to justify rebellion against them. The championing of masculine virtues for male citizens did not necessarily work to enforce conscription in the First World War. Masculinity was multi-layered, and to avoid military duty objectors found it possible to emphasise their commitment to other civic-spirited and equally masculine virtues, such as maintaining the integrity of the family household.

Communal values associated with citizenship have therefore also been used strategically and actively to promote social justice in past societies. The building of consensus even in the early Roman republic involved conflict and opposition between 'plebeians' and 'patricians'. In medieval cities, artisan and guild opposition to merchant elites and princes, based on the public good, encouraged a more demotic notion of citizenship. 'Active' and 'critical' forms of citizenship have not been the preserve of modern democratic societies, nor have they been a constant feature within them. The history of the Workers' Educational Association suggests a frequent ebb and flow in the desire for active citizenship in modern Britain, rather than a linear progression towards it.

Situating the ideas and practices of citizenship firmly within historical contexts, as this volume does, also demonstrates how fluid and fragmented they can be, even within relatively mono-cultural societies. Several contributors explore the effects on ideals of citizenship when societies are under stress, in times of political upheaval, sickness or war. Communal values prove to be shot through with division; crises have led to the enforcement of norms and conformist ideologies, as well as reaction against them; immigration and the need to accommodate other people have frequently raised questions as to what it meant to be a citizen.

It was apparently the 'multitude of citizens' that prompted new codifications in classical Athens, as well as the view that new arrivals would not fit in — as being 'worthless peg[s] in a plank'. Deciding on who to include in early Rome as it grew was part of the fraught process of forming a political community. Medieval cities had to deal with the constant arrival of newcomers in search of work. Periods of stress in Egypt produced resentment among growing Muslim majorities of protections granted to religious minorities. Movements of people were troubling to the city authorities of Aberdeen in times of plague, and sharpened demarcation between those who were permitted access to the city and citizen body and those who were not. Immigration may have accelerated with modern globalisation, but it has often been a divisive issue that has driven re-evaluations of citizenship.

Modern debates on citizenship — the roles, values and identities that citizens are to play, hold or perform — are often old debates recast. Taking a historical and comparative approach to the subject illuminates issues that have commonly been key to defining the citizen's relationship with the state. This book places these issues within their historical contexts to highlight the need to see them as part of broader social processes and problems. For instance, 'citizenship' has never quite been the all-inclusive category that the name seems to imply; defining the values and identities of citizens in the present, as it has in the past, may well be implicated in processes of power that include some and exclude others.

This book also shows, however, that the differences between past and present are just as significant as the similarities, and that these too are informative: sensitivity to the past's otherness, to citizenship in other societies, develops awareness of the contingency of modern debates on present and changing contexts. 'Critical' citizens, who engage actively with

contemporary issues, will also need to engage with the past: understanding their sense of place in society, being able to question present norms, values and identities, demands a critical perspective on the histories of their own political communities and those of others.

ENDNOTES

1. Aristotle, *The Politics*, trans. T. A. Sinclair, rev. Trevor J. Saunders (Harmondsworth: Penguin, 1982), 168 [1275a2].
2. For the following, see Peter Reisenberg, *Citizenship in the Western Tradition: Plato to Rousseau* (Chapel Hill: The University of North Carolina Press, 1992), esp. xvi–xxiv, 267–70; J. G. A. Pocock, 'The Ideal of Citizenship Since Classical Times,' in *Theorizing Citizenship*, ed. R. Beiner (Albany NY: SUNY Press, 1995), 29–52; Derek Heater, *A Brief History of Citizenship* (New York: NYU Press, 2004); Richard Bellamy, *Citizenship: A Very Short Introduction* (Oxford: Oxford University Press, 2008).
3. Aristotle, *The Politics*, 404 [1326b2]. A population of 100,000 would 'no longer be a city': Aristotle, *Ethics*, trans. J. A. K. Thomson, rev. Hugh Tredennick (Harmondsworth: Penguin, 1976/1986), 307.
4. Benjamin Constant, 'The Liberty of the Ancients Compared with that of the Moderns (1819),' in *The Political Writings of Benjamin Constant*, ed. Biancamaria Fontana (Cambridge: Cambridge University Press, 1988), 309–28. See also Emily Beausoleil, *infra*.
5. T. H. Marshall and T. Bottomore, *Citizenship and Social Class* (London: Pluto Press, 1992); and see Derek Heater, *What is Citizenship?* (Oxford: Blackwell, 1992), 17–24.
6. Jürgen Habermas, *The Structural Transformation of the Public Sphere: An Inquiry into a Category of Bourgeois Society*, trans. Thomas Burger (Cambridge MA: MIT Press, 1991), 14–5, 23–4, 30: Heater, *What is Citizenship?*, 84–5.
7. See, for instance, discussion of modern 'communitarian' views of citizenship that retains a stronger sense of 'duties': Gerard Delanty, 'Communitarianism and Citizenship,' in *Handbook of Citizenship Studies*, ed. Engin F. Isin and Bryan S. Turner (London: SAGE Publications Ltd, 2002), 159–74; Nigel Clark, 'Cultural Studies for Shaky Islands,' in *Cultural Studies in Aotearoa New Zealand: Identity, Space and Place*, eds. Claudia Bell and Steve Matthewman (Melbourne: Oxford University Press, 2004), 3–18; S. Grey, 'Citizen Engagement,' in *New Zealand Government and Politics*, ed. Janine Hayward, 6th ed. (Melbourne: Oxford University Press, 2015), 496–8. For the changing notion of citizenship between 1870 and the outbreak of the Second World War see Brad Beaven and John Griffiths, 'Creating the Exemplary Citizen: The Changing Notion of Citizenship 1870–1939,' *Contemporary British History* 22, no. 2 (2008): 203–25.
8. See, for instance, Maurice Roche, 'Social Citizenship: Grounds of Social Change,' in *Handbook of Citizenship Studies*, eds. Engin F. Isin and Bryan S. Turner (London: SAGE Publications Ltd, 2002), 69–86.
9. Derek Heater, *World Citizenship: Cosmopolitan Thinking and its Opponents* (London: Bloomsbury, 2005).
10. Engin F. Isin and Bryan S. Turner, 'Citizenship Studies: An Introduction,' in *Handbook of Citizenship Studies*, eds. Isin and Turner, 1–10; S. Hall, 'The Question of Cultural Identity,'

INTRODUCTION

in *Modernity: An Introduction to Modern Societies*, eds. S. Hall, D. Held, D. Hubert, and K. Thompson (Massachusetts: Blackwell Publishers, 1995), 611–8; Chantal Mouffe, *Dimensions of Radical Democracy: Pluralism, Citizenship, Community* (London: Verso, 1992); Will Kymlicka, 'Multicultural Citizenship,' in *The Citizenship Debates: A Reader*, ed. Gershon Shafir (Minneapolis: University of Minnesota Press, 1998), 167–88 (among other contributions in this volume).

11 Isin and Turner, 'Citizenship Studies,' 3.
12 See, for instance, contributions in *Cultural Studies in Aotearoa New Zealand: Identity, Space and Place*, eds. Bell and Matthewman.
13 'Forgetfulness, and I would even say historical error, are essential in the creation of a nation': Ernest Renan, *What is a Nation?* (1882).
14 Michael Ignatieff, 'The Myth of Citizenship,' in *Theorizing Citizenship*, ed. Beiner, 53–77.

1. TWENTY-FIRST-CENTURY CITIZENSHIP:
CRITICAL, GLOBAL, ACTIVE

Emily Beausoleil

TWENTY-FIRST-CENTURY CITIZENSHIP: CRITICAL, GLOBAL, ACTIVE

In liberal democracies like New Zealand, citizenship is often understood as reducible to bearing rights that are bestowed and protected by the state — the right to think and speak freely, irrespective of whether anyone is listening; the right to pursue one's own happiness, putting aside the question of how such capacity is shaped by background conditions and structural inequalities; the right to associate with others according to one's positions and interests, even as available sites and forms of civic association diminish in the wake of a market society; and the right to vote on who decides all remaining political decisions for us for three more years, if we're not too busy or it's not raining too hard on election day.

And yes, I'm being a little tongue-in-cheek, not because these rights are unimportant dimensions of democratic citizenship, but because they have come to eclipse far more wide-reaching and complex definitions of what citizenship has meant and might yet mean. Certainly, these rights are so significant and integral that democracy cannot exist without them. From the hard-won battles for such rights in New Zealand and abroad for women, people of colour, and indigenous communities, to current attacks on such rights for first-generation Canadian citizens and children of illegal immigrants to the US, we can see in countless ways how profoundly these fundamentals of citizenship matter.

And yet the 'liberal' in 'liberal democracy' — and the attendant emphasis on rights and rule of law — has more often than not come to dominate, so much so that we mistake liberalism as a synonym for democracy rather than its complement, counterpart, and ultimately its odd bedfellow, for 'liberalism' and 'democracy' are ever in tension even at the best of times. As Chantal Mouffe, among others, has observed, there is a 'paradoxical nature [to] modern democracy . . . [a] fundamental tension between the logic of democracy and the logic of liberalism'.[1] For the emphasis on rights that forms the bedrock of liberalism, and the reliance on established universals and the seamless rule of law such abstract and stable rights require, runs ever counter to the inescapably unruly activity of the *demos*, ever uncertain and unpredictable, ever dynamic, ever in excess of any particular political or legal constellation in which it finds itself.

In liberal democracies such as New Zealand in this period of history, the tendency is all too often to forget the particular genealogies, histories and legacies that trace their way through the language we employ if not the practices or self-perceptions we maintain. What does this 'demotic' side of democratic citizenship entail? What does it mean to enact, protect and benefit from citizenship beyond the liberal emphasis on rights and rule of law?

Benjamin Constant was, in 1819, arguably the first to delineate these competing definitions of citizenship, as the 'liberty of the ancients' in contrast to the 'liberty of the moderns'. The former is the liberty achieved and enacted through public governance or popular sovereignty — collective decision-making regarding the world we share. This is the liberty enjoyed by citizens in the general assemblies of ancient Athens: a liberty only achieved insofar as we experience ourselves as social beings and our agency and influence via participation and interaction. In the context of ancient Greece, this was understood — à la Rousseauian republicanism — as possible only when citizens put aside their individual identities and particular interests in the search for a 'common good'.

With the modern period came a change in how we conceive of democracy, not as a project of abandoning particular differences in the name of a resounding echo of the singular collective voice of '*res publica*', but as a space of contending differences and conflict. The birth of pluralism — the end of a substantive idea of 'the good life' — ushered in an emphasis on personal liberty, against the tyranny of the majority as well as the state. Hence 'the liberty of the moderns' emerged in the liberal hallowing of individual rights and freedoms — liberty achieved not through collective governance but through individual

protections against the teeming, unpredictable and unruly practices of the populace and the power of the state.

Conceptions of citizenship that emphasise this 'liberty of the moderns' tend to procedures and institutions that seek universals — stable laws, group consensus — to diffuse the potential conflict within collective decision-making in diverse societies. And so, while liberalism emerged in part through an acknowledgement of pluralism, if left unchecked its protections against the pressures and conflicts such social difference entails work to deny, suppress and fix in place the distinctly *democratic* dimensions of citizenship.

The core condition of political life is its irreducible and ineradicable plurality — as Hannah Arendt writes, a common political world is possible only because 'not one man, but men in the plural inhabit the earth'.[2] And such plurality — of needs, values, perspectives, and claims — necessarily entails uncertainty, conflict, contingency and change. This is what Claude LeFort is speaking of when he writes that democracy is a political system that is 'instituted and sustained by the dissolution of the markers of certainty':[3] it is the only system, in fact, that chastens its own claims to offer fixed and final answers, that is perpetually experimental. It is designed to be open and responsive to the productive disruption and potential transformation that characterise the messy business of rule *by* the demos and not merely *for* them via rule of law. As Sheldon Wolin writes:

> democracy should not depend on elites making a one-time gift to the demos of a predesigned framework of rights . . . rights in democracy depends on the demos winning them, extending them substantively, and, in the process, acquiring experience of the political . . . Democracy is about the continuing self-fashioning of the demos.[4]

Ultimately, a tension persists within democratic citizenship between popular sovereignty and individual rights/the rule of law, and this tension cannot be overcome because diverse positions and perspectives, irreconcilable claims, and partiality and contextual specificity will always inform, exceed and disrupt attempts to name, organise and regulate the complex world we share. In such inescapable conditions, 'pluralist democratic politics consists in pragmatic, precarious and necessarily unstable forms of negotiating its constitutive paradox'.[5]

And yet, as LeFort and John Dewey also observe, democracy always has the potential to become totalitarian, to lose this definitive uncertainty, open-endedness and conflict.[6] Groups and their values can dominate and muffle dissenting views; systems, institutions and organisations fall into place that make decisions simpler, implementation smoother, but also prevent the active nature of democratic life. And in fact, 'liberalism' — as a system that seeks through the rule of law to enhance order, coherence and certainty; as a system that seeks through personal rights to protect individuals from the unruliness of public life; as a system of impersonal formalism that dovetails easily with a managerial or bureaucratic approach to politics — is prone to such tamping down of the participatory nature of democracy.

This tamping down can be seen to characterise our current experience of citizenship in countries like New Zealand. In fact, it is one of the great contradictions of the last century that just as Western theorists heralded 'the end of history' with the triumph of democracy on the world stage, democracy has been declared to be 'in crisis', undermined and eroded from within the very liberal democracies that were thought to be at the helm of this triumph.

If democracy is understood simply in terms of the universal franchise within free and competitive elections, the twentieth century began with no democracies and ended with democracy attaining majority status, with 58.2 per cent of the world's population. 'In a very real sense, the twentieth century [was] the "Democratic Century"'[7] — described famously by Samuel Huntington as 'an almost irresistible global tide moving on from one triumph to the next',[8] as all major opposition to liberal democracy — whether fascism, communism, or military dictatorships — crumbled, the franchise and other civil and political liberties were extended to women and non-white groups within democratic countries, and industrialisation fuelled demands and

capacities for social citizenship and the welfare state.

In fact, in the 1970s, analysts on the Left and the Right declared a crisis of democracy spanning Europe, the US, and Japan, but by this was meant a very different kind of crisis than we might imagine today — insufficiencies of existing systems of governance and the capacity to govern in light of surges of activity, involvement and collective engagement — what was called 'an excess of democracy',[9] where popular participation outweighed and overburdened both democratic institutions and governmental authority.

But as democracy has spread, democratic expectations have diminished, because with the growth of large-scale, complex and diverse societies, public participation in collective decision-making, or rule *by* as well as *for* the people, appeared ever more impractical, if not impossible. Representative democracy supplanted direct democracy, heralded by James Mill, Thomas Paine and others as 'the grand discovery of modern times' and 'the solution of all difficulties', and governance was increasingly conflated with government. The notion that citizenship was reducible to key rights that included the right to vote for those who decide on our behalf had political as well as practical causes: in response to fascism and Stalinism, and solidified by the Cold War, more socialist dimensions of democracy were pushed to the margins of mainstream liberal democratic theory.

Despite the connections between communism and democracy and Marx's own identification as a democrat, the West came to downplay popular engagement and direct influence and instead (such as in elitist and realist theories of democracy) equated democracy with the presence of competitive elections. Participation equated — was reduced — to voting alone. And with the rise of liberal approaches to democracy, and liberalism's clear divide between public and private and primacy given to the latter, these sporadic elections came to be seen primarily as the means to secure and free the people to pursue what Benjamin Constant called the 'private pleasures' of modern liberty.

Over time, politics came to be understood as an exceptional activity that rarely involves everyday citizens. This minimal definition of democracy limits participation beyond the vote to either being passive respondents to opinion polls, or following political events and issues as observers. Political debate happens via tightly controlled spectacles, by rival teams of professionals expert in the techniques of persuasion, concerning a small range of issues selected by those teams; the mass of citizens play a passive, quiescent, even apathetic role, and even where the action happens politically, most is happening behind the scenes between elected governments and elites that increasingly represent business interests. As Hibbing and Theiss-Morse, authors of *Stealth Democracy*, write, 'The people want to be able to make democracy visible and accountable on those rare occasions when they are motivated to be involved. They want to know that the opportunity will be there for them even though they probably have no intention of getting involved in government or even paying attention to it.'[10]

This has meant the emergence of a different 'crisis' of democracy. In the words of Constant, 'the danger of modern liberty is that, absorbed in the enjoyment of our private independence, and in the pursuit of our particular interests, we should surrender our right to share in political power too easily'.[11] As democracy has increased in quantity worldwide in the form of competitive elections, it has experienced a crisis of quality. In 2016, the 'crisis' of democracy in the West has less to do with an 'excess of democracy' and more to do with a lack of activity among democratic publics (declining voter turnout and declining membership of parties the most cause for alarm among scholars), and a lack of faith in the formal institutions and leaders of government (long-term decline in trust in and approval of democratic institutions and in political elites in general). In short, this is a crisis of imbalance between liberal and demotic forms of citizenship — a decline in participation by the *demoi*, and decline in the trust, respect and capacity such participation requires.

The old standby explanation that such disengagement and disaffection by the public is due to its laziness, stupidity or apathy has, among political analysts, become outmoded. Yes, voter turnout and party membership are in decline; yes, this means that formal politics — the representative politics that works so well with liberalism — is experiencing a true crisis in democratic legitimacy and, in some respects, efficacy. And yet, as Colin Hay and Gerry

Stoker observe, these 'crises' cannot be addressed by 'electoral cosmetics and gimmickry',[12] such as mandatory or online voting, because they are not the problem to be solved but a sign of a more general condition of disenchantment with and challenge to formal representative politics, what Pierre Rosanvallon calls the phenomenon of 'counter-democracy'.

For Hay and Stoker, such civic disengagement is the result of a failure of political leadership and the self-interested 'rent-seeking [and] short-termism'[13] that electoral politics encourages; for Simon Tormey, it is the result of structural and technological developments of a globalised and post-industrial 'second modernity' undermining the sovereignty of the nation-state and the coherence or clarity of 'the people' the state is designed to govern. For Max Weber, Colin Crouch and others, it is the rise of bureaucracy in modern politics that reduces practical wisdom to legal formalism and calculation, and lends itself to the privatisation of public goods and institutions.

Whatever the reason, citizens do not appear apathetic so much as dissatisfied with formal politics. This is reinforced by the creative and prolific surge of what Simon Tormey calls 'post-representative politics' that we observe around the world, from Occupy to Arab Spring to Red Square to Black Lives Matter — instances of political voice and collective action that circumvent mediation by formal politics to impact on society through more direct and horizontal forms, in the streets, online, outside Parliament. Tormey observes in such practices

> less a crisis of democracy, than a crisis of a particular iteration of representative democracy, a democracy of, by and for politicians. It's a crisis that may, ironically, be the condition of possibility for the return of some of those elements once held to be indispensable to democracy: dissensus, noise, politics, and the direct involvement of *demoi* — as opposed to those who would represent them.[14]

This simultaneous disengagement with formal politics and vibrant engagement with more direct and horizontal forms of political action gestures to the insufficiency of current accounts of and opportunities for citizenship to express and fulfil the demands of the *demoi* for collective governance. For the remainder of this chapter, I would like to signal three developments in contemporary understandings and experiences of citizenship that challenge the commonly held liberal model, and in doing so offer distinct resources for the crises of democracy that characterise this moment.

Firstly, in contrast to the assumed and entrenched certainties of liberal rights and rule of law, citizenship can be understood and experienced as definitively *critical*. This lies at the heart of the unruly, unpredictable, 'excessive' nature of the demos — not to receive meekly and bear gratefully rights bestowed upon us and the identities, values and experiences these assert for us, but to embrace the open-ended nature of the democratic project. Enacting citizenship is about the agency and practice of questioning received wisdom and established orders, interrogating the underlying norms and beliefs of the world we inherit, and asking ourselves and one another, as agents of collective governance, if this is, in fact, the world as we wish it to be.

To acquire the context and tools with which to become critical citizens we may begin by asking, 'Who is the "we" that forms the citizenry? What is this context in which we find ourselves — whether geographical, historical, demographic, semiotic — that gathers, constrains and enables? Who am "I" as a citizen by virtue of all that has come before me and brought me to this place, at this moment?'

Secondly, in contrast to the statism that is integral to liberal and representative politics, contemporary citizenship is increasingly a *global* phenomenon. One of the most fundamental principles of democracy is the 'all affected' principle — all those affected by a decision should be able to influence it. Conventionally, this has meant a centralised state able to govern with authority and force over a given territory and the citizenry demarcated within, while international relations, however amicable, can largely be characterised as a Hobbesian state of war between these self-governing nation-states.

TWENTY-FIRST-CENTURY CITIZENSHIP

From the late nineteenth century, increasingly deterritorialised forms of domination as well as extensive networks and intensive flows across territorial boundaries of everything from goods and people to culture and disease have undermined the autonomy of the nation-state and its territorial definition of the civic community. Whether it is because of our individual and collective capacity to affect the lives of others across the globe or because of human-created global issues — from carbon emissions and rising ocean levels to food scarcity and overpopulation — which affect us all and create a sense of a 'single community' with a shared fate, we are clearly living in an age of global responsibility.

Granted, the debates continue unresolved on how cosmopolitan citizenship relates to local loyalties, how it might be fostered given the ease with which we deny and rationalise global responsibilities, and how it might be institutionalised in practical terms. And yet these are the questions of our times, when our interconnection, co-implication and attendant responsibilities extend in every direction across the globe. Again, as global citizens we need to ask: 'How are we connected to communities across the world, through our most quotidian practices? What are the impacts we have and roles we play in these vast, complex, and overlapping networks? How are we implicated in such global encounters, and what responsibilities does this entail?'

Finally, in contrast to the passivity of liberal notions of citizenship, to respond to the contemporary challenges we face as well as address formal politics' crisis of legitimacy, contemporary citizenship must be *active*. For at its most minimal, even the laws and rights we share and the representative system we employ falter in the absence of a robust civic culture. Argued by democratic theorists from Alexis de Tocqueville to John Dewey and evidenced in current declines in voter turnout, a thriving civil society is integral to democracy as the means to cultivate faculties of observation, reflection and deliberation as well as sensibilities of reciprocity and public-mindedness that governance requires.

There is no textbook, no law, no institution that can lay this groundwork, only the education that comes of political experience; in Benjamin Barber's words, 'Politics is its own university, citizenship its own training ground, and participation its own tutor.'[15] If this is true, then as much as demotic practices of citizenship challenge, disrupt and undermine their liberal counterparts, the latter cannot survive and thrive without an active, engaged citizenry. A further dimension of citizenship that needs exploring is therefore citizenship as agency and action, as an activity rather than a passive state, which must be fostered, practised, and continually experienced if it is to be achieved.

Meeting the set of challenges and opportunities such citizenship presents requires a tolerance for ambiguity, complexity and change, a keen-sightedness and public-mindedness in grasping the field, as well as the courage and agency to intervene in imaginative and constructive ways. In short, a critical, global, and active civil society is not only essential to liberal notions of citizenship as rights and rule of law, but also the most promising resource for addressing the central challenges that beset our democracies today.

With this brief and broad-sweeping and thus — in the company of contributions from historians in this volume — what might appear a methodologically whimsical history of citizenship in its liberal and demotic guises, I open the intellectual gates to an elucidation of how citizenship as concept and practice has morphed and changed from ancient Rome to contemporary New Zealand. For if there is anything my own inquiry into the genealogy of citizenship has made clear, it is that the range of possible meanings and significances of the term far exceeds the prevailing terms of any one context, and it is a loss to our own democracies, and our capacity as citizens to contend with the challenges of political life, to ignore this wealth of resources housed in the annals of history.

ENDNOTES

1. Chantal Mouffe, *The Democratic Paradox* (London and New York: Verso, 2000), 93.
2. Hannah Arendt, *The Origins of Totalitarianism* (Orlando and Austin: Harcourt, Inc., 1968), 476.
3. Claude LeFort, *Democracy and Political Theory*, trans. David Macey (Minneapolis: University of Minnesota Press, 1988), 19.
4. Sheldon Wolin, 'The Liberal/Democratic Divide: On Rawls's *Political Liberalism*,' Political Theory 24 (1996): 97–119, esp. 98.
5. Mouffe, *The Democratic Paradox*, 11.
6. LeFort, *Democracy and Political Theory*; John Dewey, *The Public and Its Problems: An Essay in Political Inquiry* (University Park, Pennsylvania: Pennsylvania State University Press, 2012).
7. Freedom House, *Democracy's Century: A Survey of Global Political Change in the 20th Century* (New York, 1999).
8. Samuel Huntington, *The Third Wave: Democratisation in the Late 20th Century* (Norman, OK: University of Oklahoma Press, 1991), 21.
9. Samuel Huntington, Michael Crozier, and Joji Watanuki, *The Crisis of Democracy: Report on the Governability of Democracies to the Trilateral Commission* (New York: New York University Press, 1975).
10. John R. Hibbing and Elizabeth Theiss-Morse, *Stealth Democracy: Americans' Beliefs About How Government Should Work* (Cambridge: Cambridge University Press, 2002), 2.
11. Benjamin Constant, 'Liberty of the Ancients Compared with that of the Moderns,' in *Political Writings*, trans. and ed. Biancamaria Fontana (Cambridge: Cambridge University Press, 1993), 326.
12. Colin Hay and Gerry Stoker, 'Revitalising Politics: Have We Lost the Plot?' *Representation* 45, no. 3 (2009): 225–36, 226.
13. Hay and Stoker, 'Revitalising Politics,' 229.
14. Simon Tormey, 'The Contemporary Crisis of Representative Democracy,' *Democratic Theory* 1, no. 2 (Winter 2014): 104–12, 111.
15. Benjamin Barber, *Strong Democracy: Participatory Politics for a New Age* (Berkeley and Los Angeles, CA: University of California Press, 1984), 152.

2. CITIZENS & SERPENTS IN CLASSICAL ATHENS

Daniel Ogden

CITIZENS & SERPENTS IN CLASSICAL ATHENS

In 451/450 BC Pericles, the leading politician of Classical Athens, enacted a notorious citizenship law. The scope and purpose of the law have achieved the status of a standard problem in Ancient History, to which the vagueness of the evidence denies a definitive solution.¹ Two texts are of particular importance for it. First, the Aristotelian *Constitution of Athens*, composed at the end of the fourth century BC, has this to say: 'In the archonship of Antidotus, because of the multitude of citizens [*dia to plēthos tōn politōn*], on Pericles' proposal, they determined that whoever was not born of two citizens [*ex amphoin astoin*], should not participate in the city.'²

The phrase 'because of the multitude of citizens' evidently achieved an iconic status in the recollection of the law, for in the later second century AD it was parodied by Lucian in his *Assembly of the Gods*, where Mt Olympus is portrayed as being subject to a rigorous population scrutiny 'because of the multitude of drinkers' (*dia to plēthos ton pinontōn*).³ Secondly, Plutarch, writing at the turn of the first and second centuries AD, supplies an account of the law focused more engagingly on the person of Pericles himself:

When Pericles had taken control of affairs again, and had been elected general, he asked for the law concerning bastards [*nothoi*] to be relaxed, the law which he himself had previously proposed, in order that his name and his family should not completely disappear [*or*: disappear from his house] for want of succession. The story of the law is as follows. When Pericles was at his peak in politics much earlier on, and had legitimate children, just as was said, he wrote a law that they alone should be Athenians that were born of two Athenian parents. When the king of the Egyptians sent a gift to the people of 40,000 bushels of grain and it had to be divided among the citizens, many lawsuits sprang up as a result of that law for bastards, who had been escaping notice, and many of them fell victim to informers too. Therefore a few short of 5,000 were convicted and excluded from citizenship [*or*: sold into slavery]. Those that remained in the citizenship and were judged to be Athenians were 14,040. Although it was strange that the law that had been enforced against so many should have been relaxed again by the very man that had made it, Pericles' current misfortune concerning his house distressed the Athenians, since they felt that he had paid the penalty for his arrogance and haughtiness, and they thought that he had suffered the things of Nemesis and needed humane treatment, and so they agreed that he should enrol his bastard among the men of his phratry,[4] giving him his own name. And the people subsequently executed him after the sea-battle against the Peloponnesians at Arginusae, together with his fellow generals.[5]

The implication of the way in which Plutarch introduces the law is that henceforth those who were not born of two citizen parents were not only to be debarred from citizenship but were also to be designated bastard, whatever the circumstances of their birth otherwise. One of the established debates about the law is whether bastards of two Athenian parents could nonetheless claim citizenship after it, but the answer here is certainly 'no'. The evidence for the dispensation for bastards (in general) prior to Pericles' law is intricate but ultimately decisive: they had already been debarred from citizenship from the era of Solon (ca. 600 BC).[6] And that is why it was appropriate to characterise Pericles' law, which was primarily concerned with the criteria for citizenship, as a law 'about bastards': it expanded the categories of children henceforth to be designated 'bastard' and thereby deprived of the citizenship which was already incompatible with the status.

Now, Plutarch's personalised story is slightly misleading in the form given, for the son of Pericles in question, also known (eventually, at any rate) as Pericles, had not been a bastard merely by virtue of Pericles' law (his mother,

Aspasia, was Milesian rather than Athenian). He had also been a bastard even before the passing of the law by virtue of the fact that she had not been married to his father (she was in fact a courtesan).[7]

The most powerful explanation for the making of the citizenship law probably lies above and beyond its immediate context in Athens. Analysis of the fragments of law-codes we possess from the wider ancient Greek world indicates that, while some Greek states were, at any given point, stricter than others about the criteria they enforced for legitimacy or citizenship, nonetheless there was a trend for the states in general to move towards stricter criteria in the Classical period, before moving back towards laxer ones again in the Hellenistic period.[8]

Nonetheless, we may still ask what Pericles' immediate purpose might have been in enacting the law. The words of the *Constitution of Athens*, 'because of the multitude of citizens', taken at face value, suggest that the agenda was to limit the size (or the growth in size) of the citizen body. Would it have done so? Only if Athenian men who would otherwise have married alien women did not now marry at all.[9] And presumably that would only happen if there was a relative shortage of citizen women. It is just about conceivable that there was such a shortage.

There is reason to believe the ancient Greeks did in general practise infanticide disproportionately against female babies, and at a rate greater than was normally compensated for by the losses of young men to war: 'Everyone rears a son, even if he happens to be a poor man, and exposes a daughter, even if he happens to be a rich man.'[10] But if this was the limiting device, it is worrying that we have no trace of a crisis of citizen men being unable to find (necessarily citizen) brides after the citizenship law; rather, the crisis we do find is of citizen women being unable to find husbands, a crisis addressed by a temporary provision permitting men to take on two wives (admittedly this crisis came in the wake of the Athenians' manpower-sapping military disasters in Sicily in 413 BC).[11]

But perhaps we are wrong to take the phrase 'because of the multitude of citizens' (*dia to plēthos tōn politōn*) at face value. The law itself manifestly, in view of its requirements, aimed at creating (or maintaining) a supposedly pure citizen body. This explanatory phrase may signify the same thing, for it was and remains a common phenomenon for advocates of racial purity to express their dissatisfaction with the current states of their societies by making appeal to the notion that their lands are in some way too full or overburdened.

The historian Thucydides, too, when discussing the democratic cities of Sicily, perceived a fundamental link between the size of their populations and their mixedness: 'The cities have many inhabitants because of mixed together rabbles and they have easy changes and successions of citizens (*politōn*) [or constitutions (*politeiōn*)].'[12] Closer to our own time, such notions have given succour to the extreme Right: from the Nazis' *Lebensraum* and extermination policies to the continuing protests of the United Kingdom Independence Party (UKIP) that Britain has insufficient room for its immigrants ('Immigration is not about race: it is about space').[13]

Insofar as the maintenance of a supposed racial purity was the law's intention, it will have aligned closely with an ideological and indeed religious belief that flourished in Athens before and after Pericles: this was the conviction that the Athenian people were autochthonous, which is to say that they had been born directly from the soil of their land, Attica, back in the remote mythical era, and that they had from that point maintained a pure descent group. The association between this sort of thinking and the citizenship law was made explicit by the Socratic philosopher Antisthenes, who was himself a bastard born of a citizen father and alien mother (a so-called *mētroxenos*, 'mother-alien'). As Diogenes Laertius was to tell us, 'He himself deflated the Athenians, who puffed themselves up on the basis of being earthborn, by saying that they were no better born than snails and slugs.'[14]

This notion of autochthony was celebrated in the dense bullets of state ideology that constituted the annual Funeral Orations that were given over the first of the year's war dead. These were instituted at the time of the great Persian invasion of 480–79 BC, according to Dionysius of Halicarnassus, and it is thought that from the first they are likely to have resembled in their contents and their drift the largely fourth-century BC examples and refractions of them

that survive. The best known of these is the one that the historian Thucydides puts into the mouth of Pericles himself, for the first year of the Peloponnesian war (430 BC).[15]

In these speeches the Athenian people are conceptualised as being autochthonous by virtue of the fact that the first generation of their ancestors was born en masse from the earth. Athens has always been inhabited by this same descent group, and it has never been populated by immigrants.[16] Athens is the only state of this kind; by contrast, the peoples of other states are merely 'adoptive' and unable to love their land in the way that Athenians do.[17] The condition of autochthony is accordingly one naturally resistant to foreign domination.[18] The earth is the mother of all the Athenians, and they are brothers born of the same mother.[19] Since all Athenians share this common condition of autochthony, it forms the basis of the unity of the city and its order, and it is closely identified with citizenship in itself.[20] The freedom and democracy of which the Athenians are so proud necessarily proceeds from their common autochthonous origin.

Plato observes that, 'The natural equality of our birth compels us to seek equality in law by legal means.'[21] Lysias encapsulates the link between autochthony and democracy by declaring that the Athenians are 'born finely and thinking alike'.[22] He notes further that, 'First and alone at that time [that is, the time of their autochthony] they cast out their tyrants and established democracy' (the problem of where these undemocratic tyrants might have come from is glossed over).[23] By contrast, other states, which are necessarily non-autochthonous and made up of mixed peoples, are doomed to constitutional inequality. As Plato observes, they are made up of 'men of all sorts and unequal', and accordingly have 'similarly unequal constitutions'.[24] We find similar ideas expressed also in a fragment from Euripides' tragedy *Erectheus* of 422 BC:

> One could not get a better city than this. In the first place its people are not brought in from outside, but we are born autochthonous. But other cities were founded alike by people moving from place to place like draughts, importing people from each other. Whoever comes to live in

one city from another is like a worthless peg fixed into a plank: he is a citizen in word, but not in fact.[25]

The Funeral Orations and associated literature do not tell us the precise circumstances and mechanics by which the first generation of Athenians sprang, plant-like, out of the earth of Attica. But the vignette is a familiar one from myth and the tales of the two crops of the Spartoi or 'Sown Men'. When Cadmus slew the Serpent (or Dragon: *drakōn*) of Ares with a rock at the site of his future city-foundation of Thebes in central Greece, Athene advised him to hack out the serpent's teeth and sow them in the ground. At once these marvellous seeds gave rise to a crop of fully armed warriors (given their metal cladding, it may be significant that Cadmus was considered to be the discoverer of metal, and the inventor of the process of extracting metal from the ground in mining). Again on Athene's advice, Cadmus threw a second rock among the children of the serpent, and they began to fight each other. The six surviving warriors became the first and founding 'earthborn' generation of the new city of Thebes, and it was back to these that the noblest men of the city would subsequently trace their birth.[26] (Serpent-slaying was often associated with city foundation in the Greek world: the motif appears in connection with the founding of the cities of Tripodisci in the Megarid, Sybaris in southern Italy and even with that of Alexandria in Egypt.)[27]

Athene held back half of the Serpent of Ares' teeth, however, and these she passed on to Aeetes in Colchis, at the eastern end of the Black Sea, who was the owner of the golden fleece. He deployed the teeth in a pair of challenges he imposed on Jason. First, our hero had to yoke fiery bulls so that he could sow the teeth, and then he had to defeat the warriors duly produced.[28] Viewers of Ray Harryhausen's atmospheric 1963 stop-motion animation movie *Jason and the Argonauts* will remember his take on this episode well, with Jason and his men battling a crop of skeleton warriors in the film's climactic sequence.[29]

The parallelism between Athenian thinking and the Theban story suggests that there may once have been a tradition that the first generation of Athenians was similarly created from the teeth of a serpent. We may just find a hint that such was the case in a fragment of Androtion's fourth-century BC *History of Attica*. According to Androtion, not the first generation of Athenians, but rather one of the original kings of Attica, Erectheus, was himself actually one of the Theban Spartoi. This is a curious and anomalous claim, it must be admitted, because it preserves the notion of Athenian autochthony but at the expense of self-defeatingly deriving this autochthony from somebody else's land, Boeotia rather than Attica![30] It is no accident that the teeth sown to produce autochthonous peoples should belong to a serpent: the Greeks regarded snakes as themselves the most paradigmatic of earthborn creatures.[31]

Erectheus brings us to the other and probably far more ancient way in which the Athenians understood their autochthonous condition, namely as deriving, precisely, from a single, original autochthonous king, himself sprung indeed from the soil of Attica. He was known not only as Erectheus but also as Ericthonius, the latter name signifying 'very chthonic'.[32] The notion of autochthony is associated with both names already in early epic. In the *Iliad* we find reference to 'great-spirited Erectheus, who once Athene, daughter of Zeus, reared, but the grain-giving soil bore him, and Athene set him down in Athens in her rich temple',[33] while Ericthonius seemingly appeared from the ground in the anonymous epic *Danais*.[34]

It was around the latter name that the more interesting traditions tended to develop. The earliest images of Ericthonius, of ca. 500 BC, depict him as a humanoid baby, being raised out of the ground by a female figure, Earth personified, and being handed over to his foster-mother and patron of the city, the virgin goddess Athene.[35] And so too do our only coherent narrative accounts of his birth and first days present his origin in a compatible way. Amelesagoras (fourth or third century BC) and Apollodorus (ca. AD 100) tell of Hephaestus' attempt to rape Athene. The lame god was unable to achieve congress with his fleeing quarry, despite his ardour, and his seed fell upon her leg. Athene wiped it off in disgust with wool (*eri-on*), and cast it on the ground (*chthōn*). Earth, thus fertilised, produced 'Eri-cthonius' as a result, and gave the evidently humanoid (at this point anyway) baby to Athene to rear. Athene retained her virginity still, but even so was putative mother to the child as inspirer of the ejaculate. She enclosed him in a basket and gave him over to the daughters of Cecrops (the 'Cecropids') to look after, forbidding them to look within. But curiosity got the better of Agraulos and Pandrosos, of course, and they opened the box and saw either a single serpent (*drakōn*) or a pair of them coiling around Ericthonius. The girls were either destroyed by the serpent(s) or driven mad by Athene for their disobedience, throwing themselves down from the acropolis.[36]

But this was not the only way in which Ericthonius was conceived. Parallel traditions portrayed him as a serpent in himself, and indeed such a notion makes for a rather crisper story than those preserved by Amelesagorus and Apollodorus, whose accounts may reflect a partly rationalising attempt to render the great ancestor humanoid.[37] In Sophocles' *Tympanistai*, which could have been composed at any point between 468 and 406 BC, one of the daughters of Cecrops was given the name *Drakaulos*, presumably an alternative form of *Agraulos*, to signify that Athene had put a serpent (*drakōn*) to live (*aulisai*) with the girls in question. This would be rather more meaningful if the serpent were Ericthonius himself rather than a guard for him.[38] Euripides' tragedy *Ion*, probably written between 414 and 412 BC, tells that the 'Erectheid' Athenians dressed their babies in a pair of golden bangles of serpent form; these preserve the 'custom . . . of the earthborn [*gēgenēs*] Ericthonius' and, more to the point, are '*imitations* of ancient Ericthonius' (my emphasis).[39]

Among second-century AD authors, Hyginus in his *Astronomica* describes Ericthonius himself simply as a snake (*Ericthonius anguis*), while Pausanias conjectures that the serpent integrated into the Parthenon's cult image of Athene, the famous Athene Parthenos statue of Phidias, 'could be Ericthonius'. In the following century Philostratus appears to have Ericthonius somehow in mind in making the curious assertion that Athene herself once bore a serpent (*drakōn*) to the Athenians.[40]

Almost certainly Ericthonius-as-serpent is documented already on an Attic red-figure vase of ca. 480 BC, on which the Cecropids are shown being chased by a superb bearded serpent,[41] and so too on a vase of ca. 430 BC on which a serpent emerges from a cast-down basket to pursue a fleeing Cecropid.[42] Given that one would have expected the painters of these vases by all means to incorporate the focal figure of Ericthonius into scenes of this kind in some shape or form, and given that there is no sign of any humanoid baby, we can only conclude that the serpent in both these scenes is Ericthonius himself. Later authors, starting with Hyginus again but in his *Fabulae* this time, also preserve a sub-tradition that Ericthonius was more specifically an anguipede, which is to say that he was humanoid down as far as the waist, but a serpent below, in the fashion of Cecrops himself, to whom we turn next.[43]

Ericthonius and the serpent that sired the first generation of Athenians (if such there was) were not the only serpents integral to the Classical Athenians' conceptualisation of themselves as citizens. We may point to no fewer than four more. For the Athenians, as for us, citizenship, 'sharing in the city (*polis*)', meant not merely the exercise of a birth-right by those able to do so, but also engagement with an ordered and civilised state. It was above all in the figure of Cecrops, yet another anguiform original king of Attica, that the Athenians found this social side of their citizenship to be embodied.

The earliest unrationalised account of the myth of Cecrops to survive is Apollodorus' (ca. AD 100). He tells that Cecrops was born of Earth, and was an anguipede with a body combined from man and serpent (*drakōn*). He was an original king of Attica, and he initially called the region Cecropia after himself. He took a signal role in shaping the city as it was to be known by aiding Athene against Poseidon in winning the role of its patron deity: this he did by bearing witness to the fact that it had been she who had first planted the olive upon which Attica's economy came to depend.[44] Cecrops' iconographic tradition extends from the beginning of the fifth century BC, just prior to the Persian invasions, until it peters out in the mid-fourth century. In this he is usually shown either in the form of a simple anguipede,[45] or as fully humanoid,[46] and either way sporting the attributes of beard, sceptre and tunic or cloak; the form in which he is shown tends to depend upon the conventions of the scene-type in which he is featured, and it is surely significant that he is most consistently portrayed as an anguipede when he attends the birth of Ericthonius from the earth.[47]

Cecrops' combined man-serpent form was celebrated in his familiar epithet *diphyēs* ('of two natures'). But the Athenians sought to imbue the epithet with additional significances.[48] Aristotle's pupil Clearchus of Soli explained that, 'At Athens Cecrops first yoked one woman to one man. Previously sexual relations had been held in common. This is why some decided to call him *diphyēs*, since previously men did not know their father because of the multitude of candidates.'[49] Clearchus' explanation makes Cecrops the founder not simply of the physical city of Athens, but also, via the invention of marriage, of the order of its citizenship, of its descent group, and of its canons of legitimacy.[50] The tradition of ancient scholarship represented in the scholia to Aristophanes and in the *Suda* (a Byzantine encyclopedia) builds upon the work of Clearchus, and also on the work of Philochorus. The latter had much to say of Cecrops' role both as a founder and as a lawmaker, to explain that his *diphyēs* form was emblematic more generally of the fact that he discovered many laws for (Athenian) men, and led them from a state of wildness to one of gentleness.[51] Cecrops was, then, not only the creator of Athens' citizenship, but also of its civilisation.

We have to look a bit harder to find the fourth serpent to support the ideology of citizenship in Attica. The supposedly historical (as opposed to the mythical) record famously identifies the first lawgiver of Athens as Draco (*Drakōn*), he of the notoriously 'Draconian' legislation. His floruit is given as the 39th Olympiad, i.e. 624–1 BC, and he is said to have been the author of a famous law against homicide, but also, and more importantly here, of the first Athenian constitution.[52]

As will be immediately apparent, Draco's name plainly and simply signifies 'Serpent'. Manifestly, the origin of this further first lawgiver lies either in a rationalised version of the mythical serpentine lawgiver Cecrops, or in a heavy assimilation of an actual historical lawgiver towards the paradigm offered by the mythical Cecrops. That a serpent should lurk behind the figure of Draco is acknowledged in a bon mot attributed to Herodicus or Prodicus by Aristotle: he had observed that, in view of their harshness, the laws in question were the work not of a human Draco but of an actual serpent (*drakōn*).[53] Anyway, once again, a

significant creator of the Athenian state is associated with serpent imagery.

The citizens of Athens held themselves to be under the protection of a fifth serpent, a 'house-watching snake' (*oikouros ophis*) or 'house-watching serpent' (*oikouros drakōn*). Despite its seemingly more specific title, this served in fact to guard, according to Herodotus, the acropolis and its shrines as a whole, the religious heart of Athens and indeed the ancient origin-point of the city.[54] Its best-known moment came during the great Persian invasion of 480–79 BC. Herodotus tells how the priestess of Athene Polias used to lay out monthly offerings of honey-cakes for the snake, which were ever devoured. However, as the Persians drew near, the priestess had to report to the community that the latest honey-cakes were untouched. And so the Athenians abandoned their city to be sacked by the Persians, on the basis that their patron goddess Athene had herself abandoned it. We must infer that she was understood to have taken the snake, evidently her pet or avatar, with her. (Later on, it was similarly imagined that the city of Alexandria was doomed to fall whenever her own protecting serpent, Agathos Daimon, should abandon her.)[55]

Although the ancients in other contexts certainly did keep actual sacred snakes in their shrines, most notably healing snakes in the case of shrines of Asclepius,[56] the *oikouros ophis* seems to have belonged to another religious phenomenon, namely that of the individual great sacred snake, typically tended by chaste priestesses with honey-cakes, but never actually set eyes upon.[57] Further examples of this phenomenon are found in the cult of Juno Sospita at Lanuvium,[58] and the cult of Zeus Sosipolis at Elea.[59] In both cases we are told that the priestesses entered the relevant parts of their shrines blindfolded to tend their snakes. One may well doubt, of course, that the snakes in this category ever existed: but what happened to the honey-cakes (which snakes are in any case unable to eat)?

And so the Athenians abandoned their city to the resistless Persian armies, and trusted instead in the power of their fleet, with which indeed they were able to destroy that of the Persians at the battle of Salamis. This was their greatest hour, and was ever after looked upon as such. It was only fitting that yet another serpentine figure should have come to their aid on this defining occasion. The second-century AD Pausanias was to tell of what he found on the island of Salamis adjacent to the trophy set up there by the victorious Athenian general Themistocles: 'And there is a sanctuary of Cychreus. It is said that a serpent [*drakōn*] appeared amongst the ships when the Athenians were fighting their sea battle against the Persians. The god prophesied to the Athenians that the hero was Cychreus.'[60]

The Classical Athenians imagined serpents, creatures symbolic of the earth, to define the bounds of their citizenship in almost every respect. As a people they were of serpent-descent: either they were descended from a single serpent king, in the form of Ericthonius, born of the Earth, or their first generation had risen from the soil as if, or more probably when, sown with the teeth of another serpent. Their laws, marital system and civilisation in general (including the olive) they owed to another earthborn serpent-king, Cecrops, or else to Draco, the historicised refraction of the same figure. The ancient heart of the city and the religious shrines to which they, as citizens, had unique access were under the protection of the 'house-watching snake' (*oikouros ophis*). And a serpent attended what they came to see as their greatest and most defining moment as a people, their victory over the Persian fleet at the battle of Salamis. Pericles' citizenship law was probably seen first and foremost as a populist affirmation of the Athenian people's serpent-derived autochthony and indeed of their broader serpent-derived sense of themselves as a community.

The citizenship law and the serpents of Athens introduce us to a broad range of ideas about citizenship adumbrated in the Introduction to this volume and recurring (in positive and negative forms) throughout the remainder of it: the notion of the citizen body as a strongly differentiated and strongly privileged group (the citizenship law itself); that of a relationship between citizenship and place (Ericthonius, etc.); that of a relationship between citizenship and descent (the citizenship law and Ericthonius); that of a relationship between citizenship and law (the citizenship law, Cecrops and Draco); that of a relationship between citizenship and religion (the *oikouros ophis*); that of a relationship between citizenship and history (Salamis, etc.); and finally the notion of a relationship between citizenship and civilisedness or cultural identity (Cecrops).

A NOTE ON SOURCES FOR NON-CLASSICISTS
The majority of the ancient texts referred to here — but by no means all, alas — are most conveniently found translated in Harvard University Press' Loeb Classical Library series.

ABBREVIATIONS
DK Hermann Diels and Walther Krantz, *Die Fragmente der Vorsokratiker*, 3 vols (3rd ed., Berlin: Weidmann, 1912).
FGrH *Die Fragmente der griechischen Historiker,* ed. Felix Jacoby et al., multiple volumes and parts (Berlin and Leiden: Brill, 1923).
GGM *Geographi graeci minors*, ed. Carl F. W. Müller (Paris: A. Firmin Dido, 1855–82).
IG *Inscriptiones Graecae*, multiple series, volumes and parts (Berlin, 1903–).
K-A Rudolf Kassel and Colin Austin, *Poetae Comici Graeci*, 8+ vols (Berlin: De Gruyter, 1983–)
LIMC *Lexicon Iconographicum Mythologiae Classicae*, ed. Lily Kahil et al., 9 vols in 18 parts (Zurich, 1981–1999).
PL *Patrologiae cursus completus: Series Latina*, ed. Jacques-Paul Migne (Paris: Garnier, 1884–1904).
P.Oxy. *The Oxyrhynchus Papyri*, ed. Bernard P. Grenfell et al., Continuing Series (Oxford: Oxford University Press, 1998).
TrGF Bruno Snell, Richard Kannicht, and Stefan Radt, *Tragicorum Graecorum Fragmenta*, 5 vols (Göttingen: Vandenhoeck & Ruprecht, 1971–2004).

ENDNOTES
1 My own views on the law and its context, by which I stand, are laid out in detail in *Greek Bastardy in the Classical and Hellenistic Periods* (Oxford: Oxford University Press, 1996), 32–82, where previous scholarship is cited; the literary aspects of this study are glossed by Mary Ebbott, *Imagining Illegitimacy in Classical Greek Literature* (Lanham: Lexington Books, 2003), while Salvatore Vacante, 'Nothoi in Ancient Greece: The Contribution of Epigraphy,' *Hephaistos* 31 (2014): 73–94, takes a new look at its epigraphic aspects. The single most influential discussion of the citizenship law itself remains that of Cynthia Patterson, *Pericles' Citizenship Law of 451–0 BC* (New York: Arno Press, 1981); cf. also eadem, 'Those Athenian Bastards,' *Classical Antiquity* 9 (1990): 39–73; eadem, *The Family in Greek History* (Cambridge, Mass.: Harvard University Press, 1998), 108–14, who contends that it was in effect the second paragraph of a law primarily designed to debar non-citizens from the phratries, as the Athenians came to regret their former generosity in the extension of their citizen rights. Alas, the scholium (the ancient or Byzantine commentary) that constitutes her only supposedly explicit evidence for this change of heart (schol. Thucydides 1.2, 'for the Athenians in ancient

times used to give a share in their citizenship readily, but later on they did this no longer') relates not to the periods before and after 451/450 BC respectively, but, in both cases, to Athens' prehistorical period, the period the scholium seeks to elucidate.

Other older contributions on the subject include Eberhard Ruschenbusch, *Athenische Innenpolitik im 5. Jahrhundert v. Chr.* (Bamberg: Aku Fotodruk, 1979), 83–7, arguing that the law sought to curb marriages between Athenian citizen women and alien men, Kenneth R. Walters, 'Pericles' Citizenship Law,' *Classical Antiquity* 2 (1983): 314–36, arguing that the law denied citizenship only to the children of slavewomen and Alan L. Boegehold, 'Perikles' Citizenship Law of 451/0 B.C,' in *Athenian Identity and Civic Ideology*, ed. Alan L. Boegehold and Adele C. Scafuro (Baltimore: Johns Hopkins University Press, 1994), 57–66, arguing that the law merely sought to bring statute into line with recent decisions taken by the popular courts. Study of the citizenship law has fallen out of fashion in more recent years, but among newer contributions one may consult Edwin Carawan, 'Pericles the Younger and the Citizenship Law,' *Classical Journal* 103 (2008): 383–406, focusing on the circumstances of Pericles' retrieval of his bastard for citizenship; Josine H. Blok, 'Perikles' Citizenship Law: A New Perspective,' *Historia* 58 (2009): 141–7, arguing, with much toil, that the law sought to tighten up the criteria for citizenship by assimilating them to the entry requirements of the pseudo-kinship groups known as the *genē*; unfortunately the evidence that the *genē* applied laxer requirements for entry than the state did for citizenship in the well-documented period after the passing of the law is incontrovertible) and Altay Coşkun, 'Perikles und die Definition des Bürgerrechts im klassischen Athen — Neue Vorschläge zu Inhalt, Zeitpunkt, Hintergrund und Auswirkungen des Gesetzes,' *Historische Zeitschrift* 299 (2014): 1–35, arguing that the law should be down-dated to 445/444 BC. For Pericles himself, see Philip A. Stadter, *A Commentary on Plutarch's Pericles* (Chapel Hill: University of North Carolina Press, 1989); Charlotte Schubert, *Perikles* (Darmstadt: Wissenschaftliche Buchgesellschaft, 1995), eadem, *Perikles: Tyrann oder Demokrat?* (Stuttgart: Reclam, 2012); Anthony J. Podlecki, *Pericles and His Circle* (London: Routledge, 1997); Gustav A. Lehmann, *Perikles. Staatsmann und Stratege im klassischen Athen: eine Biographie* (Munich: C. H. Beck, 2008); Vincent Azoulay, *Pericles of Athens* (Princeton: Princeton University Press, 2014), trans. of *Périclès: La démocratie athénienne à l'épreuve du grande homme* (Paris: A. Colan, 2010); Loren J. Samons, *Pericles and the Conquest of History* (Cambridge: Cambridge University Press, 2016).

2   Aristotle, *Constitution of Athens*, 26.4. Other texts offer similar brief summaries of the law: Aelian, *Historical Miscellany*, 13.24; *Suda* s.v. δημοποίητος; cf. Aristotle, *Politics*, 1278a 34–5 (without explicit mention of the law as such).

3   Lucian, *Assembly of the Gods*, 14 (cf. 1).

4   Phratries were pseudo-kinship groups that *effectively* controlled the gateway to citizenship at this time. See Ogden, *Greek Bastardy*, 83–135, 150–6 and, more generally, Stephen D. Lambert, *The Phratries of Attica* (2nd ed., Ann Arbor: University of Michigan Press, 1998).

5   Plutarch, *Pericles*, 37.2–5. Plutarch's source may be comic in origin, perhaps Cratinus' *Nemesis*

(cf. Plutarch's portentous reference to Nemesis), in which Pericles-as-Zeus raped (Aspasia-as-?) Leda/Nemesis (FF114–27 K-A), or perhaps Eupolis' *Demoi* (cf. Plutarch, *Pericles*, 24.10, quoting Eupolis F110 K-A, a joke about Pericles' bastard son); see Ogden, *Greek Bastardy*, 61.

6   This bar is entailed by, *inter alia*, the (probably Solonian) magistracy law incorporated into the so-called 'Constitution of Draco' (on which more anon) at Aristotle, *Constitution of Athens*, 4.2: 'They elected . . . as generals and cavalry-commanders those that proved that they had an unencumbered estate worth at least 100 minas and legitimate children from a married woman.' The general point here is that only those with a stake in the continued prosperity of the state can be trusted to serve as generals: if illegitimate children (as opposed to legitimate ones) do not constitute such a stake in the future of the state, it can only be because they will not be citizens in it. See Ogden, *Greek Bastardy*, 37–44, 150–6.

7   For Aspasia see in particular Plutarch, *Pericles*, 24–5, 30, 32. The evidence for her is collected in Madeleine M. Henry, *Prisoner of History: Aspasia of Miletus and her Biographical Tradition* (Oxford: Oxford University Press, 1995), and Nicole Loraux, 'Aspasie, l'étrangère, l'intellectuelle,' *Clio* 13 (2001): 17–42.

8   See Ogden, *Greek Bastardy*, 275–317.

9   As noted by Charles Hignett, *A History of the Athenian Constitution* (Oxford: Clarendon Press, 1952), 346.

10 Poseidippus, *Hermaphroditus*, F12 K-A. The evidence of the ca. 200 BC enfranchisement inscriptions of the Milesian Delphinium implies a very high rate of female infanticide across the Greek world at that time: see Ogden, *Greek Bastardy*, 106–10, 304–10.

11 Aristotle, *On Good Birth*, F93 Rose = Diogenes Laertius 2.26; Aulus Gellius, *Attic Nights*, 15.20; cf. Ogden, *Greek Bastardy*, 72–5.

12 Thucydides, 6.27.

13 UKIP General Election Manifesto, 2015. One would never have guessed that the Scottish Highlands is one of the least densely populated regions of Europe as a whole.

14 Diogenes Laertius, 6.1.

15 The surviving Funeral Orations and refractions of them are Gorgias (Hermann Diels and Walther Krantz, *Die Fragmente der Vorsokratiker*, 3 vols, DK 82 B5–6 (late fifth or early fourth century BC); Thucydides, 2.34–46 (ca. 400 BC, supposedly recreating Pericles' own Funeral Oration of 430 BC); Lysias 2 (ca. 392 BC); Plato, *Menexenus* (386 BC or after); Demosthenes 60 (338 BC, if genuinely attributed); Lycurgus, *Leocrates* 39–40 (330 BC); Hyperides 6 (322 BC); note also Dionysius of Halicarnassus, *Roman Antiquities* 5.17.4; cf. John E. Ziolkowski, *Thucydides and the Tradition of Funeral Speeches at Athens* (Salem: The Ayr Co., 1985), 20; Vincent J. Rosivach, 'Autochthony and the Athenians,' *Classical Quarterly* 37 (1987): 294–306, at 304–5; and William B. Tyrrell and Frieda S. Brown, *Athenian Myths and Institutions: Words in Action* (New York: Oxford University Press, 1991), 190.

16 Thucydides 2.36.1; Lysias 2.17; Plato, *Menexenus*, 237b; Demosthenes 60.4; Hyperides 6.7; Isocrates 4.24–5.

17 Plato, *Menexenus*, 245d2–4; Demosthenes 60.4; Lycurgus, *Leocrates*, 8; cf. Herodotus 7.161. Concomitantly, Thucydides 6.17 says of the 'mixed together rabbles' that constitute the Sicilian democracies that they 'do not fight and farm as if for their own homeland'.
18 Thucydides 2.36.1; Lysias 2.4; cf. Aristophanes, *Wasps*, 1076; Xenophon, *Hellenica*, 7.1.23, and Demosthenes 19.261.
19 Lysias 2.17; Plato, *Menexenus*, 237e4 and 239a1–2; Demosthenes 60.4 (cf. 60.6); cf. Plato, *Republic*, 414c–e; Isocrates 4.25.
20 Lysias 2.17; Plato, *Menexenus*, 244a1–3; Demosthenes 60.3–4; cf. Aristophanes, *Wasps*, 1075–80; Isocrates 4.23–5.
21 Lysias 2.17–20; Plato, *Menexenus*, 239a–b; Demosthenes 19.261; Lycurgus, *Leocrates*, 41.
22 Lysias 2.20.
23 Lysias 2.18.
24 Plato, *Menexenus*, 238e; Lycurgus, *Leocrates*, 47; cf. Thucydides 6.17.2–4, Isocrates 4.24 and 12.124. For discussions of the ideology enunciated by the Funeral Orations, see Nicole Loraux, *Les Enfants d'Athéna* (Paris, 1981), trans. Caroline Levine as *The Children of Athena* (Princeton: Princeton University Press, 1993), 36, 49–51, 65–7 and 71, 76, 130–1, and eadem, *L'invention d'Athènes: Histoire de l'oraison funèbre dans la cité classique* (Paris, 1981), trans. Alan Sheridan as *The Invention of Athens: The Funeral Oration in the Classical City* (Cambridge, Mass.: Harvard University Press, 1986), 1, 193–4, 277–8, 301–2, 331; Robert C. T. Parker, 'Myths of Early Athens,' in *Interpretations of Greek Mythology*, ed. Jan N. Bremmer (London: Barnes and Noble Books, 1987), 187–214, at 194; Rosivach, 'Autochthony'; Tyrrell and Brown, *Athenian Myths*, 195–6; and Josiah Ober, *Mass and Elite in Democratic Athens* (Princeton: Princeton University Press, 1989), 261–4, the last of whom sees the concept of mass autochthony as a democratic move to appropriate 'good birth' (*eugeneia*) for the common people from the aristocracy.
25 Euripides, *Erectheus*, F360 *TrGF*, lines 6–13.
26 See, *inter alia*, Euripides, *Phoenissae*, 238, 638–48, 657–75, 818–21, 931–41, 1010–1, 1060–6, 1315 (all with scholia); Ovid, *Metamorphoses*, 3.28–98 (the most expansive account); Apollodorus, *Bibliotheca*, 3.4.1–2, 3.5.4; Nonnus, *Dionysiaca*, 2.669–78, 4.348–463 (a good account of the fight), 5.121–89, 44.107–18, 46.364–7. Discussion in Daniel Ogden, *Drakōn: Dragon Myth and Serpent Cult in the Greek and Roman Worlds* (Oxford: Oxford University Press, 2013), 48–54; idem, *Dragons, Serpents and Slayers in the Classical and Early Christian Worlds* (New York: Oxford University Press, 2013), 109–18.
27 Tripodisci: Statius, *Thebaid*, 1.557–669; Sybaris: Antoninus Liberalis, *Metamorphoses*, 8; Alexandria: *Alexander Romance* (A) 1.32.
28 Eumelus F21 West (= schol. Apollonius, *Argonautica*, 3.1354); Pindar, *Pythians*, 4.213–19; Apollonius, *Argonautica*, 3.401–21, 1026–62, 1176–224, 1246–67; Valerius Flaccus, *Argonautica*, 7.46–72, 355–643, 8.106–8.
29 But Harryhausen does exercise considerable licence. To avoid confusion: the notion that the

warriors should take the form of skeletons is his and has no basis in ancient myth; the fiery bulls have disappeared, and Aeetes sows the teeth directly into the ground himself before Jason; his serpent's teeth derive not from the Theban Serpent of Ares, but from the Colchis Serpent, the guardian of the golden fleece, already killed by Jason at this point in the film; and the part of the original myth's single-headed Colchis Serpent is actually given over to the multi-headed Hydra (explicitly so named), which has been borrowed from the myths of the labours of Heracles (all the more teeth, one supposes) . . .

30 Androtion, *FGrH* 324 F37 = Tzetzes schol. on Lycophron, *Alexandra*, 495.

31 See, for example, Herodotus 1.78, Artemidorus, *Oneirocritica*, 2.13; many further examples in Ogden, *Drakōn*, 247–54.

32 Liliane H. Bodson, ἱερὰ ζῷα. *Contribution à l'étude de la place de l'animal dans la religion grecque ancienne* (Brussels: Académie royale de Belgique, 1978), 80–1.

33 Homer, *Iliad*, 2.547–9; cf. *Odyssey*, 7.81. The Iliadic lines may be an interpolation into Homer's seventh-century BC (?) text, but even so, it is thought that they can be no more recent than the sixth century. See Loraux, *Les Enfants d'Athéna*, 41; Parker, 'Myths of Early Athens,' 193; Rosivach, 'Autochthony,' 294; and Geoffrey S. Kirk et al., *Homer: The Iliad. A Commentary* (Cambridge: Cambridge University Press, 1985–1993), I, 179–80, 205; cf. Pierre Brulé, *La Fille d'Athènes: La religion des filles à Athènes a l'époque classique. Mythes, cultes et société* (Paris: Les Belles Lettres, 1987), 13–8.

34 *Danais*, F2 West.

35 For the iconography of Ericthonius, see *LIMC* Erechtheus and Kron 1976, 249–59; 1988, 945–6. In addition to the scenes with Earth (*LIMC* Erechtheus 1–27), note also the British Museum *pelikē* of 440–30 BC (*LIMC* Aglauros 18 = Athena 480 = Erechtheus 36 = Ellen D. Reeder, 'Erichthonios,' in *Pandora*, ed. Ellen D. Reeder (Princeton: Princeton University Press, 1995), 250–66, no. 69), on which baby Ericthonius is watched over by a pair of snakes in a round basket, with Athene standing by, and the late fifth-century BC *loutrophoros* fragment (*LIMC* Erechtheus 32) that preserves an image of a baby Ericthonius with a single rampant snake, though there may also have been a second one when the vase was complete.

36 Amelesagoras, *FGrH* 330 F1 and Apollodorus, *Bibliotheca*, 3.14.6. For further texts on the Ericthonius figure see Sophocles, F643 *TrGF* (*apud* Hesychius s.v. Δράκαυλος); Euripides, *Ion*, 16–28, 267–82, 1427–32; Amelesagoras, *FGrH* 330 F1 = Antigonus of Carystus, *Mirabilia*, 12; Eratosthenes, *Catasterismi*, 13; Ovid, *Metamorphoses*, 2.552–64; Pausanias 1.18.2, 1.24.5–7; Hyginus, *Fabulae*, 166, *Astronomica*, 2.13; Lactantius, *Divinae Institutiones*, 1.17; schol. Germanicus, *Aratea*, pp. 394–5 Eyssenhardt; Servius on Virgil, *Georgics*, 3.113; Augustine, *City of God*, 18.12; Nonnus, *Dionysiaca* 41.58–64; Fulgentius, *Mitologiae*, 2.11; First Vatican Mythographer 2.26; Second Vatican Mythographer 48; schol. Plato, *Timaeus*, 23e; Tzetzes, schol. on Lycophron, *Alexandra*, 111; *Etymologicum Magnum* s.v. Ἐρεχθεύς. Discussions at: Benjamin Powell, *Erichthonius and the Three Daughters of Cecrops* (Ithaca: Cornell University Press, 1906), with a repertorium of sources at 56–86; Arthur B. Cook, *Zeus: A Study in Ancient*

Religion, 3 vols (Cambridge: Cambridge University Press, 1914–1940), iii, 181–8, 218–23, 237–61; Murray Fowler, 'The Myth of ἘΡΙΧΘΟΝΙΟΣ,' *Classical Philology* 38 (1943): 28–32; Walter Burkert, 'Kekropidensage und Arrhephoria,' *Hermes* 91 (1966): 1–25; idem, *Homo Necans: The Anthropology of Ancient Greek Sacrificial Ritual and Myth*, trans. Peter Bing (Berkeley: University of California Press, 1983), trans. of *Homo Necans* (Berlin: De Gruyter, 1972), 150–4; Uta Kron, *Die zehn attischen Phylenheroen: Geschichte, Mythos, Kult und Darstellung* (Berlin: Mann, 1976), 32–83; eadem, 'Aglauros, Herse, Pandrosos,' in *LIMC*, 283–98; eadem, 'Erechtheus,' in *LIMC*, iv.1, (1988), 923–51 (NB this article is out of sequence in *LIMC*); Noel Robertson, 'The riddle of the Arrhephoria at Athens,' *Harvard Studies in Classical Philology* 87 (1983): 241–88; idem, 'The Origin of the Panathenaea,' *Rheinisches Museum* 128 (1985): 231–95; Brulé, *La fille d'Athènes*, 13–79; Emily Kearns, *The Heroes of Attica, Bulletin of the Institute of Classical Studies Suppl.* 57 (London: Institute of Classical Studies, 1989): 110–5, 160–1; Parker, 'Myths of Early Athens'; Tyrrell and Brown, *Athenian Myths*, 133–51; Timothy Gantz, *Early Greek Myth: A Guide to Literary and Artistic Sources* (Baltimore: Johns Hopkins University Press, 1993), 233–7; Loraux, *Les Enfants d'Athéna*, cf. eadem, *Born of the Earth: Myth and Politics in Athens* (Ithaca: Cornell University Press, 2000), trans. (Selina Stewart) of *Né de la terre: Mythe et politique à Athènes* (Paris, 2000) — somewhat frustrating; Reeder, 'Erichthonios'; H. Alan Shapiro, 'The Cult of Heroines: Kekrops' Daughters,' in *Pandora*, ed. Reeder, 39–48; Laurent Gourmelen, *Kékrops, le roi-serpent. Imaginaire athénien, représentations de l'humain et de l'animalité en Grèce ancienne* (Paris: Les Belles Lettres, 2004), esp. 329–40; Christiane Sourvinou-Inwood, *Athenian Myths and Festivals: Aglauros, Erechtheus, Plynteria, Panathenaia, Dionysia* (Oxford: Oxford University Press, 2011), 24–134; Ogden, *Drakōn*, 263–7.

37 Bodson, ἱερὰ ζῷα, 81–3, argues that Ericthonius was originally a pure serpent (*drakōn*) in form.
38 Sophocles F643 *TrGF apud* Hesychius s.v. Δράκαυλος.
39 Euripides Ion 1427–31, Ἐριχθωνίου γε τοῦ πάλαι μιμήματα. Discussion at Bodson, ἱερὰ ζῷα, 79–80; Gourmelen, *Kékrops*, 125–41, 341.
40 Hyginus, *Astronomica*, 2.13; Pausanias 1.18.2, 1.24.5–7 (*LIMC* Erechtheus 46); Philostratus, *Apollonius*, 7.24.
41 *LIMC* Kekrops 13 = Aglauros, Herse, Pandrosos 15 = Erysichthon ii 1 = Gourmelen, *Kékrops*, fig. 5.
42 *LIMC* Aglauros 19 = Reeder, 'Erichthonios' no. 66.
43 Hyginus, *Fabulae* 166 (*inferiorem partem draconis habuit*), *Astronomica* 2.13; Servius on Virgil, *Georgics* 3.113 (*puer draconteis pedibus*); Nonnus, *Dionysiaca*, 41.58–64 ('Erechtheus' described as an anguipede and explicitly paralleled with Cecrops in this); Fulgentius, *Mitologiae*, 2.11 (where the phrase *cum draconteis pedibus* is excised as an interpolation by Helm); First Vatican Mythographer 2.26 (*draconteis pedibus*); schol. Plato, *Timaeus*, 23e (δρακοντόπους), *Etymologicum Magnum* s.v Ἐρεχθεύς (δρακοντόπους). See Kron, 'Erectheus', 925, 947 for contention that this sub-tradition simply confuses Ericthonius with Cecrops.

44 Cecrops' autochthony: Hermippus of Smyrna F82 Wehrli = *FGrH* 1026 F3 (γηγενής); Lycophron, *Alexandra*, 110–1 (γηγενής; cf. Tzetzes *ad loc.*); Apollodorus, *Bibliotheca*, 3.14–5 (αὐτόχθων); Hyginus; *Fabulae*, 48 (a son of Terra); Antoninus Liberalis; *Metamorphoses*, 6 (αὐτόχθων); Eusebius, *Praeparatio evangelica*, 10.9.9. Further texts on Cecrops: Herodotus 7.44; Aristophanes, *Wasps*, 438, *Wealth*, 773, with schol.; Eupolis; *Kolakes*, F159 K-A; Euripides, *Ion*, 1163–5; 'Antiochus-Pherecydes', *FGrH* 333 F1; Thucydides 2.15; Xenophon, *Memorabilia*, 3.5.10; Philochorus, *FGrH* 328 F93–8; Clearchus of Soli F73 Wehrli (*apud* Athenaeus 555d); Callimachus, *Iambi* 4 F194 line 68 Pf.; *Marmor Parium* (264/263 BC), *FGrH* 239 A1; Varro *apud* Augustine, *City of God*, 18.9; Diodorus 1.28.7; Cicero, *Laws*, 2.63; Ovid, *Metamorphoses*, 2.555; Pliny, *Natural History*, 7.194; Plutarch; *Moralia*, 551ef; Tacitus, *Annals*, 11.14.2; Hyginus, *Fabulae*, 48, 158 (in the latter chapter making Cecrops a son of Vulcan/Hephaestus, seemingly in confusion with Ericthonius); Pausanias 1.5.3, 8.2.2–3; Justin 2.6.7; Nonnus, *Dionysiaca*, 41.58–64; Hesychius, s.vv. Δράκαυλος, ἐν δ' Αἴθυια (the younger Cecrops?); Georgius Harmatolus, *Chronicon*, 1.30 (ix AD); *Suda* s.vv. Δράκαυλος, Κέκροψ, *Etymologicum Magnum* s.v. ἐπακρία χώρα. For discussion of Cecrops see above all Gourmelen, *Kékrops*; cf. also Carl Robert, *Die griechische Heldensage*, 4th ed., 3 vols (Berlin: Verlag der Akademie der Wissenschaften, 1920–1926), i, 137–40; Kron, *Die zehn attischen Phylenheroen*, 84–103; Kearns, *The Heroes of Attica*, 80–91, 110–2, 175–6; Parker, 'Myths of Early Athens'; Irmgard Kasper-Butz, Ingrid Krauskopf and Brigitte Knittlmayer, 'Kekrops,' in *LIMC*, vi.1 (1992), 1085–91 (NB this article is out of sequence in *LIMC.*); Gantz, *Early Greek Myth*, 223–9; Jan Bollansée, *Hermippos of Smyrna*, in *FGrH*, iv.3 (Leiden: Brill, 1999), 121–4; Yulia Ustinova, 'Snake-Limbed and Tendril-Limbed Goddesses in the Art and Mythology of the Mediterranean and the Black Sea,' in *Scythians and Greeks: Cultural Interactions in Scythia, Athens and the Early Roman Empire (sixth century BC – first century AD)*, ed. David B. Braund (Exeter: University of Exeter Press, 2005), 75; Ogden, *Drakōn*, 259–63.

45 *LIMC* Kekrops, 1–3, 6 (490–80 BC), 7–10, 16, 24–5, 28, 34; cf. Gourmelen, *Kékrops*, figs 9–12, 14–6. For the iconography of Cecrops in general, see *LIMC* Kekrops, Kron 1976: 259–62 and Gourmelen, *Kékrops*, 457–66.

46 *LIMC* Kekrops, 13–4, 17–22, 23 (ca. 480 BC), 26–7, 29, 30 (480–70 BC), 31, 33, 36–40.

47 See Gourmelen, *Kékrops*, 317–21.

48 Cecrops was probably familiarly associated with the epithet already by the time (ca. 425 BC) that Herodotus (4.9) applied the term to the identically anguipede Scythian Echidna. Gourmelen, *Kékrops*, 31–8, 43, is too sceptical in his pious insistence that we cannot be sure that the term was applied to Cecrops pior to the first century BC Caster of Rhodes *FGrH* 250 F4.

49 Clearchus of Soli F73 Wehrli apud Athenaeus 555d; cf. Nonnus, *Dionysiaca*, 41.383–4.

50 Discussion at Ogden, *Greek Bastardy*, 32–216, esp. 180–8; Gourmelen, *Kékrops*, 43, 100–5.

51 The *Suda* s.vv. Κέκροψ, Προμηθεύς and schol. Aristophanes, *Wealth*, 773 (cf. Philochorus *FGrH* 328 F93–8; *diphyēs* at 96). Curiously, the *Suda* and the scholia also offer the variant

theory that Cecrops embodied the institution of marriage he invented by virtue of being a man above and not a snake but a woman below. For Cecrops as Athens' first lawmaker see further Hermippus of Smyrna F82 Wehrli = FGrH 1026 F3, Xenophon, *Memorabilia*, 3.5.10; Callimachus *Iambi*, 4 F194 line 68 Pf. and Pausanias 8.2.2–3. Discussion at Gourmelen, *Kékrops*, 239–45; Phillip Harding, *The Story of Athens: The Fragments of the Local Chronicles of Attica* (London: Routledge, 2008), 194.

52 Cratinus F300 K-A, *IG* i³ 104 (decree of 409 BC referring to the homicide law); Lysias F40b Carey; Andocides 1.83 (quoting decree of 403 BC); Xenophon, *Oeconomicus*, 14.4; Aristotle, *Politics*, 1274b, *Rhetoric*, 1400b; Aristotle, *Constitution of Athens*, 4.1, 7.1, 41.2 (clear statements of Draco's role as the first writer of laws for Athens; his homicide law and his constitution); Demosthenes 23.51 (homicide law), 47.71; Demades F23 de Falco; Plutarch, *Solon*, 17 (homicide law); Tatian, *Against the Hellenes*, 41; Pausanias 9.36; Clement of Alexandria, *Stromateis*, 1.80.1; Pollux, *Onomasticon*, 8.42, 8.125, 9.61. See Eberhard Ruschenbusch, '*Phonos*. Zum Recht Drakons und seiner Bedeutung für das Werden des athenischen Staates,' *Historia* 9 (1960): 129–54; Ronald S. Stroud, *Drakon's Law on Homicide* (Berkeley: University of California Press, 1968); Michael Gagarin, *Drakon and Early Athenian Homicide Law*, Yale Classical Monographs 3 (New Haven: Yale University Press, 1981); Peter J. Rhodes, *Commentary on the Aristotelian Athenaion Politeia* (Oxford: Oxford University Press, 1981), 109–18; Edwin Carawan, *Rhetoric and the Law of Draco* (Oxford: Clarendon Press, 1998).

53 Aristotle, *Rhetoric*, 1400b. On the other side of the equation, we may note Plutarch's observation (*Moralia*, 551ef) that 'the ancients called Cecrops *diphyēs*, not, as some say, because from being a good king he became a fierce and *drakōn*-like tyrant, but for the opposite reason, because he was originally twisted and fearsome, but later on ruled gently and humanely'.

54 Herodotus 8.41. Hesychius and Photius, *Lexicon* s.v. οἰκουρὸν ὄφιν, Eustathius on Homer, *Odyssey*, 1.357 and perhaps, too, schol. Aristophanes, *Lysistrata*, 759 make the creature more specifically the guardian 'of [sc. Athene] Polias', whose shrine was located in the Erectheum. Discussion at Bodson, ἱερὰ ζῷα, 78-9, eadem, 'Nature et fonction des serpents d'Athéna,' in Pierre Lévêque hon., Marie-Madeleine Mactoux and Evelyne Geny, eds., *Mélanges Pierre Lévêque*, 9 vols (Paris: Belles Lettres, 1988–95), iv, 45–63; Jean-Marie Pailler, 'La vierge et le serpent. De la trivalence à l'ambiguïté,' *Mélanges de l'École française de Rome. Antiquité* 109 (1997): 535–49; Gourmelen, *Kékrops*, 342–8.

55 *P.Oxy.* 2332 lines 51-3; cf. Tom W. Hillard, 'The *Agathos Daimon* abandons Alexandria: the Potter's Oracle and possible Roman Allusions,' in *Ancient History in a Modern University: 1. The Ancient Near East, Greece and Rome*, ed. Tom W. Hillard et al. (Grand Rapids: Eerdmans, 1998), 160–72.

56 The evidence is collected at Ogden, *Drakōn*, 350–9.

57 Ogden, *Drakōn*, 347–50.

58 Propertius 4.8.2–14; Aelian; *Nature of Animals;* 11.16; cf. *De promissionibus* (*PL* 51, 835) for an intriguing Christian take on the fate of the blindfolded girls in this cult.
59 Pausanias 6.20.2–6.
60 Pausanias 1.36.1. Aeschylus' reference to 'Cychrean shores' at *Persae* 570 may already express an awareness of this tale; so thinks Gourmelen, *Kékrops*, 401. But the traditions of Cychreus more generally are complex: sometimes he is portrayed rather as the (humanoid) keeper of a serpent; at other times actually as the (humanoid) slayer of a destructive serpent. See Hesiod F226 MW; Euphorion F30 Powell = 32 Lightfoot; Lycophron, *Alexandra*, 110–4 (curiously merging Cychreus with Cecrops); Diodorus 4.72.4; Strabo C393; Plutarch, *Solon*, 9; Apollodorus, *Bibliotheca*, 3.12.7; Stephanus of Byzantium *s.v.* Κυχρεῖος πάγος of B; Tzetzes, schol. on Lycophron, *Alexandra*, 110, 175, 451; Eustathius, *Commentary on Dionysius Periegetes*, 506–7 (*GGM* ii, 314). For discussion, see Harrison, *Themis*, 286–8; Marie Delcourt, 'Cychreus,' *Revue de l'histoire des religions* 148 (1955): 129–40; Kearns, *The Heroes of Attica*, 180; Gourmelen, *Kékrops*, 401–3; Ogden, *Drakōn*, 267–9.

3. THE PEOPLE & THE STATE IN EARLY ROME

James H. Richardson

THE PEOPLE & THE STATE IN EARLY ROME

Countries and states — that is, sovereign states under a single government — are today by and large synonymous, and they are also both generally taken for granted. This is still the case, even though the country, which is actually a relatively recent invention, is arguably starting to look out of date in some respects (think, for instance, of the exploitation by multinational companies of workers in countries with a low, or no, legal minimum wage; think too of the moving of profits offshore, and of tax havens and what their use means; or, for a positive example, think of the European Union). In antiquity, there were no countries. The main political structure in the Classical world, or at least the one which is the most prevalent in modern discussion and in the modern imagination more generally, was the individual city-state. The most famous of those are of course Athens, Sparta and Rome, although there were a great many others. Each of these cities was a state in its own right, with its own laws and customs, its own citizen populace, its own territory and so on.

When it comes to the question of how cities came into existence, the Romans had really quite specific ideas, and since, in antiquity, cities were usually city-*states*, these Roman ideas were as much concerned with the establishment of states as they were with the actual cities themselves. First of all, cities were usually founded at a precise moment in time and usually by one individual, or so the Romans believed (and they were not alone in this). In the case of Rome, that individual was Romulus, and the moment in time was 21 April, 753 BC.[1]

In order to found his city (and founders were usually, although not always, men), the founder needed to perform a variety of rituals, the precise details of which differ somewhat from account to account. What appears to have been the most important of these rituals required the founder to plough a ditch around the site where the city was to be built, using a pair of oxen, one male and one female, and a plough fitted with a bronze ploughshare.[2] Since this ditch supposedly marked out the location of the walls of the city (and, some said, it also marked out the city's sacred boundary, the *pomerium*), the founder had to lift the ploughshare out of the ground wherever he wanted to have a gate in the city wall, and carry it over to where the wall was to begin again. This idea led to the questionable derivation of the word for a gate, *porta*, from the verb to carry, *portare*.[3]

According to the account of Marcus Terentius Varro, a Roman antiquarian of the first century BC, this ploughing ritual was, it would appear, absolutely fundamental to a city being a city. Varro's argument, however, is scarcely persuasive. He supposed that cities (*urbes*) were so-called after the circle (*orbis*) made by the furrow that the founder ploughed around the site of his city, and after the *urvum*, the curved part (the plough-beam) of the plough that he used to make this furrow.[4]

What this particular ritual presupposes, obviously enough, is a very clear idea from the outset, not only of where the city itself should be built and where its boundaries should be (and consequently how big it would be), but also where the gates, and so also the roads that went through them, should be located. All this requires a considerable amount of planning, as well as some awareness of the wider geographical, political and even economic landscape.[5] More than that, it probably also requires a certain manner of thinking and a certain type of knowledge, that is, the sort of thinking and knowledge which can readily be expected of an urban dweller, but which are perhaps less easily expected of someone used only to life in some sort of pre-urban settlement, and which are hardly to be expected at all of someone who does not even lead a sedentary life.

After his furrow had been ploughed, the founder — since he was founding a city-*state* — would usually draw up a law-code, create a senate, perhaps establish a political assembly of some kind, create a citizen populace, enrol an army and so on.[6] In the case of Rome, various developments of a constitutional nature took place during the course of the regal period and during republican times too, but the Roman state itself nonetheless clearly started with Romulus.[7]

THE PEOPLE & THE STATE IN EARLY ROME

Indeed, some ancient writers took for granted the existence of citizenship, elections and even magistracies during Romulus' reign.[8] Once again, all this presupposes a significant amount of planning, as well as the existence of a range of sometimes fully developed social and political ideas, including of course the very idea of a state and, along with it, the idea of citizenship.

If these Roman ideas about the formation of city-states are assessed in the context of much later times and of the founding by the Romans of something like an autonomous colony, there are no significant difficulties with them. But if they are assessed in the context of the origins of the earliest city-states of Italy, of which Rome was one, they are quite obviously problematic. How could the very first founders have come to possess all the knowledge and expertise that these ideas presupposed they had? Recently, Andrea Carandini — an Italian archaeologist who has managed to convince himself that the foundation myth of Rome is actually historical — has hit upon a possible solution.[9]

According to Varro, the ploughing ritual was — despite Varro's various Latin etymologies — actually Etruscan, and the Greek writer Plutarch, in his biography of Romulus, says that Romulus summoned people from Etruria to instruct him.[10] Carandini says: 'Romulus sent for priests from Etruria, from whom he learned how to found an *urbs* (which implies the prior foundation of *urbes* on the right bank of the Tiber [that is, in Etruria, since Etruria was to the north of Rome and so on the Tiber's right bank]).'[11] This, however, only really pushes the problem back in time: when and how did the Etruscans learn how to found an *urbs*? Moreover, since the ritual was believed — rightly or wrongly — to be Etruscan, it would be a very easy assumption to make that Romulus must have turned to the Etruscans for help (as the Romans in later times did on occasion for various issues). This is actually an unnecessary assumption, since the city of Alba Longa, from whose kings Romulus was said to have been descended, was also an *urbs*.[12] It would, therefore, be comparable (certainly as far as the value of the evidence goes) to suppose that Romulus could have learnt how to found an *urbs* from his own family.[13] Furthermore, the ruling house of Alba Longa was allegedly descended from the Trojan hero Aeneas and, according to Virgil, in his epic poem the *Aeneid*, Aeneas certainly knew how to perform the ploughing ritual, as did — or so it is implied — the settlers from Tyre who founded the north African city of Carthage.[14] It would seem that the details of this supposedly Etruscan ritual were very widely known, or so the Romans could assume; clearly they just took the performance of this ritual for granted, no matter how improbable the results.

When it comes to the supposed foundation of Rome, none of this evidence, the story of the Etruscan priests included, is of any historical value whatsoever, not least because the very idea of a 'foundation', prior to which Rome did not exist and after which Rome did, is unhistorical. And, it hardly needs to be said, Romulus is himself an entirely mythical figure. He simply did not exist. What this evidence does show, however, is just how ingrained the idea of the city-state was in the Roman mindset (as the country perhaps is in the contemporary mindset), and this has quite significant implications for the nature of the evidence (see below).

It may come as no surprise that it has long been argued that Roman ideas about the way cities were founded actually developed at a much later date. It appears that they developed out of Roman colonising activities (and note in the fully developed version of the story, Rome was a colony, of Alba Longa). While the Romans may have come to believe that they founded their colonies in the same way Romulus had supposedly founded Rome, it is much more likely that they simply assumed that the rituals they used to found their colonies had been performed when Rome was founded.[15] Although, it must be said, not everyone agrees with that.[16]

In contrast to the idea that Rome was founded at a specific moment — indeed on a specific day — sometime in the mid-eighth century, the archaeological evidence shows that the site of Rome had actually been inhabited from a considerably earlier date and, more importantly, that the settlement and later city had developed over a long period.[17] Even without such evidence, it is reasonable enough to expect that the city and state of Rome took some time to develop, although that expectation is obviously difficult to reconcile with the ancient idea of a precise and dateable act of foundation. Under these circumstances, the only way in which the cake can be had and

eaten too is to reduce the act of 'founding' a city to little more than a ritual and/or political undertaking, something that could even be carried out inside an existing settlement, thus potentially marking out some part of that settlement from the rest of the surrounding community.

So it is that Carandini, who very much wants to have his cake as well as eat it (and in more ways than one, since his approach involves defending certain, selected ancient accounts of the foundation of Rome, while also effectively rewriting those accounts to solve all the problems that that initial defence creates), claims that the founding of Rome essentially amounted only to 'the invention of a new form of organization and government'.[18] Thus — contrary to what the ancient sources imagine — what Romulus did, Carandini claims, 'involved not the realization of any plans for a city but a series of ceremonial acts and sacred prohibitions that instilled into the soil and the people a will to power expressed from the start in forms that we might term "modern" — that is, juridical, political, governmental, constitutional — masked but not negated by sacred and holy institutions'.[19]

But this approach just does not work. The story has Romulus found his city on essentially uninhabited land.[20] The literary evidence for his supposed foundation of Rome on the Palatine hill in the mid-eighth century BC cannot, therefore, be made to fit with the archaeological evidence for the much earlier and more extensive inhabitation of the site of Rome. Carandini's response to this objection is, typically, to dismiss those details in the literary evidence that do not fit with his reconstruction; hence, in this instance, he claims that 'Rome had to have arisen from nothingness [in the Roman accounts] so that Romulus's achievement could appear to have happened without prior groundwork and constitute a miracle: the founding'.[21] That, however, directly contradicts the ancient story (which Carandini, in this particular case, wants to retain) that Romulus had to call on the Etruscans to show him what to do. Why was that detail also not completely excised? There is nothing miraculous in following someone else's instructions.[22]

As for the political and, it could almost be said, 'constitutional' side of things, and the supposed establishment of the state, the details are quite clearly anachronistic. The very idea of a state — that is, of an organised political community under a single government — also had to develop, and there is similarly evidence which suggests that this too was something that took time, and, moreover, was something that was variously asserted and contested in a number of different ways (see below).

What all this means is that, unfortunately, what the Romans have to say about the origins of their city-state is largely unusable, simply because it takes for granted the existence of the city-state from the moment of Rome's supposed foundation and, even more improbably, presupposes the existence of the very idea of the city-state even before the creation of the city or state itself (although these are not the only reasons why the use of the literary evidence is extremely difficult). Once Rome had been founded, as far as later Romans were concerned — at least, those who wrote and whose works have survived — Rome existed as a city-state, with a citizen body, various political structures and so on. There are further consequences of this approach too.

At the time when the first city-states of central Italy were starting to come into existence, other social groupings and political organisations already existed in the region, and indeed continued to exist. The first city-states did not, after all, appear from nowhere and out of nothing, as the archaeological evidence shows. It is not unreasonable to suppose that some of these other groupings and organisations may have been directly threatened by the emergence of the city-state, and that some may have also even threatened the first, fledgling city-states.

In the Roman literary tradition, however, the city-state is not just taken for granted, it generally predominates (and this is something which has, in turn, cast a long shadow over modern scholarship, and continues to do so in some quarters even to this day). Not only does Rome simply come into existence when Romulus founds it but, as noted earlier, Romulus himself is also connected with another, much older city-state, Alba Longa. Alba Longa was said to have been founded by Ascanius who, like his father Aeneas, had come from the city of Troy.[23] Furthermore, when it came to his education, the young Romulus supposedly went to school in the nearby city of Gabii (note, as well, that this presupposes that there was no school where he was raised, presumably because the site of Rome was, according to the story, essentially all pasture).[24] It is no wonder, then, that Romulus can so easily conceive of founding a city, and subsequently do so; he supposedly lived in a world where city-states had long existed and were the norm. This is obviously because later Romans just took the idea of the city-state for granted.

The almost inevitable result of all this is that, should the literary evidence happen to contain any material that may potentially shed some light on those various social groups and political organisations that predated and possibly even rivalled the earliest city-states (and this is an extremely difficult proposition: no one wrote history at Rome until the late third century BC), that material is quite likely to have been reshaped in various ways on account of later Roman assumptions and to conform with later expectations.[25] There is a further difficulty: any attempt to identify such material and to take that reshaping into account will usually and almost unavoidably result in a circular argument. Fortunately, however, there is some helpful archaeological evidence, and this evidence has the distinct advantage that it is contemporary.

In the late 1970s, archaeologists carrying out excavations at the site of the temple of Mater Matuta in Satricum, a city that lay to the south of Rome, found a slab of stone on which an inscription had been written. The stone had been reused in the construction of the temple, and that reuse means that the inscription must date to some time earlier than the construction work, so to about 500 BC at the latest.[26]

The inscription is a dedication to the god Mamars (Mars) by a group of individuals who called themselves the *suodales* of Poplios Valesios (the *sodales* of Publius Valerius, in Classical Latin). The word *sodales*, 'companions', could be used in a number of contexts including, perhaps most significantly, the military. Whatever the precise context of the word's use in the inscription (which does, note, record a dedication to Mars), the inscription provides evidence for a group of individuals who defined themselves with reference simply, and entirely, to another person.[27]

There is a small body of further evidence which seems to fit with this idea of an individual and his companions. The bulk of it is literary, and so from much later times, which means that its value and use are extremely problematic. Much of it consists of stories of prominent individuals who move from one city to another (usually their destination is Rome, but that is doubtless because the literary evidence focuses on Rome), and who take with them large numbers of followers. If these followers thought of themselves in any way as belonging to, or even as citizens of, the city-state they were leaving behind, then presumably their ties to their leader were greater.

It is on account of this and other evidence for mobility that archaic Rome has been called an 'open city',[28] although it may be anachronistic to make anything much of this. When city-states were still comparatively new, and indeed still developing, and when urban lifestyles were new along with them, and when the concept of citizenship, of belonging to a city-state, was equally new, or only starting to emerge,[29] the idea that a city could be 'closed', in the sense of having a definite and fixed body of citizens or of simply refusing to admit immigrants, may conceivably have been more novel than the idea that one could be 'open'.

One such story of mobility which, it has recently been argued by Fausto Zevi may have been recorded in a near-contemporary source, involved a man called Lucumo. Lucumo was said to have been the son of a Corinthian merchant called Demaratus who had settled in the Etruscan city of Tarquinii. After his father died, Lucumo left Tarquinii and moved to Rome, taking with him all his family's wealth and all his followers.[30] Another equally famous but much more difficult story involved a man called Attus Clausus. He was also said to have migrated to Rome, in his case from Inregillus, a Sabine town, and he similarly took with him very large numbers of followers.[31]

The story of Lucumo has further significance because, after he moved to Rome and after the incumbent king of Rome, Ancus Marcius, had died, Lucumo managed to succeed him. He became Rome's fifth king, Lucius Tarquinius. ('Lucumo' was Romanised as 'Lucius', and Lucumo took the name 'Tarquinius' from the city of his birth.)[32] As far as the Romans were concerned,

this was nothing extraordinary. Their monarchy, they believed, had never been hereditary, and most of their kings had supposedly come from elsewhere.[33] It may be that the model of powerful men (men like Poplios Valesios, Attus Clausus, as well as Demaratus, and obviously also Lucumo) and their followers provides an explanation for any number of Rome's kings.[34]

It is in this same context that the word *sodalis* reappears too, although it does so in a text from the first century AD, so extreme caution is needed.[35] The emperor Claudius gave a speech, the text of which has been partially preserved in an inscription that was found in Lyons in 1528, in which he argued in favour of allowing Gauls from Gallia Comata into the Senate. As part of his case, he pointed out that Rome had always been open to outsiders, and he illustrated this with several examples, one of which is particularly important. According to Claudius:

> If we follow our Roman sources, [Servius Tullius, Rome's sixth king] was the son of Ocresia, a prisoner of war; if we follow Etruscan sources, he was once the most faithful companion (*sodalis fidelissimus*) of Caelius Vivenna and took part in all his adventures. Subsequently, driven out by a change of fortune, he left Etruria with all the remnants of Caelius' army (*Caelianus exercitus*) and occupied the Caelian hill [in Rome], naming it thus after his former leader. Servius changed his name (for in Etruscan his name was Mastarna), and was called by the name I have used, and he obtained the throne (*regnum*) to the greatest advantage of the state (*res publica*).[36]

In this story too there is a prominent individual, Caelius Vivenna (or Caeles Vibenna, as he is usually known), and his followers, at least one of whom, Mastarna, is called a *sodalis*. Like Lucumo, Mastarna allegedly became king at Rome after moving there from Etruria; in his case, he changed his name to Servius Tullius, who was Rome's sixth king (which makes him Mastarna Lucumo's successor). It has been argued that Caeles Vibenna may have ruled Rome too, for a time, although he is not included in the canonical list of kings.

But that list unrealistically had a total of just seven kings, even though Rome's regal period supposedly lasted for two and a half centuries, so there are good grounds for supposing that Rome had other, otherwise unknown rulers.[37]

Claudius also speaks of Caeles' army, and it may be that the term *sodales* is applicable here too, to the soldiers in that army, or at least to some of them, those who were closest to their leader. The army, in any case, was *Caeles'* army (*Caelianus exercitus*, says Claudius), and what was left of it following a setback of some kind and the death of Caeles — both of which are usually inferred from Claudius' account — appears to have been passed on to Mastarna. This is quite clearly not the army of the city-state of Vulci, the 'hometown' of Caeles Vibenna; it is Caeles Vibenna's own personal army. These are his men, and subsequently they become Mastarna's.[38]

What Claudius has to say about Caeles Vibenna and his most faithful companion, by chance, gets some support from a fourth-century BC Etruscan tomb painting from Vulci, which depicts a naked and bound 'Caile Vipinas' being freed by 'Macstrna' (the figures are identified by inscriptions).[39] This certainly fits perfectly well with the Etruscan context that Claudius mentions and seems to confirm the friendship between the two men, although it does not necessarily verify anything else, or even those details. The painting is still more than two hundred years later than the purported events.[40]

As the city of Rome developed, another type of group appears to have emerged, if it did not already exist; these were the *gentes* (the singular form is *gens*; the word is often translated as 'clan'). A *gens* was essentially a group of people who shared a common *nomen*, which is the second part of a Roman's name (so, in the case of Gaius Julius Caesar, Julius is the *nomen*, so Julius Caesar belonged to the *gens Julia*). There was a notional idea that each *gens* ultimately originated from one individual, but these individuals are usually mythical (the *gens Julia*, for instance, claimed descent from Iulus, who was Ascanius, the son of Aeneas), and the extent to which individuals from different branches of the same *gens* were actually biologically related to one another is unclear. It is, however, unlikely that they were.[41]

It used to be believed that the *gentes* existed before the city-state, but the more prevalent view today is that they probably developed at about the same time.⁴² That does not mean, however, that they were necessarily all developing in the same direction.⁴³ It may also be the case that clear distinctions should not be imposed between individuals and their *sodales* and the *gentes*.⁴⁴ *Gentes* too, or at least some of them, may perhaps have once also had individual leaders. Attus Clausus, the man who took all his followers to Rome, changed his name once he got there to Appius Claudius. The story explains the origins of the *gens Claudia* at Rome. Having said all that, the evidence does generally suggest that the *gentes* were acephalous, certainly in historical times.

The *gentes* were powerful groups who appear to have long been able to pursue their own agendas, and even behave in ways that may have been contrary to the idea of the state. The best example is found in the story of the private war that was said to have been waged by the *gens Fabia* with the Etruscan city of Veii (or, more likely, just with a rival group based in that city). The evidence for this war is, however, deeply problematic, and it has long been recognised that the story of the Fabii's expedition has been modelled on the famous, and essentially contemporary, exploits of the 300 Spartans at Thermopylae; like the Spartans, the Fabii were 300 or so in number and, like the Spartans, they were all killed, and the parallels do not stop there.

Whether or not it is possible to strip away all the parallels between these two episodes, and whether or not anything of value would be left if they were removed, is anyone's guess.⁴⁵ Yet it may be that the story is not wholly fabricated, simply because it fits so poorly with all those assumptions about the Roman state and its army (namely that both had been created by Romulus, and so existed from his day onwards). It is telling that it is also possible to detect various attempts to harmonise the story of the Fabii's campaign with those assumptions. In the account of the historian Diodorus, for instance, the Romans fought a great battle with the people of Veii in which they were defeated; among the dead were the 300 Fabii.⁴⁶ The private war of the Fabii is thus effectively made, in Diodorus' version, into an affair of the state.

The power and influence of the *gentes* can be seen as well in the Roman tribal system. Rome's territory came to be divided up into regions called *tribus* ('tribes'). The earliest of these were named after *gentes*. One was called the *tribus Fabia*, the Fabian tribe, and it has been suggested that this tribe should be located in the direction of Veii, on the principle that the 300 Fabii were fighting to defend their own land. It is reasonable to infer that the tribes were named after those who dominated the land in question, and that cannot have been the state.[47] Later on, however, when Roman territory expanded and new tribes were created, they were instead named after geographical features.

The first of these new tribes seems to have been the *tribus Clustumina*, following the defeat of Crustumeria; it was perhaps created in 495 BC, if the literary evidence can be trusted.[48] Whether or not it can, it is significant that no further tribes were said to have been added for over a century, which is a considerable period of time. Four were created in 387 BC, then two each in 358, 332, 318, 299 and 241, and these tribes were almost all given geographical names.[49] Clearly, by this time, the state had become more powerful and so tribes ceased to be named after *gentes*.

From this necessarily brief and patchy overview it is possible to see that, alongside the developing city-state of Rome, there appear to have existed other social and political groups, and it seems that these groups could, for some time, act entirely independently of the state, if they so chose, even when they were based at Rome. The most obvious conclusions to draw from this are that the Roman state was at first under-developed and comparatively weak, and also that not everyone subscribed to the idea of it.

The difficulty then is working out why, how, and when the state and the idea of being a part of it and belonging to it — so, essentially, citizenship — became firmly established and more influential than, say, adherence to a man like Poplios Valesios or Attus Clausus, and also why, how and when those men themselves came to commit to the idea of the state, and to the idea that they too were citizens of it.

These questions are, not surprisingly, unanswerable in any precise way, not just because the city and state of Rome were not 'founded' at some particular moment in time, but also because the evidence is simply insufficient

to answer questions of this kind in anything other than the most general of terms. The only contemporary evidence is the archaeological evidence, and archaeological evidence can only very rarely be used to answer questions about political ideas and practices. This is part of the reason why Carandini has ended up having to draw increasingly on the literary evidence for Romulus' foundation of Rome, although he thinks that that evidence is reliable, or at least that some of it is. Not only does Carandini's selective handling of the literary evidence and his need to reconcile it with the archaeological evidence (which points in a different direction) undermine his approach, but the basic assumption that the literary evidence for Romulus and the foundation of Rome sheds light on the origins of Rome is simply untenable.

Contemporary textual evidence is what is really needed, but barely a handful of inscriptions from archaic Rome have been discovered and only two of those are relevant to questions pertaining to the state, and even then only vaguely so. What makes those two inscriptions relevant is simply that some form of the word *rex* ('king') appears on them. Moreover, one of the inscriptions was carved on a stone stele that was set up in the Forum, and the very act of setting up such a monument is in itself highly significant, while the other inscription is on a fragment of a bucchero cup that was found at the site of a building known as the Regia (the regal connotations are clear from the name).[50] Nonetheless, while this evidence confirms that Rome had in fact once been ruled by kings,[51] and while it also helps to reveal something of the wider context, its value is somewhat more limited than it may seem at first sight.

The ideas associated with the word '*rex*' evidently changed over time,[52] and this makes it very difficult to use any of the evidence (viz. the writings of Rome's historians, antiquarians and so on) for the king's position in the state, simply because that evidence dates to the second and first centuries BC and, in some cases, even later still. That evidence was also written under the belief that the Roman state, of which the king was said to have been a central part, existed from the time of the city's foundation and that Rome's first king was Romulus. The inscriptional evidence certainly proves that Rome had once been ruled by individuals whose title was *rex*, but it does not prove that these kings had the powers, status or position in the state that later writers claimed they had, nor that the state itself existed to the extent or in the way that those writers assumed it did.

A further piece of evidence, which can to a certain extent be treated as contemporary, lends some support to this conclusion. Some time supposedly in the late sixth century BC the Romans made a treaty with the city of Carthage. The treaty itself does not survive but, fortunately enough, the Greek historian Polybius saw the text of it on a bronze tablet and — with the help of some learned Romans who were able, for the most part, to decipher the archaic Latin in which it was written — included a translation of it in his work.[53] The treaty shows that, by this time, Roman influence spread over parts of Latium, the region to the south of Rome. More significantly, the oath that was sworn when this treaty was made was sworn by only one individual and the divine punishment envisaged in that oath, should the treaty be broken, was to be meted out only to that same individual. Polybius' account of the oath has been rejected by modern scholars, precisely because it does not involve the state, but that is to beg the question. The account Polybius provides fits perfectly with the evidence discussed so far, which suggests that individuals could dominate Rome and that the state was weak by comparison.[54]

The difficulties involved in tracing the emergence of the Roman city-state have also been made worse by problems of methodology. One approach for identifying the moment when Rome qualifies as a city-state has been to begin with questions of definition and with establishing a set of criteria that will allow for that moment to be identified.[55] As these criteria are themselves a matter of debate, the date inevitably changes with the criteria. Under these circumstances, the value of any attempt to identify some point in time when Rome can be called a city-state is naturally limited. The same applies, *mutatis mutandis*, to trying to identify the moment when some sense of allegiance to the state came to the fore, and when the idea of citizenship developed.

Despite all these difficulties (and equally, because of them) a good number of hypotheses about the formation of the Roman city and state have been entertained.[56] Outside influences, such as trade, warfare and the influence of

the cities of the Greek world (which included southern Italy) on the development of the Italic city-states in general have been frequently discussed. The role of internal factors has also been included in the debate, although the evidence for them is often especially difficult.

Trade with outside peoples usually leaves traces in the archaeological record, the context of which often also reveals something of the distribution of wealth and of social stratification, while something like the construction of defensive works or the destruction of a settlement is also often visible archaeologically. Evidence for developments driven by internal social, political or economic factors, on the other hand, can be much more difficult to detect,[57] where such evidence even happens to exist, and more often than not it is unlikely to do so. Again, contemporary textual evidence is what is needed, but there is none from those early times, while the much later literary evidence takes the existence of the city and state from the very outset for granted. Arguments about internal developments and processes are usually therefore of a considerably more theoretical and conjectural nature.

Nicola Terrenato, for instance, has recently argued that it was actually the *gentes* who were responsible for the creation of the Roman state, a proposition which inevitably requires him to address the big question of why they, of all groups, might have done this. To answer this, Terrenato considers the various roles that a city-state could have played in diplomacy, politics, trade and religion, as well as in warfare and domestic conflict. In his view, the state was simply 'one of many political tools that clans [*gentes*] had at their disposal', although, for this argument to work, Terrenato inevitably has to depict Rome as long an extremely weak state. Indeed, he views it as 'a weak and fragile entity' which suffered from 'congenital frailty' and 'inherent instability'; it was in fact nothing more than a puppet of the *gentes*. But this is a picture that may start to seem at odds with Rome's growth and military success.

Moreover, Terrenato's model is entirely top-down, so much so that the state can be described as the *gentes*' 'toy' which 'they felt fully entitled to tear ... apart whenever they grew tired of it'.[58] It may be asked, however, why the Roman people should have gone along with this, and why they should have tolerated the idea that the nascent city-state where they lived and with which they may have identified, and of which they were or were becoming citizens, was little or nothing more than a plaything of the powerful, and potentially a transitory plaything at that, one that could be cast aside at any moment.

The views of the Roman people are, of course, unknown, since there is hardly any evidence for them, and certainly none that is anywhere near contemporary. Even apart from the question of what they may have been prepared to put up with, it would nonetheless be rash simply to deny them any role in the formation of the Roman state, and to suppose that the state's formation was due entirely, or even largely, to the activities of the powerful few, and even more so when the powerful few were the ones who stood to lose the most (even if there were also some potential gains to be made).

As it happens, it may just about be possible to detect something of the role that the people may have played in the formation of the Roman state. The argument does require that all ideas of a 'foundation' moment are dismissed entirely,[59] and much greater prominence be given to the evidence which suggests that the formation of the Roman state was the result of a very lengthy process, one which saw advances as well as steps backwards (or even sideways), and one which was affected in various ways by conflicting needs and ideas. If the case that has been made so far has been at all persuasive, such an approach should not seem problematic in the least.

The main theme, according to the Romans' own accounts, of Roman social and political history during the fifth and fourth centuries BC is the so-called 'conflict (or struggle) of the orders'. The Roman citizen body was, or so the Romans believed, neatly divided into two groups, the patricians and the plebeians; the division is, however, over-schematic and quite probably unhistorical.[60] From the beginning of the republican period (that is, after the kings had been expelled and replaced with elected annual magistrates), the patrician families allegedly dominated the state, as only patricians could hold the magistracies and priesthoods of the state. The phrase 'the conflict of the orders' refers to the struggles of the plebs to gain protection from abuse

at the hands of the rich and powerful, to gain representation in the state, and subsequently to gain access to the state's magistracies and priesthoods.

According to the ancient accounts, the plebs — who made up at least some part of the Roman army and the bulk of the labour force more generally — organised several 'secessions', in which they withdrew from the city, effectively going on strike, in order to force concessions from the patricians. The result of the first of these secessions (in the mid-490s BC) was the creation of a new magistracy, the plebeian tribunate, whose role seems to have been to protect the plebeians and represent their interests.[61] This magistracy was one to which people were elected, and so its creation required the organising of a suitable electoral assembly, one for plebeians only. The plebs supposedly also began to keep official records, although that claim may be anachronistic, for the fifth century at least, but probably for the early fourth too. It was the plebeian movement as well that was said to have been responsible for getting Rome's first ever law-code drafted and set up in public. That was in the mid-fifth century BC.[62]

As far as later writers were concerned, the activities of the plebs looked like they amounted to a state and, since these writers took the existence of the Roman state for granted (it had, after all, been created centuries earlier by Romulus), they conceived of the plebeian movement as leading to the formation of a state within the state. This idea has been carried over into modern scholarship, most notably by Theodor Mommsen in the nineteenth century, and it has been more recently defended by Timothy J. Cornell in his important and influential book *The Beginnings of Rome*.[63]

Cornell's defence of the idea focuses on the question of whether or not the plebeian movement can be viewed as something that can reasonably be called a state. He takes the existence of the wider Roman state for granted.[64] On the one hand, he is absolutely right to do so — it would be extremely difficult, if not even perverse, to argue that the Roman state simply did not exist at all by the early fifth century BC — but, on the other, it may be premature to think that it existed in an uncontested or straightforward manner, or that it was an idea to which everyone fully subscribed.

The private war of the *gens Fabia* was supposedly fought in the early 470s BC, some thirty years after the expulsion of the kings (that was in 510/509 on traditional chronology, with the first elected magistrates supposedly holding office in 509). It has been said that the campaign of the Fabii 'represents one of the last vestiges of an archaic form of social organisation which was probably already in an advanced state of obsolescence'.[65] This may very well be so, although the phrase 'advanced state of obsolescence' is probably something of an overstatement.[66] When it comes to the matter of private wars of this kind, the argument is to a certain extent one from silence; but that silence pertains to earlier times as well as to later, thanks no doubt in part to Roman assumptions about the establishment by Romulus of the Roman army. The argument from silence is therefore an especially difficult one to make. There is, moreover, evidence for behaviour that is not entirely unrelated.

When it comes to those powerful individuals and their followers, they did not just disappear with the Roman monarchy. Attus Clausus was said to have migrated to Rome in the early years of the republican period.[67] There are also various stories of individuals who allegedly sought to establish themselves as kings of Rome, even in republican times. The evidence is, as always, extremely difficult, and it is clear that many of these stories have been heavily modified (if not, in some instances, perhaps even invented outright) at a later date and in light of later events. As with the expedition of the 300 Fabii, it is impossible to know what, if anything, lies behind the evidence as it currently stands, or whether or not it is possible to try to put aside that subsequent manipulation and shaping. Nonetheless, the evidence does have a certain cumulative force and, more significantly, not all of what it suggests fits quite so neatly with the expectations that the literary evidence may otherwise engender.[68]

The most famous of the would-be kings were Spurius Cassius, Spurius Maelius and Marcus Manlius Capitolinus, each of whom was in the end killed for his activities and alleged aspirations, but there were others.[69] Also relevant in this context is the story of Appius Herdonius. Herdonius was a Sabine, like Attus Clausus; like Clausus, he too was said to have gone to Rome although, in his case, he was said to have seized the Capitoline hill in a bid to take over

the city (this was in 460 BC).⁷⁰ He supposedly had with him 2500 followers (or perhaps more), according to the Roman historian Livy, and it may be tempting to think of Caeles Vibenna, his faithful *sodalis* Mastarna, and his army, or of Poplios Valesios and his *sodales*. By 460, however, Rome had been a republic for nearly half a century and the rule of kings was a thing of the past. Herdonius, the aspiring monarch, was out of date; he was automatically bad, and his followers are all cast by Livy as exiles and slaves.⁷¹

It is also possible to think of someone like Marcius Coriolanus, who has been made so very famous in the modern world by Shakespeare's play. Cornell has argued that Coriolanus' career should perhaps be understood in the same general context of powerful, independent individuals who do their own thing, look out only for their own interests, and do not think of themselves as under the authority of any government, or anyone. Consequently, when Coriolanus' activities in Rome did not work out, he simply left and went to join the Volscians.⁷² This too was supposedly in the early fifth century.

The literary evidence for all these individuals and events is extremely problematic. The point does need to be stressed. Nonetheless, this evidence does fit very well with the circumstances implied by the inscription from Satricum and with the evidence (likewise problematic) for powerful individuals from the regal period and for *gentes* that appear to have once been more powerful than the state. The evidence certainly suggests some element of continuity with those times.

While the difficulties with basing an argument on textual evidence written centuries after the events in question need always to be kept in mind, it is worth giving careful consideration to the plebeian movement in the context of state formation. To what extent did the activities of that movement — restricting the actions of the powerful, creating magistracies and an assembly, keeping records, campaigning to get a law-code drafted and published,⁷³ and so on — play a role in the formation of the Roman state? Developments of this kind are just the sort of thing that ought to be expected when a state comes into existence. And, although it is the view of later writers who were drawing on an anachronistic literary tradition, the idea that the plebeian movement itself amounted to a state (albeit within a state) is nevertheless suggestive.

The nature of the evidence, unfortunately, may not allow for the argument to go much further than this, that is, beyond simply suggesting that 'the conflict of the orders' was not just about securing and advancing plebeian rights, but that it may well have also played a role in the formation of the Roman state, in its early stages at least. This possibility is certainly significant, not only in itself and for what it may reveal about the origins of at least one state, and, on its own terms at least, one extremely successful state. It is also significant for contemporary discussion, about states in the twenty-first century, about the roles that they should play, and about their duties and responsibilities, as well as the duties and responsibilities of their citizens. For, in the case of Rome, it may be possible to see something of how the state was created — to some extent — by the people, and for the people, for their protection, to rein in those wealthy and powerful individuals who were concerned only with their own agenda and interests, to get them to adhere to the idea of the state and to behave responsibly towards it and their fellow citizens, as well as to try to address at least some of the inequalities in Roman society.

THE PEOPLE & THE STATE IN EARLY ROME

ENDNOTES

1. According to some, at least; the Greek historian Timaeus put the foundation of Rome in 814 BC, while the Roman historian Q. Fabius Pictor put it in 747 BC, L. Cincius Alimentus in 728, and Cato the Elder in 751 (see Dionysius of Halicarnassus, *Roman Antiquities*, 1.74.1–2). The Roman poets Naevius and Ennius made Romulus the grandson of the Trojan hero Aeneas (Servius Danielis, *Commentary on the Aeneid*, 1.273), while the historian Sallust claimed that Rome was founded by Trojans under the leadership of Aeneas (*The Catilinarian Conspiracy*, 6.1); on that sort of chronology Rome would have been founded in something like the twelfth century BC. See T. Peter Wiseman, *Remus: A Roman Myth* (Cambridge: Cambridge University Press, 1995), 160–8 for 61 different versions of the foundation myth of Rome. These dates, the better known one of 753 included, are all unhistorical; they are not based on evidence, but on various calculations and synchronisms; see Denis Feeney, *Caesar's Calendar: Ancient Time and the Beginnings of History* (Berkeley: University of California Press, 2007), 86–100. Elias Bickerman's classic paper, 'Origines gentium,' *Classical Philology* 47 (1952): 65–81 is also relevant in this context.

2. See Cato, *Origins*, fragment 66 (*FRHist* 5 F 66 = Serv. *Aen.* 5.755; Isid. *Orig.* 15.2.3); Varro, *On the Latin Language*, 5.143. For the performance of this ritual by Romulus, see Dionysius of Halicarnassus, *Roman Antiquities*, 1.88.2; Plutarch, *Life of Romulus*, 11.2–3. Further evidence can be found in Andrea Carandini, ed., *La leggenda di Roma, volume I: dalla nascita dei gemelli alla fondazione della città* (Milan: Arnoldo Mondadori Editore, 2006), 183–219, and also 433–4 on the ritual itself.

3. Isidore, *Origins*, 15.2.5: *ubi portam vult esse, aratrum sustollat et portet, et portam vocet* ('where [the founder] wants there to be a gate, let him lift the plough and carry [*portet*] it, and call it a gate [*portam*]'). Varro, however, thought that gates were named from the carrying of goods through them (*On the Latin Language*, 5.142). See further Robert Maltby, *A Lexicon of Ancient Latin Etymologies* (Leeds: Francis Cairns, 1991), 486.

4. Varro, *On the Latin Language*, 5.143. For further ideas along these and other lines, see the evidence collected in Maltby, *Lexicon*, 655.

5. See the entirely anachronistic discussion in Cicero, *On the State*, 2.5–11 of Romulus' choice of site. But then, Cicero's Romulus lived in a literate and enlightened age, see *On the State*, 2.18–9; cf. T. Peter Wiseman, *Unwritten Rome* (Exeter: Exeter University Press, 2008), 125–6.

6. See, for instance, Virgil's imaginative depiction of the founding of Carthage in book one of the *Aeneid*; at 1.425 there is an allusion to the ploughing ritual; the very next line reads: *iura magistratusque legunt sanctumque senatum* ('they choose laws and magistrates and a venerable senate').

7. Note especially Dionysius of Halicarnassus, *Roman Antiquities*, 2.3–29 (on which, see T. Peter Wiseman, *Remembering the Roman People: Essays on Late-Republican Politics and Literature* [Oxford: Oxford University Press, 2009], 81–98); also Plutarch, *Life of Romulus*, 13; Livy 1.8.1 on

Romulus' establishment of law, 1.8.4–5 on the big, and consequently empty, city that Romulus supposedly built. The literary evidence is collected in Andrea Carandini, ed., *La leggenda di Roma, volume III: la costituzione* (Milan: Arnoldo Mondadori Editore, 2011); see also Gennaro Franciosi, ed., *Leges regiae* (Naples: Jovene Editore, 2003), 3–57.

8   According to Servius, *Commentary on the Aeneid*, 7.709, the Sabines (who came to Rome during Romulus' reign) were made Roman citizens, although they were not given the right to vote, and so they could not elect magistrates; for the election of magistrates in Romulus' day, see also Junius Gracchanus, in Ulpian, *Digest of Justinian*, 1.13.1.*pr.*

9   An overview of Andrea Carandini's ideas about the origins of Rome can be found in his book *Roma: il primo giorno* (Rome-Bari: Editori Laterza, 2007), translated as *Rome: Day One* by Stephen Sartarelli (Princeton: Princeton University Press, 2011). The significance of the title is obvious. For further work by Carandini on this topic in English, see his papers 'Urban Landscapes and Ethnic Identity of Early Rome,' in *Landscape, Ethnicity and Identity in the Archaic Mediterranean Area*, ed. Gabriele Cifani and Simon Stoddart (Oxford: Oxbow Books, 2012), 5–23 and 'The Myth of Romulus and the Origins of Rome,' in *The Roman Historical Tradition: Regal and Republican Rome*, ed. James H. Richardson and Federico Santangelo (Oxford: Oxford University Press, 2014), 17–33.

10 Varro, *On the Latin Language*, 5.143; Plutarch, *Life of Romulus*, 11.1.

11 Carandini, *Rome: Day One*, 50 (= *Roma: il primo giorno*, 44).

12 For Alba Longa as an *urbs*, see, for example, Cicero, *On the State*, 2.4; Livy 1.3.3, 1.29.4–6; Virgil, *Aeneid*, 8.47–8.

13 See Livy 1.7.3 for Romulus performing rituals 'in the Alban manner' (*Albano ritu*).

14 See, for example, *Aeneid*, 5.755: *interea Aeneas urbem designat aratro* ('meanwhile Aeneas marks out the city [*urbem*] with a plough'); for the Tyrians and Carthage, see note 6 above.

15 Some time ago, for example, Ferdinando Castagnoli, 'Roma antica,' in *Topografia e urbanistica di Roma*, ed. Ferdinando Castagnoli et al. (Bologna: Licinio Cappelli Editore, 1958), 3–186, at 9; more recently, Jörg Rüpke, *Religion of the Romans*, trans. Richard Gordon (Cambridge: Polity Press, 2007), 181–2; T. Peter Wiseman, *The Myths of Rome* (Exeter: Exeter University Press, 2004), 141, and 'The Palatine, from Evander to Elagabalus,' *Journal of Roman Studies* 103 (2013): 234–68, at 248. For another example of the Roman tendency to imagine that rituals performed in much later times had been performed from a very early date, see James H. Richardson, 'The Development of the Treaty-Making Rituals of the Romans,' *Hermes*, forthcoming.

16 Carandini aside, see, for instance, Alexandre Grandazzi, '*Vrbem condere*: de la linguistique à l'histoire? À propos de Varron, *ling.*, V, 143,' in *Varietates Fortunae: Religion et mythologie à Rome. Hommage à Jacqueline Champeaux*, ed. Dominique Briquel, Caroline Février, and Charles Guittard (Paris: Presses de l'université Paris-Sorbonne, 2010), 159–73 on the ritual itself.

17 See, for example, Francesca Fulminante, *The Urbanisation of Rome and Latium Vetus, from the Bronze Age to the Archaic Era* (Cambridge: Cambridge University Press, 2014), chapter 3,

THE PEOPLE & THE STATE IN EARLY ROME

although the influence of the work of Carandini and his followers is palpable; on Rome's earliest walls, see Seth G. Bernard, 'Continuing the Debate on Rome's Earliest Circuit Walls,' *Papers of the British School at Rome* 80 (2012): 1–44; the reconstruction and identification of several of the buildings Fulminante discusses are optimistic to say the least; see, for instance, Eric M. Moormann, 'Carandini's Royal Houses at the Foot of the Palatine: Fact or Fiction?' *Bulletin Antieke Beschaving* 76 (2001): 209–12; Wiseman, *Unwritten Rome*, 271–92. See note 56 below as well.

18   Carandini, *Rome: Day One*, 22 (= *Roma: il primo giorno*, 19).
19   Carandini, *Rome: Day One*, 28 (= *Roma: il primo giorno*, 25).
20   See, for example, Livy 1.4.5–9 and 1.6.3, 1.7.3; Tibullus 2.5.55–6: *carpite nunc, tauri, de septem montibus herbas/ dum licet: hic magnae iam locus urbis erit.* ('Graze now, bulls, on the grass from the seven hills/ while it is permitted: this will be the site of a great city.')
21   Carandini, *Rome: Day One*, 27 (= *Roma: il primo giorno*, 25).
22   It may come as no surprise that Carandini's views are extremely controversial; see, for instance, T. Peter Wiseman, 'Reading Carandini,' *Journal of Roman Studies* 91 (2001): 182–93, Wiseman, 'Andrea Carandini and *Roma Quadrata*,' *Accordia Research Papers* 10 (2004–2006): 103–25, and also his *Unwritten Rome*, 271–92; Jonathan M. Hall, *Artifact & Artifice: Classical Archaeology and the Ancient Historian* (Chicago: University of Chicago Press, 2014), 119–43; Moormann, 'Carandini's Royal Houses'.
23   See Livy 1.3.3; Dionysius of Halicarnassus, *Roman Antiquities*, 1.66.1–2. Romulus' grandfather was Numitor, the rightful heir to the throne of Alba Longa; Numitor's position as king of Alba Longa was secured by Romulus and his brother, Remus (for a succinct account, see Livy 1.3.10–6.2). As noted above (see note 14), Virgil has Aeneas found cities using the appropriate ritual.
24   Dionysius of Halicarnassus, *Roman Antiquities*, 1.84.5; Plutarch, *Life of Romulus*, 6.1. For Gabii as an *urbs*, see Livy 1.53.4.
25   On the tendency for Roman writings about the past to be anachronistic, see, for example, T. Peter Wiseman, *Clio's Cosmetics: Three Studies in Greco-Roman Literature* (Leicester: Leicester University Press, 1979), 42–5; Timothy J. Cornell, 'The Value of the Literary Tradition Concerning Archaic Rome,' in *Social Struggles in Archaic Rome: New Perspectives on the Conflict of the Orders*, 2nd edition, ed. Kurt A. Raaflaub (Malden, MA: Blackwell Publishing, 2005), 47–74, at 59–60; Kurt A. Raaflaub, 'From Protection and Defense to Offense and Participation: Stages in the Conflict of the Orders,' in *Social Struggles in Archaic Rome: New Perspectives on the Conflict of the Orders*, 2nd edition, ed. Kurt A. Raaflaub, 185–222, esp. 187–8; James H. Richardson, 'Ancient Historical Thought and the Development of the Consulship,' *Latomus* 67 (2008): 328–41, at 330–3. See also note 15 above.
26   For the inscription, see Conrad M. Stibbe et al., *Lapis Satricanus: Archaeological, Epigraphical, Linguistic and Historical Aspects of the New Inscription from Satricum* (The Hague: Nederlands Instituut te Rome, 1980).

27 The inscription reads: [. . .]IEI STETERAI POPLIOSIO VALESIOSIO SVODALES MAMARTEI ('The companions of Poplios Valesios set this up [?] to Mars'); on *sodales*, see Henk Versnel, 'Historical Implications,' in *Lapis Satricanus: Archaeological, Epigraphical, Linguistic and Historical Aspects of the New Inscription from Satricum*, 97–150, at 108–27, and more recently Versnel, 'IUN]IEI: A New Conjecture in the Satricum Inscription,' *Mededelingen van het Nederlands Instituut te Rome* 56 (1997): 177–97, esp. 181–2.
28 See the classic study of Carmine Ampolo, 'Demarato: Osservazioni sulla mobilità sociale arcaica,' *Dialoghi di Archeologia* 9–10 (1976–77): 333–45; also, for example, Timothy J. Cornell, *The Beginnings of Rome: Italy and Rome from the Bronze Age to the Punic Wars (c. 1000–264 BC)* (London: Routledge, 1995), 157–9, and 'Coriolanus: Myth, History and Performance,' in *Myth, History and Culture in Republican Rome: Studies in Honour of T. P. Wiseman*, ed. David Braund and Christopher Gill (Exeter: University of Exeter Press, 2003), 73–97, at 86–7; Guy Bradley, 'Investigating Aristocracy in Archaic Rome and Central Italy: Social Mobility, Ideology and Cultural Influences,' in *'Aristocracy' in Antiquity: Redefining Greek and Roman Elites*, ed. Nick Fisher and Hans van Wees (Swansea: Classical Press of Wales, 2015), 85–124, at 102–5. Rome's nobility actually long remained open to outsiders; much of the evidence was assembled long ago by Friedrich Münzer, *Römische Adelsparteien und Adelsfamilien* (Stuttgart: J. B. Metzlersche Verlagsbuchhandlung, 1920), 46–97; this openness may have been more extensive than the evidence suggests: most people are usually not visible.
29 As Cornell, *Beginnings*, 158 says, 'such concepts as nationality and citizenship are anachronistic in the context of the seventh and sixth centuries BC'.
30 Livy 1.34; Dionysius of Halicarnassus, *Roman Antiquities*, 3.46.3–48.2. See Fausto Zevi, 'Demaratus and the "Corinthian" Kings of Rome,' in *The Roman Historical Tradition: Regal and Republican Rome*, ed. James H. Richardson and Federico Santangelo (Oxford: Oxford University Press, 2014), 53–82 also for further references to the ancient evidence.
31 Livy 2.16.4–5; Dionysius of Halicarnassus, *Roman Antiquities*, 5.40.3–5; Suetonius, *Life of Tiberius*, 1.1. For references to further evidence and an analysis of the various differences in the several accounts, see Wiseman, *Clio's Cosmetics*, 59–64.
32 Livy 1.34.10, 1.35.1–6; Dionysius of Halicarnassus, *Roman Antiquities*, 3.48.2, 3.49.1.
33 Succinctly stated by the emperor Claudius, *ILS*, 212: *quondam reges hanc tenuere urbem, nec tamen domesticis successoribus eam tradere contigit. supervenere alieni et quidam externi* ('Kings once held this city, yet they were not able to pass it on to successors of their own line. Strangers intervened, and even some foreigners').
34 See, for example, Arnaldo Momigliano, 'The Origins of Rome,' in *The Cambridge Ancient History, Volume VII, Part 2: The Rise of Rome to 220 B.C.*, 2nd edition, ed. F. W. Walbank et al. (Cambridge: Cambridge University Press, 1989), 52–112, at 97–8; Cornell, *Beginnings*, 141–50.
35 See Versnel, 'Historical implications,' 120–1 and Daniele Maras, 'Ancora su Mastarna, *sodalis fidelissimus*,' in *La grande Roma dei Tarquini*, ed. Giuseppe M. Della Fina (Rome: Edizioni Quasar, 2010), 187–200 for optimistic assessments.

36 Claudius, *ILS*, 212: *Servius Tullius, si nostros sequimur, captiva natus Ocresia, si Tuscos, Caeli quondam Vivennae sodalis fidelissimus omnisque eius casus comes, post quam varia fortuna exactus cum omnibus reliquis Caeliani exercitus Etruria excessit, montem Caelium occupavit et a duce suo Caelio ita appellita[vit], mutatoque nomine (nam Tusce Mastarna ei nomen erat) ita appellatus est, ut dixi, et regnum summa cum rei p(ublicae) utilitate optinuit.* The translation is Cornell's (*Beginnings*, 133–4).

37 For Caeles as a possible king, see Andreas Alföldi, *Early Rome and the Latins* (Ann Arbor: University of Michigan Press, 1965), 212–31 (Claudius' story implies that Caeles had died, but there were other versions); a slightly stronger case can be made in favour of Caeles' brother, Aulus Vibenna, see Alföldi's discussion; Cornell, *Beginnings*, 144–5. On the problems in the king-list and the chronology of the regal period see, for example, Olivier de Cazanove, 'La détermination chronographique de la durée de la période royale a Rome,' in *La Rome des premiers siècles: Légende et histoire* (Florence: Leo S. Olschki Editore, 1992), 69–98; Cornell, *Beginnings*, 121–6; Gary Forsythe, *A Critical History of Early Rome, from Prehistory to the First Punic War* (Berkeley: University of California Press, 2005), 98–9; Feeney, *Caesar's Calendar*, 90; various problems were already observed in antiquity, see Cicero, *On the State*, 2.28–9 and Dionysius of Halicarnassus, *Roman Antiquities*, 4.6–7.

38 Cf., for example, Cornell, *Beginnings*, 144, and 'Coriolanus,' 88; Mario Torelli, '*Bellum in privatam curam* (Liv. II, 49, 1). 'Eserciti gentilizi, sodalitates e isonomia aristocratica in Etruria e Lazio arcaici,' in *Miti di guerra, riti di pace. La guerra e la pace: un confronto interdisciplinare*, ed. Concetta Masseria and Donato Loscalzo (Bari: Edipuglia, 2011), 225–34, at 230.

39 For the frescoes, see Anna Maria Moretti Sgubini, ed., *Eroi etruschi e miti greci: gli affreschi della Tomba François tornano a Vulci* (Calenzano: Edizioni Cooperativa Archeologia, 2004), and especially the chapter in the same volume by Bernard Andreae, 'La Tomba François ricostruita,' 41–57, at 52–4; further bibliography can be found in James H. Richardson, 'Andreas Alföldi and the Adventure(s) of the Vibenna Brothers,' in *Andreas Alföldi in the Twenty-First Century*, ed. James H. Richardson and Federico Santangelo (Stuttgart: Franz Steiner Verlag, 2015), 111–30.

40 On the handling of the evidence for Caeles Vibenna, see Richardson, 'Adventure(s)'.

41 See Christopher Smith, *The Roman Clan: The Gens from Ancient Ideology to Modern Anthropology* (Cambridge: Cambridge University Press, 2006), on the *gentes* in general, and 32–44 on mythical ancestors; see also Christian Kvium, 'Identifying Identities: Some Thoughts about *gentes* and *gentiles* in Archaic Rome,' in *Religion and Society: Rituals, Resources and Identity in the Ancient Graeco-Roman World. The BOMOS-Conferences 2002–2005*, ed. Anders Holm Rasmussen and Susanne William Rasmussen (Rome: Edizioni Quasar, 2008), 267–85 for a different approach.

42 Momigliano, 'The Origins of Rome,' 99; Cornell, *Beginnings*, 84–5; Smith, *The Roman Clan*; and see below for the approach of Terrenato.

43 Cf., for instance, Torelli, '*Bellum in privatam curam*,' 226–7, and below for the hypotheses of Terrenato.

44 See Momigliano, 'The Origins of Rome,' 98–9; Versnel, 'A New Conjecture,' 182; and the hypotheses of Kvium, 'Identifying Identities'. See note 45 as well.
45 For the various issues, see, for example, James H. Richardson, *The Fabii and the Gauls: Studies in Historical Thought and Historiography in Republican Rome* (Stuttgart: Franz Steiner Verlag, 2012), 81–3, 106–7, 119–20, 139–42, 150–1; Jean-Claude Richard, 'Les Fabii à la Crémère: grandeur et décadence de l'organisation gentilice,' in *Crise et transformation des sociétés archaïques de l'Italie antique au Ve siècle av. J.-C.* (Rome: École Française de Rome, 1990), 245–62 (note 255–6 on the Fabii and their *sodales*).
46 Diodorus, 11.53.6. Cf. Richard, 'Les Fabii à la Crémère,' 248–51.
47 Lily Ross Taylor, *The Voting Districts of the Roman Republic: The Thirty-five Urban and Rural Tribes*, reprinted with updated material by Jerzy Linderski (Ann Arbor: University of Michigan Press, 2013), which was first published in 1960, remains the classic study of the Roman tribes; on the location of the *tribus Fabia*, see Taylor, *Voting Districts*, 40–1 and Linderski's defence (p. 363) in his essay in the reprinted edition. On the tribes named after *gentes*, see Taylor, 4–6, 35–7; Cornell, *Beginnings*, 173–9; Wiseman, *Myths of Rome*, 56.
48 See Livy 2.19.2 for the capture of Crustumeria; at 2.21.7, Livy says only that 21 tribes were created (*tribus una et viginti factae*), which is an ambiguous phrase. Among Livy's 21 tribes was presumably the *tribus Clustumina*.
49 Livy 6.5.8 (387 BC), 7.15.11 (358), 8.17.11 (332), 9.20.6 (318), 10.9.14 (299), *periocha* 19 (241); Taylor, *Voting Districts*, 47–68. The *tribus Poblilia* appears to have been named after the Publilii; this may be the result of political circumstances, see Taylor, *Voting Districts*, 50–2.
50 See Mauro Cristofani, ed., *La grande Roma dei Tarquini, catalogo della mostra* (Rome: «L'Erma» di Bretschneider, 1990), 22–3, 58–9 for the evidence. On the symbolic value that an inscription could have, cf. the discussion in Callie Williamson, 'Monuments of Bronze: Roman Legal Documents on Bronze Tablets,' *Classical Antiquity* 6 (1987): 160–83.
51 It is telling that even this could have once been doubted, as it famously was by the Italian scholar Ettore Pais, who argued in his *Storia di Roma*, I.1 of 1898 (Turin: Carlo Clausen) that Rome's kings were in effect just euhemerised gods (e.g., bluntly 378: 'i sette re di Roma non sono altro che divinità'); unfortunately for Pais the inscription from the Forum was discovered in 1899, so just after his book had appeared. That Pais could have even argued what he did at all is nonetheless a reflection of the immense difficulties that exist in the literary evidence. It is worth noting as well that ancient authors who mention the stele from the Forum had absolutely no idea what it was, and offered all manner of explanations for it (see Dionysius of Halicarnassus, *Roman Antiquities*, 2.54.2, 3.1.2 on the inscription).
52 Cf., for example, Andrew Erskine, 'Hellenistic Monarchy and Roman Political Invective,' *Classical Quarterly* 41 (1991): 106–20.
53 Polybius 3.22, 3.25.6–9.
54 Most explicitly, Jyri E. Vaahtera, 'Roman Religion and the Polybian *politeia*,' in *The Roman Middle Republic: Politics, Religion, and Historiography, c. 400–133 B.C.*, ed. Christer Bruun

(Rome: Institutum Romanum Finlandiae, 2000), 251–64, at 257; more recently, John Rich, 'The *fetiales* and Roman International Relations,' in *Priests and State in the Roman World*, ed. James H. Richardson and Federico Santangelo (Stuttgart: Franz Steiner Verlag, 2011), 187–242, at 194; for an attempt to put aside assumptions about the state and to take Polybius' evidence seriously, see James H. Richardson, 'The Oath *per Iovem lapidem* and the Community in Archaic Rome,' *Rheinisches Museum für Philologie* 153 (2010): 25–42. In the same context of treaty-making, assumptions about the existence and nature of the Roman state have also led to anachronistic retrojections being accepted as historical, see Richardson, 'Treaty-Making Rituals'.

55 See the discussion in Carmine Ampolo, 'Sulla formazione della città di Roma,' *Opus* 2 (1983): 425–30 and Cornell, *Beginnings*, 97–103.

56 See the various discussions (some of which are now out of date in some respects) on the formation of the Roman city and state (the two need not go together and may, in fact, have not) in, for example, Carmine Ampolo, 'Le origini di Roma e la «cité antique»,' *Mélanges de l'École française de Rome. Antiquité* 92 (1980): 567–76 and 'Sulla formazione della città'; Robert Drews, 'The Coming of the City to Central Italy,' *American Journal of Ancient History* 6 (1981): 133–65; Timothy J. Cornell, 'La guerra e lo stato in Roma arcaica (VII–V sec.),' in *Alle origini di Roma. Atti del Colloquio tenuto a Pisa il 18 e 19 settembre 1987*, ed. Enrico Campanile (Pisa: Giardini Editori, 1988), 89–97 and *Beginnings*, chapter 4; Forsythe, *Critical History*, 82–93; Hall, *Artifact & Artifice*, 138–41; Fulminante, *Urbanisation of Rome and Latium Vetus*, especially chapter 1 for a discussion of various approaches to urbanisation and state formation (but see the comments in note 17 above).

57 Does some indication of increasing specialisation in the production of pottery, for instance, reflect internal developments or external influences?

58 Nicola Terrenato, 'The Versatile Clans: Archaic Rome and the Nature of Early City-States in Central Italy,' in *State Formation in Italy and Greece: Questioning the Neoevolutionist Paradigm*, ed. Nicola Terrenato and Donald C. Haggis (Oxford: Oxbow Books, 2011), 231–44 (see 236, 237 and 243 for the several quotes).

59 The influence of such ideas is still detectable in recent work; even apart from Carandini's own work (where the influence is obviously predictable), note, for instance, Terrenato, 'Versatile Clans,' 235, who talks of 'the time when the decision to create a city-state was taken'; 241, 'cities were the result of conscious decisions made by individuals'. But it is most unlikely that, at least as far as the earliest city-states are concerned, individuals did indeed make conscious decisions at some particular moment in time to create a city-state: this is the ancient model, which is entirely unsatisfactory.

60 The division was, predictably enough, said to have first gone back to Romulus' time: Cicero, *On the State*, 2.14 and 2.23; Livy 1.8.7; Dionysius of Halicarnassus, *Roman Antiquities*, 2.8; Plutarch, *Life of Romulus*, 13.1–3. The reality may very well have been much more complex; see, for instance, Timothy J. Cornell, 'The Failure of the Plebs,' in *Tria corda. Scritti in onore di Arnaldo*

Momigliano, ed. Emilio Gabba (Como: Edizioni New Press, 1983), 101–20; Cornell, *Beginnings*, 242–58.

61 Livy 2.32.2–33.3; Dionysius of Halicarnassus, *Roman Antiquities*, 6.45–89. On the tribunate, see recently Christopher Smith, 'The Origins of the Tribunate of the Plebs,' *Antichthon* 46 (2012): 101–25 in which references to earlier work can also be found.

62 Assembly: the evidence is difficult; Livy says that a law was passed in 471 BC to allow plebeian tribunes to be elected in the tribal assembly (2.56.2–58.2; also Dionysius of Halicarnassus, *Roman Antiquities*, 9.41–9), but Livy does not say how they had been chosen previously; some sources say that they had been elected in the curiate assembly (Asconius 76C; Dionysius of Halicarnassus, *Roman Antiquities*, 6.89.1, 9.41.2); for different reactions, see, for example, Robert M. Ogilvie, *A Commentary on Livy Books 1–5* (Oxford: Clarendon Press, 1965), 380–1; Cornell, *Beginnings*, 260–1; Forsythe, *Critical History*, 177–9. For the keeping of records, see Livy 3.55.13; Pomponius, *Digest of Justinian*, 1.2.2.21; Zonaras 7.15. For the plebeians' efforts to get a law-code drafted, see Livy 3.9.2–32.7 *passim*; there are, as usual, numerous difficulties in the evidence; see, for example, Ogilvie, *Commentary*, 411–3, 449–54; Cornell, *Beginnings*, 272–6; Forsythe, *Critical History*, 202.

63 Livy 2.44.9: *duas civitates ex una factas, suos cuique parti magistratus, suas leges esse* ('Two states had been created out of one; each faction had its own magistrates, its own laws'), also, for example, 2.24.1, 3.19.9; see Dionysius of Halicarnassus, *Roman Antiquities*, 6.88.1 for the concern that two states may be formed in one (μή ποτε δύο πόλεις ποιήσωμεν ἐν μιᾷ); Theodor Mommsen, *Römisches Staatsrecht* III.1, 3rd edition (Leipzig: Verlag von S. Hirzel, 1887), 145 ('die Gemeinde in der Gemeinde'); Cornell, *Beginnings*, 258–65; see also Arnaldo Momigliano, 'The Rise of the *plebs* in the Archaic Age of Rome,' in *Social Struggles in Archaic Rome: New Perspectives on the Conflict of the Orders*, 2nd edition, ed. Kurt A. Raaflaub (Malden, MA: Blackwell Publishing, 2005), 168–84, at 178–80. For arguments against this idea, see Forsythe, *Critical History*, 176.

64 Note Cornell, *Beginnings*, 265, for example: 'The later vestiges of the [plebeian] movement ... were gradually recognised and integrated with the institutions of the state ... What is remarkable is not only the way in which plebeian institutions matched those of the state, but the fact that their organisation was in many ways more advanced and sophisticated. In the period down to 367 BC the plebeian institutions were either integrated into the constitution, or were themselves imitated by the "patrician state".'

65 Cornell, *Beginnings*, 311; see also Richard, 'Les Fabii à la Crémère'.

66 Compare Cornell's comments in 1987/88, in 'La guerra e lo stato,' 94: 'Si può, però, facilmente sospettare che guerre gentilizie di questo genere fossero un fenomeno comune e forse caratteristico dell'epoca.'

67 See note 31 above. There was another version, which put his migration in Romulus' time; but on this, see Wiseman, *Clio's Cosmetics*, 59–61.

68 As Ernst Badian, 'Diskussion, Sektion II: Quellen und Quellenkritik,' in *Staat und Staatlichkeit in der frühen römischen Republik*, ed. Walter Eder (Stuttgart: Franz Steiner Verlag, 1990), 208–17 notes (p. 215), with reference to the inscription from Satricum, 'the inscription calls into question the whole interpretation of the Roman social and political structure that we get in Livy: the *suodales* cannot be plausibly matched, or fitted into the background we are given. They point to a social organization plausible in itself, but irreconcilable with the late Republican version of the "Struggle of the Orders" that we have come to take for granted.' This is perhaps something of an exaggeration, since there is other evidence which seems to fit with the circumstances implied by the inscription, but it is true that such evidence only rarely accords, and never easily, with what is implied and assumed by Livy.

69 See, for example, Christopher Smith, '*Adfectatio regni* in the Roman Republic,' in *Ancient Tyranny*, ed. Sian Lewis (Edinburgh: Edinburgh University Press, 2006), 49–64; and also Forsythe, *Critical History*, 193–5, 239–41, 259–62 for a sceptical assessment of the evidence.

70 Livy 3.15.5–18.10; Dionysius of Halicarnassus, *Roman Antiquities*, 10.1–16.

71 Livy 3.15.5: *exsules servique, ad duo milia* [Ogilvie, *OCT*: *quattuor milia*] *hominum et quingenti* ('exiles and slaves to the number of 2500 [Ogilvie: 4500] men'); Dionysius of Halicarnassus, *Roman Antiquities*, 10.14.1, in contrast, has Herdonius gather together his clients and the most courageous of his attendants (συνήθροιζε τοὺς πελάτας καὶ τῶν θεραπόντων οὓς εἶχε τοὺς εὐτολμοτάτους; on θεράποντες, see Versnel, 'Historical implications,' 117); Herdonius' plan, however, Dionysius says (10.14.3), nonetheless involved calling on exiles, slaves, those in debt, and the like. Cf. Torelli, '*Bellum in privatam curam*,' 232. Livy's choice of words may, however, be due to first-century influences, see Ogilvie, *Commentary*, 423–5, also Forsythe, *Critical History*, 205.

72 Cornell, 'Coriolanus,' 84–91.

73 Note Maras, 'Ancora su Mastarna,' 189, 195 for the evidence that the XII Tables (Rome's first law-code) contained legislation aimed at restricting the actions of *sodalitates* with respect to public law.

4. MEDIEVAL CITIZENSHIP:
BRUGES IN THE LATER MIDDLE AGES

Andrew Brown

MEDIEVAL CITIZENSHIP: BRUGES IN THE LATER MIDDLE AGES

Within his account of events in Bruges in the late fifteenth century, a local clerk included description of two oaths sworn within the city.[1] On 6 July 1483, according to the 'old custom', an oath was declaimed from the Belfry (*Halle*) in the market place (*markt*), on behalf of Bruges' ruler Philip, the young count of Flanders. It was received by the 'common belly' of the town; and in the neighbouring *burg* (central town square) it was also heard by the guild headmen and deans, various high-ranking lords, and the magistrates of the city, who were seated on benches arranged into a square and covered with cloths bearing the city's coat of arms.[2] With this oath, wrote the clerk, 'God and Mary will bring us good. Amen.'

The clerk's trust in divine help, however, was not shared by everyone in Bruges. He also describes how, in the following year, one Martine, the wife of a burgher named Pieter Prysbier, was caught swearing during a game of dice that she would win despite God and his mother. For this blasphemous oath, on 23 August 1484 she was brought to the same market place, pierced with a 'glowing iron' to within an inch of her life, and from there paraded past the Belfry, round the back of St Donatian's church and into the *burg* where she was placed on a scaffold, bound to a stake, and had a piece of her tongue extracted. She was then banished from Flanders for six years.

Behind the clerk's description of these events lie assumptions about what it meant to be a citizen (or 'burgher') of Bruges. His reference to groups participating in political processes, to a sense of space that defined the city, as well as to vices deemed to have no place within its walls, all point to key ideas that underpinned the construction of burghership in Bruges. These will be explored more fully here, and also in relation to modern debates on the meaning of citizenship. However, the relevance of medieval views to modern, and vice versa, is not immediately apparent. Present-day debates have often focused on the rights of individuals and their duties in relation to the state, or more recently on their sense of belonging and identity in societies unsettled by migration and globalisation.[3] These issues appear to have little to do with the Bruges clerk's focus in the 1480s on hierarchy, urbanity and spirituality as markers of citizen identity and practice.

Concern with citizenship in the medieval world has even been called 'peripheral'.[4] After all, the Bruges clerk offers no clear definition of what a burgher was, and tracts dealing directly or exclusively with the nature of citizenship were rarely written in the Middle Ages. Few medieval writers, these usually churchmen, considered 'citizenship' in this world, preferring to privilege links forged with the next. In discussing origins of the modern idea, it seems appropriate to begin with Aristotle or Cicero, and then leap a millennium and a half to Machiavelli, with perhaps a steadying toe being placed on the special case of medieval Florence where 'Renaissance' men reworked Ciceronian ideals.[5] The non-Christian beliefs of ancient thinkers and the proto-secularity of early modern theorists have more immediate contemporary resonance.

Moreover, citizenship before the rise of nation-states (excepting the Roman empire) was small-scale. Aristotle seems to have thought that the ideal body of citizens would not exceed 40,000. The majority of late medieval towns had only a few thousand inhabitants, although there were exceptions — Paris contained 200,000, and Venice 100,000 in the early fourteenth century. Venice also lay in northern Italy, the most urbanised part of Europe, and city-states in this region did generate tracts from the thirteenth century onwards that theorised on the nature of citizenship. Yet even these remained limited to an urban context.[6] Medieval citizens (burghers) lived in cities, and outside northern Italy they usually fell under the jurisdiction of 'feudal' lordships, lay and ecclesiastical. At the same time, the polities of these lordships hardly resemble the structures of modern states, at least not in scale and scope.[7]

There are alternative perspectives, however. Reflecting on the 'otherness' of medieval citizenship, for instance, draws out the contingent nature of

MEDIEVAL CITIZENSHIP

modern perceptions and definitions. But in certain respects, medieval citizenship was not so 'other': differences with the modern world can be exaggerated, and some of the patterns in the relationship between citizen and city in the medieval period have modern parallels. How an individual was encouraged to become a citizen *was* important in the later middle ages; and far from being peripheral, the question of citizenship was of vital concern to the inhabitants of late medieval towns. This concern becomes more obvious if we look beyond theoretical tracts to sources that reveal political theory in practice: town chronicles (such as the Bruges city clerk's), legislation, treasury accounts, and even evidence relating to urban topography. But a wider perspective beyond the city also needs to be taken: medieval citizenship usually involved a relationship with an overlord and even a 'state', and historians have no difficulty discerning the lineaments of governmental structures approximating modern states, and even ideologies of statehood, within late medieval Europe.[8]

Bruges provides a useful case study to pursue these issues. The city lay in Flanders, the most urbanised region in Europe outside northern Italy. Although not the biggest Flemish city (its peak of 50,000 inhabitants in the fifteenth century was exceeded by Ghent's), it punched well above its demographic weight because of its importance as a gateway city of international commerce and banking, linking trade from the Baltic to the Mediterranean. It marketed itself as a great emporium, and consequently it was the residence (and sometimes home) of many hundreds of foreign merchants. They congregated around the *Beurse* square, which not for nothing has lent its name to the modern French stock exchange, *la Bourse*. Such was the intensity of commercial enterprise in the city that Bruges has even been dubbed the 'cradle of capitalism'.[9]

Besides its commercial networks, medieval Bruges bore other hallmarks said to define modern urbanity. It was also 'industrialised' in that it had (until the early fourteenth century) a large textile industry, fed by immigrants from the countryside and beyond, who worked in the medieval equivalent of sweatshops. In the thirteenth century, the tide of immigration meant that the city's population began to lap alarmingly over its first ramparts, which had been erected in 1127. Later immigrants were housed in areas outside the original city boundaries; for instance, in marshland to the south of the city, probably bought up by speculators, who divided it into narrow parallel streets, and rented out one-room houses to low-paid workers. Within these peripheral areas, civic authorities also placed the more polluting elements of the textile industry, such as dyeing processes.[10]

The resulting social inequalities created tensions: major upheavals of discontented craftsmen and artisans occurred, particularly from the 1280s onwards, culminating in a revolt in 1302 that weakened the hold of commercial elites on the city and allowed greater representation of craft guildsmen in government and city councils.[11] These underlying tensions remained unresolved: even in the fifteenth century four rebellions broke out, in which rebels, led by middling groups in society, aimed at similar political goals.[12] Demographic pressures had eased because of catastrophic mortality after the Black Death and subsequent plagues, but urban society faced other difficulties. Because of wider regional change, Bruges underwent a profound and (for the artisan workforce) devastating shift in its 'industrial' base, away from cloth production towards specialisation, by the fifteenth century, in luxury goods (fashion items of clothing, furniture, arms, glass and the highly prized 'new art' of Jan van Eyck and others). New immigrants were lured to the city in the fifteenth century by the promise of new opportunities.[13] Bruges was therefore a complex environment in which identities were multiple; where both cosmopolitanism and xenophobia could thrive; where social relations were tense; where city governments wrestled with problems of social disorder and alienation, managing the aspirations of citizens, but facing challenges to their authority.

Citizenship in Bruges was also about a relationship with an overlord, the counts of Flanders (who were themselves subject to the kings of France). The county was acquired through marriage by the Valois dukes of Burgundy who ruled Flanders from 1384 to 1477. Though accepted as 'natural' lords, the dukes were French rather than Flemish in origin, and as most historians argue they

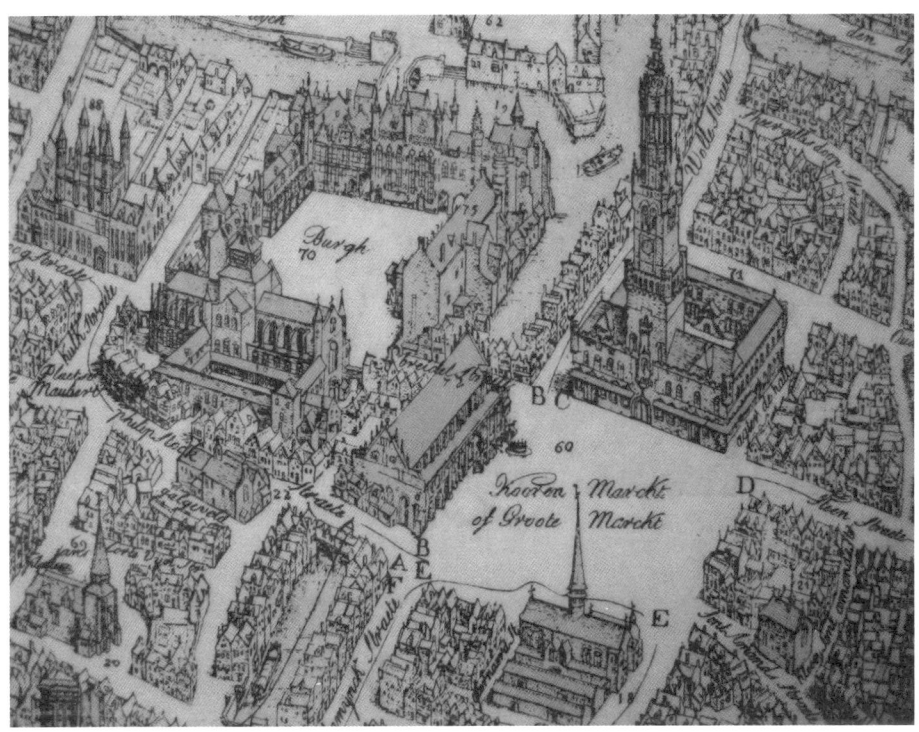

The centre of Bruges, showing the *burgh* (burg) square with St Donatian's church, and the *markt* with the Belfry.
FROM THE CITY MAP BY MARCUS GERARDS, 1562

began forging their territories into a centralised polity, treating its subjects as part of a state.[14] The autocratic inclinations of the dukes (and their Hapsburg successors after 1477) contributed to rebel discontent and factional dispute within Flemish cities.[15] Citizenship in Bruges was not therefore a simple construct, nor indeed just about cities, but an amalgam of ideas that are both familiar and alien to the modern world.

The legal definition of a burgher could vary greatly across medieval cities,[16] and in Flanders its precise meaning changed over time.[17] In the earliest privileges granted by the count of Flanders to towns in the twelfth century, the right of burghership (*poorterschap*) was a broadly inclusive category: it could be gained simply by residing in the town for a year and a day, though by the end of the thirteenth century it could also be claimed by birthright. Residence began to need confirmation by registration, the swearing of an oath, and the payment of a fee. The Flemish word for burgher — *poorter* (from *poort* meaning gate) — implied someone who lived within city limits, and a sense that 'burghership' meant all inhabitants of the city was never lost. Throughout the later middle ages, it was also a right that could be gained by immigrants, while a special category of 'out-burghership' (*buitenpoorter*) was granted to people who lived in rural regions outside the city gates.

By the fourteenth century, in the wake of social upheaval and diversification, the term could also be used in senses that were more exclusive. A narrower definition of the *poorter* emerged, as a member of a specific group of well-off, property-owning families, often associated with the commercial elite. Following a period of craft-guild revolt, by 1360 the *poorterij* were also designated as a specific body, alongside groups of craft guilds, who had voting rights on to the benches of city aldermen. The wider definition of the burgher as the town-dweller persisted, but it too became associated with a preferred kind of inhabitant, the economically productive craftsmen. Burghership became a prerequisite for becoming a member of a craft guild, in turn allowing access to retail trade, skilled labour and better wages, and craft guilds were monitored more strictly by the city government.

MEDIEVAL CITIZENSHIP

New immigrants hoping for burghership required official registration.[18] The privilege could be bought relatively easily and cheaply (the equivalent of ten days of a skilled craftsman's wages), and fees were lowered in 1440, following a disruptive rebellion in the city and the need to repopulate the city with a skilled workforce. It was also a mechanism for city governments to attract the right kind of newcomer.[19] In marketing the city as an emporium, Bruges' authorities also encouraged purchase of burghership by foreign merchants, who could thereby access retail and craft trade (and fees could be waived if the applicant offered the city a particular set of skills). Women too could acquire rights of burghership, but there were limitations to their ability to work within the guild structure, and they were excluded from political office.[20] Those workers who were outside the guild structure did not necessarily purchase burghership; thus it was not always clear whether all town inhabitants, especially those who had immigrated in search of artisanal work and paid piece-rate, were legally burghers. Craftsmen, under the authority of craft guilds and ultimately of the city government, were the ideal new citizens. Even so, the notion that all the city's inhabitants were burghers in a wider sense did not disappear; and certainly from the city government's perspective, as we shall see, the city and all its denizens could be treated as a single community.

Becoming a citizen was therefore more than a legal process: built into these legal requirements were ideas about what the citizen should ideally be. The new burgher was required to swear a sacred oath of allegiance to uphold urban 'liberties' (or rather 'privileges') and above all urban 'peace'.[21] To be a citizen partly meant being part of a corporate community. From the twelfth century, in what historians have called the 'communal movement', many towns asserted a greater independence from local lords, demanding charters of liberties, central to which was the right of the burgher to be justiciable only by his urban peers.[22] The communal movement used to be celebrated as a key moment in European if not (ultimately) global history: these towns were in effect breaking out of the straitjacket of lordly control, sowing the seeds of individual freedoms, democratic rights, and of capitalism. More recent historiography has cautiously pulled back from these claims, emphasising the more exclusive and privileged aspects of urban 'freedoms'.[23] Yet there remains a strong case for arguing that this period of urban renewal left an important legacy, not just economic but also political; in particular, a culture of negotiation and experimentation in collective political life that had been such a strong feature of medieval communes.[24]

The communal model, as a sworn association with common interests, power-sharing and self-regulation, did become a mode of government for many later European towns. With this sworn association came also a notion of the 'public' or 'common good': in the early struggles against the count in 1127–8, burghers in Flanders fiercely presented themselves as defenders of a 'common good'.[25] The ideal proved remarkably resilient, despite the pressures to which it was subjected: urban society did become more stratified; 'patricians' emerged in the thirteenth century to dominate town government; and a commercial elite, though it was challenged, held sway over town councils in the later middle ages. Yet a notion persisted that the few had to govern for the benefit of the many, while the craftsmen and artisans who sought greater representation in government invariably used the 'common good' as a war-cry to justify acts of rebellion.[26]

The ideal of the common good was underwritten with religious imperatives. Ruling for the many included obligations to the poor and weak: according to the Church, charity to the poor was one of the seven works of mercy. In the late twelfth century, St John's Hospital was founded in Bruges: hospitals for the sick and the passing traveller and pilgrim had been founded in other towns before, but St John's was one of the first in Europe to be placed under the specific supervision of the town government.[27] Other institutions that formed part of a network of 'social services' were also founded in Bruges, as elsewhere, and these also involved municipal authority: houses for lepers, and by the fourteenth century, specialised almshouses for the sick, the old, or the mentally ill.[28] Charity targeted at a parish level was also put in place: poor 'tables' were set up to distribute food weekly. The five main parish poor-tables in Bruges fed some 900 people a year in the fifteenth century — though these were for a category of poor called 'shamefaced', in other words those considered

MEDIEVAL CITIZENSHIP

'respectable'.[29] The poor-tables had their own 'table-masters', and were placed under the guardianship of the city aldermen, who were all required to swear an oath, on assuming office, that included an obligation to support the poor, widows and orphans.[30] The narrow, legal definition of the 'citizen', as well as its broader ideal, thus had implications for the construction of citizenship.

The oaths sworn by new aldermen and burghers were sacred: a civic identity was intertwined with a religious one. There were complications, though. Being a good citizen did not necessarily mean being a good Christian. Ingrained in the minds of medieval churchmen was a suspicion that cities were bad places for Christians to be. The Bible was full of monstrous cities of sin, Babylon, Sodom and Gommorah being only the most notorious: withdrawal from city life might even be a first step towards a more elevated citizenship in heaven.

Yet there were more positive views of cities even among clerics. Some theologians, drawing from classical celebrations of urbanity, considered the Church itself to be in some sense a 'city';[31] the earthly city meanwhile could also aspire to be a New Jerusalem.[32] It could be imagined as a fortress of civilisation against the rustic pagan (*paganus*), and it could earn heavenly protection.[33] In early hagiographies and chronicles, bishops can be found calling upon the saints for help, and marshalling their city's inhabitants into supplicatory processions. The adoption of patron saints or cults by townspeople, and veneration of them in ceremony and procession, became commonplace in western Europe,[34] and these practices became especially elaborate in the later middle ages.

Bruges had its own special cult, venerating no less a protector than Jesus Christ himself. By the thirteenth century, the city possessed a reliquary, containing Christ's blood collected from the Cross, which quickly became identified as a symbol of civic liberties. In 1297 the city authorities implored the king of France (who was in conflict with the count and poised to invade Flanders) not to remove their relic from Bruges. Shortly after the revolt of 1302 (and the victory of the Flemish militia over the French army at Kortrijk) a procession carrying the relic began to be funded by the city treasury.[35] It is probable that the specific use of the relic was linked to the triumph of rebellious guildsmen who claimed to represent 'the whole commune of the city'.[36] Their ascendancy was shortlived, and the procession would to some extent often serve hierarchy or the oligarchic rule of city councils who orchestrated it. Yet it was celebrated annually on 3 May, whatever the regime or faction in power, even when more radical rebels seized control of urban government: the communal idealism and potential of the event, and the claim of craft guilds to represent these ideals, was perhaps never lost to sight. From the mid-fourteenth century, the procession invariably involved all the official 54 craft guilds, many other workers' groups, as well as the city's ecclesiastical institutions.

The sacred city required citizens to be equipped with particular virtues. In this context, there was no incompatibility between the virtuous Christian and the virtuous citizen. Striving for communal peace and the common good might also merit divine love. As the burgomaster, aldermen, headman of the '*poorters*', deans and sworn men of all crafts, and all the 'common people' ('*commun ghemeenlike*') of the town collectively declared in 1360: 'We know and acknowledge that where peace is, so God is', and that 'unpeace, quarrels and dispute are destructive of every town and country, as holy scripture tells us'.[37] Divine peace was an aspiration that urban authorities began to nurture in the city's inhabitants by ordering them to observe or participate in processions — not just annual ones focused on the city's main cult, but also *ad hoc* ones, carrying a variety of other relics, called when occasion or crisis demanded. Propitiatory processions, imploring or thanking God and the saints for their help, were drawn from ecclesiastical tradition and well-established liturgical procedures, but from the late thirteenth century, first in towns of Tuscany and Lombardy, and later in many places north of the Alps, city magistrates also began to launch such processions, with the guidance of clergy but on their own initiative.[38] In Bruges by the late fifteenth century, twenty or more could be mustered in any one year: most of them included the call for peace.[39] For instance, on 6 July 1491 the city magistrates ordered a special procession of their Holy Blood relic to pray for peace in Flanders, and also for the health of its rulers; and 'so that their prayers would be better heard and received by the

MEDIEVAL CITIZENSHIP

Almighty', all town dwellers ('priests and lay people, old and young, men and women') were to go beforehand to mass and confession, while the city streets were to be cleaned, and the craft guilds were to assemble in good order.[40]

Such urban appeals for divine help seem far removed from the secular demands of modern citizenship, but they arguably foreshadow modern trends. The increasing control exercised by municipal powers over the sacred might well be viewed as part of a longer-term trend to modern secularisation.[41] Some historians have categorised these processions and cults of medieval towns as forms of 'civic religion',[42] and this with a deliberate sense that it contributed to the emergence of 'civil religion' (as most famously formulated by Jean-Jacques Rousseau).[43] The emphasis on the need for 'virtuous' citizens, educated in the values and tasks of citizenship, has also enjoyed a much longer tradition dating back to the Greek *polis*, and has re-emerged in current debate: how to encourage identification with the community, and participation in political life, is partly a question of developing values that promote these processes.[44]

In Bruges, these values were both civic and religious, and they were values that city authorities took many steps to promote. In 1483 the city council established a new musical endowment for the public and daily singing of the *Salve Regina* (in praise of the Virgin Mary), which it considered beneficial for every 'devout' person to attend.[45] 'Rhetoricians' (poets and playwrights) were employed to stage drama competitions, sometimes with 'virtues' as their theme; they also organised the 'dumbshows' for entry ceremonies, and wrote poems for general processions.[46] The rhetorician Anthonis de Roovere was subsidised from 1466 by the city treasury to remain in Bruges to write his 'morality plays' for 'the honour and happiness of the community of the town'.[47]

Processions connected Bruge's inhabitants to the urban landscape. Citizenship in modern societies is often conceived as a process of engagement, or shared identity, with a land or physical space,[48] and in medieval cities the townscape acted as a strong focus and generator of identity.[49] The annual Holy Blood procession took participants past important civic landmarks (from the heart of the city in the *burg* square, near the aldermen's townhouse and the chapel of the Holy Blood, then past the Belfry and major churches), before perambulating around the city walls, pausing at each gate for prayers. The townspeople remaining inside were alerted to the procession's progress by the chime of bells timed to be rung when the relic reached certain gates.[50] In effect, the procession described the city as a sacred kind of territory under the patronage of Christ. Other processions delineated other routes as *via sacra*: the general processions, which often emerged from St Donatian's church, carried relics or the Sacrament from the *burg*, across the *markt*, round the back of the church to the *burg*, thereby keeping to the perimeter of the original count's castle and *burg*, inside the first city ramparts built in the twelfth century.[51]

The Holy Blood procession had also emerged during a period when the urban landscape was undergoing considerable change. From the late thirteenth century, in the throes of commercial and demographic expansion, the Bruges authorities (like those contemporaneously of other Flemish and north Italian towns) had been conducting massive building campaigns that reshaped the infrastructures of their cities. The huge *Waterhalle* (where canal boats carrying merchandise from the coast could dock) and the *Halle* or Belfry (burnt down during a rebellion in 1280) were rebuilt, and became iconic statements of local pride and patriotism.[52] The population of Bruges, spilling over the original city ramparts, also prompted the civic authorities to construct new walls. The route taken by the Holy Blood procession reflected these changes: the new walls were completed in the early fourteenth century at exactly the time when the procession around them began to be funded by the civic treasury.[53]

The processors carrying the Holy Blood relic around the walls exited and re-entered the city through one of the seven gates (the Boeverie gate). To pass through the city gates was to pass through a threshold into a special kind of space.[54] Gates served prosaic purposes: they marked the place where those bringing food and articles for sale in city markets would pay a toll. But they also emphasised the heavenly protection sought by the city: they were variously decorated with niches for images of saints; some incorporated small chapels (the Boeverie gate contained the chapel of the painters' guild from 1440). The gates themselves could even be invested with particular virtues: an

early fifteenth-century poem in the 'Gruuthuse manuscript', probably written after restoration work undertaken on the city walls, praised the seven gates as guardians of the city, each of which represented a pair of virtues strongly associated with civic values: Justice and Brotherhood, Freedom and Unity.[55] These values, if maintained by citizens, would also protect the city: as Anthonis de Roovere wrote in an allegorical poem in 1480, upholding charity and divine service would help restore the ruined condition of the city, and of its gates and walls.[56] Those outside the city did not necessarily share these values: another poem in the Gruuthuse manuscript, following a well-worn topos, ridicules the boorishness of country dwellers outside the city.

Space has power to divide as well as unite. Some citizens of Bruges had a very different experience of belonging to the city compared with others — particularly the newly arrived immigrants, confined to certain areas, many of whom were not registered officially as 'burghers'. The idea of the whole city as a community also carried implications that were not necessarily inclusive. Developing a notion of the ideal city and citizen meant developing an idea of their opposites. The phrase 'bad citizenship' appears in the earliest urban charters of the twelfth century, and so also a conception of how to treat those who fell into this category. A citizen could be bad simply by failing to fulfil the required economic function: he could be expelled for being 'useless' and 'unprofitable'.[57] The beggar, or the roving journeyman and artisan, not tied to a craft guild, was potentially perilous to the community; and women too, however excluded from political office, could be included among the dangerous.[58]

This community was also a sacred body, occupying a sacred space, in which members were expected to uphold key virtues, peace especially. Those found wanting could therefore expect discrimination or punishment. As in many other towns, the Bruges authorities could choose to expel miscreants from the city; some of them were sent 'outside the peace' of the town on pilgrimage to distant shrines.[59] Somatic punishment was often meted out to those who attacked the 'common body' of the town: tongues were removed from blasphemers (male and female), heads of traitors attached to gates or the town Belfry. Other forms of punishment also made it clear that the city was a sacred and clean space in a way that the area outside its walls was not. For instance, leper houses in Bruges were situated (as they often were in medieval towns) on city boundaries — leprosy being a disease particularly associated with sinfulness. Some sins were thought to be more unclean than others. In fifteenth-century Bruges, sodomy was considered a crime that polluted the city like no other:[60] in contrast to other types of criminal, executed in public and exemplary fashion in the central town square (the *burg*), those convicted of sodomy were often taken outside the city gates for execution.[61] Those paraded for punishment within the city could also follow routes that heightened the spiritual significance of their crimes against civic virtues: the blaspheming Martine in 1484 was brought along the route, from *markt* to *burg*, that was often followed by general relic processions out of St Donatian's.

In these cases, the 'otherness' of medieval citizenship, compared with modern variants in democratic societies, appears at its most pronounced. Even so, modern definitions of citizenship still raise sharp questions about who is to be excluded from and included in society, and why.[62] In medieval Bruges, the excluded were simply defined by different criteria. The sorry tale of one bad townsman, Corneille van Poorten, tried in 1491, exemplifies the point.[63] He was an immigrant cook from Tournai (south of Bruges), and had come to Bruges to serve in the households of various leading burghers, but he was caught thieving, and also posting bills denouncing the city as a place where 'sodomy reigned daily in secret and in public'. This denunciation was not received well by the city authorities. Corneille was interrogated, and duly confessed to a string of crimes that amount in effect to an identikit profile of the bad burgher. He revealed himself guilty of sodomy (and bestiality), vagabondage, and sacrilege (having stolen a rosary). He became in effect the mirror image of the good citizen, that is the Christian, clean and stable craftsman that civic authorities had been so keen to encourage, not least in the many 'general' processions they had launched.

Citizenship in Bruges was not just about a relationship with the city and its normative values. The new burgher and office holder in Bruges also swore

MEDIEVAL CITIZENSHIP

oaths of allegiance to the counts of Flanders. The communal idea of the burgher, and the town as a privileged corporate body, had emerged in the struggles against the counts in the early twelfth century, and throughout the thirteenth century counts had been unable to curb the power of their burgeoning towns, although they profited from urban wealth and without ceding rights of jurisdiction.[64] But the liberties and judicial autonomy of burghers would be challenged by the gradual assertion of comital authority and the building of an apparatus of state government, particularly under the Valois dukes of Burgundy (from 1384).[65]

The rebellions in Bruges during the fifteenth century were not simply internal tussles for power but also reactions by groups or factions to the assertion of state control. The building of state power was partly based on ideas derived from Roman law, in which notions of the 'public good' allowed the prince greater scope to develop an authoritarian style of rule.[66] It therefore challenged the claims of townsmen to be the prime defenders of the 'common good'.[67] Under princely pressure, the good burgher was increasingly repositioned as the good subject, while state power encroached on all the spaces, physical and conceptual, that had come to define citizenship in late medieval Bruges.

City gates and walls were eroded and pierced by princely authority. As part of the punishment of Bruges for its revolt in 1436–8, in which the duke's man, Lord Lilleadam, had been killed just before the Boeverie gate, the duke ordered the gate to be bricked up, and a mass was founded, to be celebrated by the painters' guild and with municipal support, for the soul of the dead lord in perpetuity.[68] Processions were diverted for princely needs. The first general procession that appeared in the city accounts as funded by the town, in 1407, was in fact to pray for the duke in his war against the rebellious city of Liège, and many later processions were evidently launched at the instigation of the state authorities.[69] The order for the procession made in July 1491 came from the prince. Prosecutions of 'bad citizens' could also be conducted under the jurisdiction of courts presided over by princely deputies. Sodomy was a crime that the prince increasingly claimed as lying within his special jurisdiction as guardian of the public good: the case of Corneille van Poorten was heard before the court of the sheriff of Bruges, the representative of the prince.[70] The crime of breaking city peace was elided with defiance of state authority.

In 1492 the urban court dealing with criminal cases tried people who defied the prince and the Peace of Tours, which was imposed by the Hapsburg ruler Maximilian on Flemish towns after a long period of revolt. Some were punished by being forced to attend general processions in penitential clothing and carrying candles; others were banished 'in the name of the sheriff, burgomaster and the whole body (*gheheele lichame*) of the town' for disrupting the 'peace of the town' and 'the welfare of the land', or in line with 'God's way and the lawful way of the land'.[71] Speaking out against the prince was tantamount to blasphemy: it was for 'horrible and injurious words' uttered against the prince and the Peace that Margaret, the widow of Jan de Madevenis, was banished from Flanders.[72] State control of Bruges meant that in the sixteenth century there were far fewer rebellions of burghers against princely rule than there had been in the past; even so, the processes by which citizens were transformed from being inhabitants of towns to subjects of states were already in place before the early modern period.[73]

The concerns of medieval burghers were different from those of modern citizens: the Bruges city clerk's admiration of piety, order and hierarchy among the city's inhabitants jars with democratic values and notions of citizenship. Yet issues and patterns in medieval burghership resonate with present-day concerns. Even if modernity is defined as industrialisation, capitalism, secularisation, democracy and diversity, these are also to be found to some degree in late medieval towns — creating familiar problems of 'citizenship' in relation to identity, to a sense of belonging, and to civil management of them.

Legal definitions of citizenship are as important to study in the medieval city as they are in the modern world, above all because they have implications for the inclusiveness or otherwise of their societies, and for the values that underpin them. Debates on modern citizenship no longer focus narrowly on

MEDIEVAL CITIZENSHIP

legal rights, but medieval citizenship was never simply about these either. The norms, practices and identities that now inform 'citizenship studies' are equally relevant to the study of burghership in the medieval city. Despite the strength of hierarchy and of elite social groups in late medieval Bruges, citizenship was a 'social process' through which other groups engaged in 'claiming rights': oppositional demands from lower orders for greater political representation, and against state authority, persisted throughout the late medieval period.

Similarities can be taken too far, and applied too anachronistically. Some recent shifts of interest in modern citizenship studies may take us even further away from the medieval city: the place of the nation-state as the primary authority on citizenship has been challenged by 'postmodernisation', and by a globalisation unimagined in the medieval period.[74] Yet even these changes of perspective do not represent a complete break with the past. In a sense the 'global' citizen is also an urban one: without urban infrastructures, globalisation is inconceivable. The study of 'global history' has also emphasised the importance of cities, especially port cities, and the movement of people, ideas and commodities as part of an international urban network of exchange.[75] This is one area where the term 'citizenship' retains an association with 'urbanity'; and why also reflecting on urban-based citizenships of the past is relevant to modern debate.

ENDNOTES

1. The anonymous writer was probably a town official and a clerk in holy orders. For the following: *Het boeck van al 't gene datter geschiet is binnen Brugge sichent Jaer 1477, 14 Februarii, tot 149*, ed. C. L. Carton (Ghent, 1859), 55–6, 66–7.
2. The common 'belly' or 'body' was a phrase often used to refer to the body of townspeople, as opposed to the aldermen, councillors, deans of craft guilds and other town officials. There was a tense political context in which this oath was sworn: the young count was under the guardianship of his father, Maximilian of Hapsburg, whose rule not all townspeople in Flanders accepted. For an overview, see Wim Blockmans and Walter Prevenier, *The Promised Lands: The Low Countries Under Burgundian Rule, 1369–1530* (Penn. State University Park, Philadelphia: University of Pennsylvania Press, 1999), 199–203.
3. See Emily Beausoleil, in this volume; Engin F. Isin and Bryan S. Turner, 'Citizenship Studies: An Introduction,' in *Handbook of Citizenship Studies*, ed. Engin F. Isin and Bryan S. Turner (London: Sage Publications, 2002), 1–10; Anthony Elliott, 'The Reinvention of Citizenship,' in *Culture and Citizenship*, ed. Nick Stevenson (London: Sage Publications, 2001), 47–61; Richard Bellamy, *Citizenship: A Very Short History* (Oxford: Oxford University Press, 2008).
4. Derek Heater, *A Brief History of Citizenship* (New York: NYU Press, 2004), 42.
5. Most well known is Leonardo Bruni's *Laudatio florentinae urbis* (ca. 1403–4), celebrating Florence as a latter-day Rome, whose constitution sought the good of all, where even members of the lower class could proudly claim to be a 'citizen of Florence'. For an extended immersion into citizenship within Italian city-states, to the relative exclusion of other regions of Europe, see Peter Riesenberg, *Citizenship in the Western Tradition: Plato to Rousseau* (Chapel Hill and London: University of North Carolina Press, 1992), 87–199 ('Part II: Citizenship in the Medieval Italian City').
6. Heater, *Brief History*, 43.
7. For a modernist view of the limitations of medieval 'states' and 'nations', see John Breuilly, 'Changes in the Political Uses of the Nation: Continuity or Discontinuity,' in *Power and the Nation in European History*, ed. Len Scales and Oliver Zimmer (Cambridge: Cambridge University Press, 2005), 67–101.
8. See, for instance, Rees Davies, 'The Medieval State: The Tyranny of a Concept?' and Susan Reynolds, 'There Were States in Medieval Europe: A Response to Rees Davies,' *Journal of Historical Sociology* 16 (2003): 280–99, 550–5.
9. James M. Murray, *Bruges, Cradle of Capitalism 1280–1390* (Cambridge: Cambridge University Press, 2005).
10. For recent archaeological research on early Bruges, see *Op het raakvlak van twee landschappen, de vroegste geschiedenis van Brugge*, ed. Bieke Hillewaert et al. (Bruges: Van de Wiele, 2011).
11. Jan Dumolyn, 'Economic Development, Social Space and Political Power in Bruges, c. 1127–1302,'

MEDIEVAL CITIZENSHIP

in *Contact and Exchange in Later Medieval Europe: Essays in Honour of Malcolm Vale*, ed. Hannah Skoda, Patrick Lantschner and R. L. J. Shaw (Woodbridge, 2012), 33–57.

12   Jan Dumolyn and Jelle Haemers, 'Patterns of Urban Rebellion in Medieval Flanders,' *Journal of Medieval History* 31 (2005): 369–93.

13   Peter Stabel, 'Guilds in Late Medieval Flanders: Myths and Realities of Guild Life in an Export-Driven Environment,' *Journal of Medieval History* 30 (2004): 187–212.

14   In general, see Blockmans and Prevenier, *The Promised Lands*, 72–3, 92–6, 103, 116–23.

15   Jelle Haemers, *For the Common Good: State Power and Urban Revolts in the Reign of Mary of Burgundy (1477–1482)* (Turnhout: Brepols, 2008) and *De strijd om het regentschap over Filips de Schone. Opstand, facties en geweld in Brugge, Gent en Ieper (1482–1488)* (Ghent: Academia Press, 2015).

16   For an overview of this variety, see Sheilagh C. Ogilvie, *Institutions and European Trade: Merchant Guilds, 1000–1800* (Cambridge: Cambridge University Press, 2011), 51–8.

17   For the following, see Philippe Godding, *Le droit privé dans les Pays-Bas méridionaux du 12e au 18e siècle* (Brussels: Académie Royale de Belgique, 1987); Marc Boone, 'Droit de bourgeoisie et particularisme urbain dans la Flandre bourguignonne et hapsbourgeoisie (1384–1585),' *Revue Belge de philologie et d'histoire* 74 (3–4) (1996): 707–26.

18   Marc Boone and Peter Stabel, 'New Burghers in the Late Medieval Towns of Flanders and Brabant: Conditions of Entry, Rules, Reality,' in *Neubürger im späten Mittelalter: Migration und Austausch in der Städtelandschaft des alten Reiches (1250–1550)*, ed. Rainer C. Schwinges et al. (Berlin: Duncker & Humblot, 2002), 317–32.

19   Marc Boone, 'The Desired Stranger: Attraction and Expulsion in the Medieval City,' in *Living in the City: Urban Institutions in the Low Countries, 1200–2010*, ed. Leo Lucassen and Wim Willems (New York: Routledge, 2012), 32–45.

20   See, for instance, Shennan Hutton, *Women and Economic Activities in Late Medieval Ghent* (New York: Palgrave Macmillan, 2011); Martha Howell, *Women, Production and Patriarchy in Late Medieval Cities* (Chicago: University of Chicago Press, 1986).

21   For the early formulation of towns as 'places protected by a special peace', see Raoul C. Van Caenegem, 'Notes on Galbert of Bruges and His Translators,' in *Peasants and Townsmen in Medieval Europe*, ed. Adriaan Verhulst, Jean-Marie Duvosquel, and Erik Thoen (Ghent: Snoeck-Ducaju & Zoon, 1995), 619–29.

22   See, for instance, Jean Lestocquoy, *Les villes de Flandre et d'Italie sous la gouvernement des patriciens (Xie–XVe siècles)* (Paris: Presses universitaires de France, 1952); Albert Vermeesch, *Essai sur les origines et la signification de la commune dans le Nord de la France* (Heule: UGA, 1966); John K. Hyde, *Society and Politics in Medieval Italy: The Evolution of the Civil Life, 1000–1350* (New York: St Martin's Press, 1973).

23   For a discussion of these trends, see Patrick Boucheron and Denis Menjot, *La ville médiévale: Histoire de l'europe urbaine 2* (Paris: Seuil, 2003), 289–311; Peter Blickle, *Kommunalismus: Skizzen einer gesellschaftlichen Organisationsform* (Munich; Oldenbourg Verlag, 2000).

24 See generally, John Watts, *The Making of Polities: Europe 1300–1500* (Cambridge: Cambridge University Press, 2009), 98–116; Marc Boone, *À la recherche d'une modernité civique: La société urbaine des anciens Pays-Bas au bas Moyen Âge* (Brussels: Éd. de l'Université de Bruxelles, 2010).

25 *Galbertus Brugensis: De multro, traditione, et occisione gloriosi Karoli comitis Flandriarum* ed. Jeff Rider (Turnhout: Brepols, 1994); Marc Ryckaert and James M. Murray, 'Bruges in 1127,' in *The Murder, Betrayal, and Slaughter of the Glorious Charles, Count of Flanders, Galbert of Bruges*, ed. Jeff Rider (New Haven/London, 2013), lvii–lxxv.

26 Marc Boone, 'La construction d'un républicanisme urbain: Enjeux de la politique municipale dans les villes flamandes au bas Moyen Âge,' in *Enjeux et expressions de la politique municipale (XIIe–XXe siècles)*, eds. Denis Menjot and Jean-Luc Pinol (Paris: L'Harmattan, 1997), 41–60; Jan Dumolyn, 'Het corporatieve element in de Middelnederlandse letterkunde en de zogenaamde laatmiddeleeuwse burgermoraal,' *Spiegel der Letteren* 56 (2014): 123–54.

27 Griet Maréchal, 'Het Sint-Janshospitaal in de eerste eeuwen van zijn bestaan,' in *Sint-Janshospitaal Brugge 1188–1976* (Bruges: Sint-Janshospitaal, 1976), 41–75.

28 Griet Maréchal, *De sociale en politieke gebondenheid van het Brugse hospitaalwezen in de Middeleeuwen* (Kortrijk: UGA, 1978). For the wider context, see *Serving the Urban Community: The Rise of Public Facilities in the Low Countries*, ed. Manon van der Heijden (Amsterdam: Amsterdam University Press, 2009).

29 Michael T. Galvin, 'Credit and Parochial Charity in Fifteenth-Century Bruges,' *Journal of Medieval History* 28 (2002): 131–54.

30 For the aldermen's oaths, see Stadsarchief [SB], Bruges, 114: i, fo. 10v (1398); ii, fo. 163r–v (1432).

31 Claudia Rapp, 'City and Citizenship as Christian Concepts of Community,' in *The City in the Classical and Post-Classical World: Changing Contexts of Power and Identity*, ed. Claudia Rapp and H. A. Drake (Cambridge: Cambridge University Press, 2014), 153–66.

32 This was a topos later played out in scenes of entry ceremonies staged to welcome rulers into their towns in the late middle ages: Gordon Kipling, *Enter the King: Theatre, Liturgy, and Ritual in the Medieval Civic Triumph* (Oxford: Oxford University Press, 1998), 24–6, 36–7, 50–1, 58–9.

33 In general, see Ulrich Meier, *Mensch und Bürger: Die Stadt im Denken spätmittelalterlicher Theologen, Philosophen und Juristen* (Munich: R. Oldenbourg, 1994); Keith D. Lilley, *City and Cosmos: The Medieval World in Urban Form* (London: Reaktion Books, 2009).

34 André Vauchez, 'Saints and Pilgrimages: New and Old,' in *The Cambridge History of Christianity: Christianity in Western Europe c.1100–c.1500*, ed. Miri Rubin and Walter Simons (Cambridge: Cambridge University Press, 2009), 324–39.

35 See Thomas A. Boogaart II, *An Ethnogeography of Late Medieval Bruges: Evolution of the Corporate Milieu 1280–1349* (Lewiston: Edwin Mellen Press, 2004), chapter 6; Andrew Brown, *Civic Ceremony and Religion in Medieval Bruges c.1300–1520* (Cambridge: Cambridge University Press), 39; Noël Geirnaert, 'De oudste sporen van het Heilig Bloed in Brugge

(1255–1310),' *Handelingen van het genootschap voor geschiedenis te Brugge* 147 (2010): 247–55.

36 According to charters issued in July 1302: Louis Gilliodts-Van Severen, *Inventaire des archives de la ville de Bruges*, 9 vols. (Bruges: E. Gailliard, 1871–85), vol. I, 93, 98. The victory of craftsmen came as part of an alliance with a faction representing some of the merchants and 'patricians'.

37 SB, 96, 1, fo. 48r–v.

38 André Vauchez, 'Liturgy and Folk Culture in the *Golden Legend*,' in idem, *The Laity in the Middle Ages*, trans. Margery J. Scheider (Notre Dame: Notre Dame UP, 1993), 129–39; Andrea Löther, *Prozessionen in Spätmittelalterliche Städten* (Cologne: Böhlau, 1999); Rita Tekippe, 'Pilgrimage and Procession: Correlation of Meaning Practice and Effects,' in *Art and Architecture of Late Medieval Pilgrimage in Northern Europe and the British Isles: Texts*, ed. Sarah Blick and Rita Tekippe (Leiden: Brill, 2005), 693–751.

39 Brown, *Civic Ceremony*, 73–99.

40 SB, 96, i, fos. 63v–4v.

41 For the classic overview of secular 'rationalisation' in relation to cities, see Max Weber, *The City*, trans. D. Martindale and G. Neuwirth (New York: The Free Press, 1958).

42 See, for instance, André Vauchez, 'Patronage of Saints and Civic Religion in the Italy of the Communes,' in idem, *The Laity in the Middle Ages*, 153–68; Nicholas Terpstra, 'Civic Religion,' in *The Oxford Handbook of Medieval Christianity*, ed. John Arnold (Oxford: Oxford University Press, 2014), 148–65.

43 The risk of anachronism and teleology in this argument has to be acknowledged, however: Patrick Boucheron, 'Religion civique, religion civile, religion séculière: L'ombre d'un doute,' *Revue de synthèse* 134, 6th series, no. 2 (2013): 161–83.

44 Derek Heater, *A History of Education for Citizenship* (New York: RoutledgeFalmer, 2003); David Burchell, 'Ancient Citizenship and its Inheritors,' in Isin and Turner, *Handbook*, 89–104; Richard Dagger, 'Republican Citizenship,' in ibid., 145–58; Sandra Grey, 'Citizen Engagement,' in *New Zealand Government and Politics*, 6th edition, ed. Janine Hayward (Melbourne: Oxford University Press), 496–8.

45 Reinhard Strohm, *Music in Late Medieval Bruges* (Oxford: Oxford University Press, 1990), 33, 39, 85–6; Willem Vorsterman, ed., *Dits die excellente cronike van Vlaenderen* (Antwerp, 1531), fo. 220r.

46 Anne-Laure Van Bruaene, *Om beters wille: Rederijkerskamers en de stedelijke cultuur in de zuidelijke Nederlanden 1400–1650* (Amsterdam: Amsterdam University Press, 2008); Johan Oosterman, 'Anthonis de Roovere. Het werk: overlevering, toeschrijving en plaatsbepaling,' *Jaarboek De Fonteine* 45/6 (1995/6): 9–88.

47 SB, 96, 14, fos. 208v–9r.

48 See, for instance, various contributions in Claudia Bell and Steve Matthewman, eds., *Cultural Studies in Aotearoa New Zealand: Identity, Space and Place* (Melbourne: Oxford University Press, 2004).

49   For space ('perceived', 'conceived' and 'lived') as a productive force that shapes identities, see Henri Lefebvre, *The Production of Space*, trans. Donald Nicholson-Smith (Oxford: Blackwell, 1992); Marc Boone and Martha Howell, 'Introduction,' in *The Power of Space in Late Medieval and Early Modern Europe: The Cities of Italy, Northern France and the Low Countries*, ed. Marc Boone and Martha C. Howell (Turnhout: Brepols, 2013), 1–10.
50   A foundation endowed by the burgher Jan Craycieter ca. 1360 required the great bell of Our Lady's church to be rung as the Holy Blood was processed to and from the Boeverie gate, and as it passed between the Ghent gate and St Katherine gate (OCMW, Bruges archive, Register 178, fo. 64r).
51   The relics of St Donatian sometimes took a longer route closer to the larger outlines of the twelfth-century walls: Brown, *Civic Ceremony*, 97.
52   Peter Stabel, 'The Market-Place and Civic Identity in Late Medieval Flanders,' in *Shaping Urban Identity in Late Medieval Europe*, ed. Marc Boone and Peter Stabel (Leuven: Garant, 2000), 43–64.
53   On the wall building, see Murray, *Cradle of Capitalism*, 55–61, 63–7. In 1303 measures were taken to improve the route near the Boeverie city gate to allow the procession to pass there (SAB, 216, 1303, fo. 24r).
54   See use of 'thresholds' from a social-anthropological perspective (borrowed from van Gennep's 'rites of passage') to describe transformative processes in the medieval period: V. Turner and E. Turner, *Image and Pilgrimage in Christian Culture* (New York: Columbia University Press, 1978). Are modern visitors, immigrants or returning citizens at Auckland International Airport, passing through the Arrivals marae-style gate, with its sensory experience of native bird-song, signalled entry into a 'clean and green' New Zealand?
55   Jan Dumolyn, 'Une idéologie urbaine "bricolée" en Flandre médiévale: les sept portes de Bruges dans le manuscrit Gruuthuse,' *Revue Belge de philologie et d'histoire* 88 (2010): 1031–83; James D. Tracy, ed., *City Walls: The Urban Enceinte in Global Perspective* (Cambridge: Cambridge University Press, 2000), 88–116.
56   *De gedichten van Anthonis de Roovere*, ed. Jacobus J. Mak (Zwolle: Tjeenk Willink, 1955), 360–5.
57   Boone, 'The Desired Stranger'.
58   See, for instance, the city decrees in 1496 against the 'many young strong and healthy men and women' who begged in this city rather than worked; and in 1497 against *rouckloose knechten* who, having no good craft, daily caused trouble (SB, 120, Hallegeboden, i, fos. 262v, 340v).
59   The phrase '*buiten den paeys vande stede*' appears in some of the banishment sentences (e.g. SB, 157, Civiele Sententiën Vierschaar (1491–2), fo. 40r. Craft guild authorities could also expel their guildsmen from the town. Jan van Herwaarden, *Opgelegde bedevaarten: Een studie over de praktijk van opleggen van bedevaarten (met name in de stedelijke rechtspraak) in de Nederlanden gedurende de late middleeuwen (ca. 1300–1550)* (Amsterdam: Van Gorcum, 1978).

60 Marc Boone, 'State Power and Illicit Sexuality: The Persecution of Sodomy in Late Medieval Bruges,' *Journal of Medieval History* 22 (1996): 135–53.
61 SB, 192 (Verluydboek), fos. 38v, 47r, 60v, 75r, 77r.
62 For the various ways in which modern citizenship can be a category of exclusion, see Isin and Turner, 'Citizenship Studies: An Introduction,' 5–7.
63 SAB, 192 (Verluydboek), fos. 10r–12r. See also Boone, 'State Power,' 137–8.
64 Raoul C. Van Caenegem, 'Considerations on the Customary Law of Twelfth-Century Flanders,' in idem, *Law, History, the Low Countries and Europe* (London: Hambledon Press, 1994); Henri Pirenne, *Les villes et les institutions urbaines* (Paris: Alcan, 1939).
65 For example, the dukes began to challenge the right of town governments to grant 'out-burghership' to people residing out of towns (Boone, 'Droit,' 715–21).
66 Jan Dumolyn, 'Justice, Equity and the Common Good: The State Ideology of the Councillors of the Burgundian Dukes,' in *The Ideology of Burgundy: The Promotion of National Consciousness*, ed. D'Arcy J. D. Boulton and Jan R. Veenstra (Leiden: Brill, 2006), 1–20.
67 Jan Dumolyn and Élodie Lecuppre-Desjardin, 'Le Bien Commun en Flandre médiévale: Une lutte discursive entre princes et sujets,' in *De Bono Communi: The Discourse and Practice of the Common Good in the European City (13th–16th c.)*, ed. Anne-Laure Van Bruaene and Élodie Lecuppre-Desjardin (Turnhout: Brepols, 2010), 253–66.
68 SB, 96: 2, fo. 159r; 11, fo. 326. It was reopened only in 1452, after Bruges had helped the duke against 'the rebels of Ghent'. Marc Boone, 'Destroying and Reconstructing the City: The Inculcation and Arrogation of Princely Power in the Burgundian-Hapsburg Netherlands (14th–16th Centuries),' in *Propagation of Power in the Medieval West*, ed. Martin Gosman, Arie Johan Vanderjagt, and Jan R. Veenstra (Groningen: Egbert Forsten, 1997), 1–33.
69 Brown, *Civic Ceremony*, 260–7.
70 Boone, 'State Power'.
71 SB, 157, Civiele Sententiën Vierschaar (1491–2), fos. 2v–4r, 41r–4r, 45r–6r, 91r–3r, 106v.
72 Ibid., fo. 3v.
73 But note also the defiant stand of Dutch cities against Hapsburg power in the late sixteenth century. For an overview of this perspective on urban history in the region, see Blockmans and Prevenier, *The Promised Lands*, 235–41.
74 Isin and Turner, 'Citizenship Studies,' 1, 3.
75 Cf. *The Oxford Handbook of Cities in World History*, ed. Peter Clark (Oxford: Oxford University Press, 2013).

5. JEWS & CHRISTIANS AS SECOND-CLASS CITIZENS IN ISLAMIC EGYPT

Christopher J. van der Krogt

JEWS & CHRISTIANS AS SECOND-CLASS CITIZENS IN ISLAMIC EGYPT

In November 641, Cyrus, the Byzantine governor of Egypt, agreed to surrender Alexandria to the Arab commander 'Amr ibn al-'As the following September. For nearly a thousand years, the city founded by and named after an earlier conqueror, Alexander the Great, had been the capital of Egypt. Though overwhelmingly Coptic Christian, it also had a large Jewish population that traced its origins back to one of Alexander's early successors, Ptolemy I (305–282 BCE), who had encouraged immigration from Judaea.[1]

'Amr had been in the country two years and, having overcome almost all resistance, he now became its new governor, answerable only to Caliph 'Umar ibn al-Khattab (d. 644), who ruled from Medina. Following the latter's instructions, 'Amr kept his Muslim troops separate from Christian influences in Alexandria by setting up a new capital, Fustat, in the area known today as Old Cairo, centring on the mosque that still bears his name.[2] Such separation could not last, and eventually Egypt would become an overwhelmingly Muslim country. It still has the largest Christian minority in the Middle East and North Africa, but the Jewish population all but disappeared in the twentieth century as a by-product of the conflict with the new state of Israel.

This chapter examines the legal status of non-Muslims in Islamic Egypt, focusing on the medieval period (ending with the Ottoman occupation of 1517). It begins with the conquest, arguing that the primary purpose of asserting Islamic rule over non-Muslims was to tax them. Jews and Christians, however, moved into Arab settlements and were naturally attracted to the religion of their rulers — whether out of religious conviction or personal ambition. From the eighth century, Muslim rulers and scholars were no longer content with the relatively generous rights accorded to indigenous non-Muslims by the original conquerors, and they sought to assert more forcefully the superiority of Islam and Muslims. Unbelievers were accorded an elaborately defined legal status subordinate to that of believers: Jews and Christians were effectively second-class citizens. After briefly sampling the implementation of Islamic law concerning religious minorities in medieval Egypt, the chapter will conclude by showing how modern discussions about the status of non-Muslims as citizens have continued to draw on this legal heritage and the attitudes it enshrines. In other words, despite adopting the language of citizenship and human rights, understandings of citizenship in modern Egypt are still heavily influenced by medieval assumptions about inequality based on religion.

The subjugation of Egypt was part of a larger movement of Islamic conquest that established Arab-Muslim rule from the Atlantic to Central and South Asia in little more than a century after the death of the Prophet Muhammad in 632. With the unification of Arabia under Islamic rule by 634, the only outlet for the Arabs' traditional practice of raiding was to attack the neighbouring Byzantine and Sasanian (Persian) territories.[3] Beyond demonstrating one's martial valour, the purpose of raiding was to plunder and acquire captives.

Islam accommodated these motives and facilitated an unprecedented unity among the Arabs, giving them an ideology of conquest: according to the Qur'an (21:105), God's righteous servants will inherit the earth.[4] Reflecting on Muhammad's victory over a Jewish tribe, the Qur'an (33:27) reminded the believers that Allah (God) had made them heirs to the Jews' lands, houses and wealth in a place where they had not set foot before. The Muslim historian al-Tabari (d. 923) presents an Arab commander, Zuhrah ibn al-Hawiyyah, explaining to the Persian general Rustam that God had told the Prophet, 'I have given to this community dominion over those who did not embrace my religion.'[5] With the coming of Islam, inter-tribal Arab fighting was transformed into a religious war of conquest, and those who did not survive to reap worldly rewards would be welcomed into paradise instead.

Although the conquests were a religious venture, enriching the believers was a higher priority than adding to their number. Addressing two Egyptian envoys, 'Amr is said to have invited the Christians either to become Muslims

or pay *jizyah* (an annual levy) in exchange for protection.[6] Presumably, it was only the Muslims from whom they needed protection, however: the Prophet had allegedly promised his followers that they would conquer Egypt, while admonishing that they should avoid harming its people because of their kinship.[7] 'Umar evidently wrote to 'Amr that prisoners were to be given the choice of joining the Muslims or returning to their own people. He also declared that *jizyah* was preferable to plunder because the former would provide revenue for future generations of Muslims whereas booty, once shared, was quickly dissipated.[8] In practice, *jizyah* did not preclude plunder: the Christians of Alexandria knew that, in addition to the agreed annual levy, they should also offer the occupiers an initial tribute in gold.[9] For a century after the conquest of Egypt, the small population of perhaps 100,000 Arabs, mostly settled in Fustat, but with garrisons in Alexandria and Aswan, was not interested in sharing its wealth and status with newcomers, whether Arab Muslims or indigenous converts.[10]

Eventually, however, Egypt developed into an Arab-Muslim country. Egyptians who wanted to convert initially had to give up their lands and livelihood to become clients (*mawali*) of Arabs, but conversion was encouraged after the 'Abbasids replaced the Umayyads as the caliphal dynasty in 750.[11] Michael Brett argues that the shift from a predominantly Christian to a predominantly Muslim population probably occurred in the later eleventh century. Within a relatively stable population hovering around a norm of four or five million people, the transition was caused less by Christian conversion than by Arab immigration. It was further promoted by the marriage of Arab men to Christian women (whose progeny were Muslims) and the higher relative fertility of Muslims (to which Christian monks and nuns effectively contributed).[12] Shaun O'Sullivan similarly emphasises Coptic demographic decline, attributable to 'a cycle of repression, failed revolts, and aggravated repression', that made space for Arab settlement and led to the 'Islamization of Egypt . . . by the ninth century'.[13]

In traditional Islamic law, the Shari'ah, legal status depends on one's religion. According to Islamic teaching, Muhammad is the final prophet sent by Allah to mankind, so the revelation he received, the Qur'an, supersedes all earlier scriptures, notably the Torah of Moses, the Psalms of David, and the Gospel of Jesus. Despite their failure to recognise Muhammad and his revelation, not accepting that his coming had been foretold in the Bible, Jews and Christians remained 'People of the Book' — recipients of genuine scriptures and adherents of divinely revealed religions. They therefore merited a greater degree of legal protection than those who worshipped many gods and had no scripture — the idolaters or polytheists (*mushrikun*, literally those guilty of *shirk*, associating other divinities with Allah). On the basis of a late passage of the Qur'an (9:1–37, especially verses 5 and 29) and reported precedents of the Prophet and Abu Bakr, the first caliph ('successor' to the Prophet), Muslim scholars determined that polytheists, at least if they were Arabs, were to be given a choice between Islam and death. By contrast, the People of the Book could keep their religions but were required to pay *jizyah*.[14] In their treaties with the conquered Egyptians, the Arabs demanded annual *jizyah* payments, sometimes specifying a rate of two dinars for each adult male (except for the poor) as well as other goods, such as food supplies, in return for military protection and the right to continue practising Judaism and Christianity.[15]

Looking back over the period of conquest, Muslim legal scholars elaborated an idealised interpretation of *jihad*, a word that literally means 'striving' but which, following a number of passages in the Qur'an (e.g., 2:216–8), they applied to war in the cause of Allah. Offensive *jihad* was premised on a distinction between the Dar al-Harb (the land of war) and the Dar al-Islam (the land of submission, Arabic *islam*, where Muslims ruled, and the Shari'ah was supposed to be applied). Among Muslim scholars, *jihad* was understood primarily as an obligation on the community or its representatives to extend the Dar al-Islam by conquering the Dar al-Harb. In principle, the jurists taught, the Muslim leader (the caliph or *imam*) should offer People of the Book on the borders of the Dar al-Islam the choice of adopting Islam or accepting a covenant (*dhimmah*) by which they agreed to live under Islamic rule while retaining their own religion. Jews and Christians under Islamic rule were therefore known as People of *Dhimmah* or *dhimmi*s.

Peace agreements between Muslim conquerors and their new non-Muslim subjects reflected the situation at the time, but within a century or so they proved inadequate as increasing numbers of Arabs immigrated, non-Muslims moved into Muslim settlements, and *dhimmi*s converted to Islam. Al-Tabari records the Treaty of Misr in which 'Amr granted the Christians 'immunity for themselves, their religion [*millah*, religious community], their possessions, churches, [and] crucifixes, as well as their land and their waterways', adding that 'Nothing of these will be interfered with or decreased.'[16] Bishop John of Nikiu confirms that when Alexandria surrendered, the Muslims promised 'to desist from seizing Christian Churches' and declared they would not 'intermeddle with any concerns of the Christians'.[17]

As it became impossible to segregate believers from unbelievers, and ethnic Arab hegemony gave way to Islamic religious hegemony, new norms were developed for communal interaction that demonstrated the superiority of Islam and Muslims. 'Umar ibn 'Abd al-'Aziz ('Umar II), an Umayyad caliph who ruled from Damascus (717–20), declared *mushrikun* (including Jews and Christians) to be 'impure since God has made them the army of Satan'. Non-Muslim scribes (*khatib*s, a generic term for state officials from lowly clerks to powerful financial administrators) were therefore to be dismissed from official employment and replaced by Muslims since 'the annihilation of their deeds is the annihilation of their religions'. It was fitting that they be reduced to 'humility and contempt' (recalling Qur'an 2:61) as indicated by distinctive clothing.[18] The same reasoning was used in an 850 edict asserting the superiority of Islam promulgated by the 'Abbasid Caliph al-Mutawakkil (847–61), who ruled from Samarra. He added the further justification that *dhimmi*s in power were prone to oppressing and exploiting Muslims, and he imposed a number of restrictions on *dhimmi*s that would be reasserted by later rulers.[19]

In principle, however, Islamic jurisprudence (*fiqh*) was not grounded upon governmental decrees but developed by scholars drawing primarily on the Qur'an and the exemplary tradition (*Sunnah*) of the Prophet and, less often, his Companions. This tradition was expressed in numerous reports (*hadith*s) authenticated by accompanying lists of transmitters going back to the original witnesses.

A comprehensive and influential early attempt to draw up a code expressing the status of non-Muslims is attributed to al-Shafi'i, the founder of one of the four recognised Sunni schools of law. Al-Shafi'i (d. 820) studied and taught in Arabia and Iraq before finally settling in Fustat and teaching in the mosque of 'Amr. His huge legal compendium, the *Kitab al-Umm*, includes a model treaty of protection that a Muslim ruler could adapt when a city inhabited by unbelievers submitted 'to the authority of Islam and to no contrary authority'.[20] The offer of protection to the signatory and his fellow Christians, said to have requested it, was binding on all Muslims as long as the *dhimmi*s upheld the conditions listed in the treaty — though it included a stipulation that the Christians would carry out any further obligations imposed subsequently.

The most influential text on Muslim–*dhimmi* relations was the Pact (*'ahd* or *'aqd*) of 'Umar, also known as the Stipulations or Conditions of 'Umar (*al-Shurut 'Umar* or *al-Shurut al-'Umariyyah*). A number of versions were preserved, but the best known is that of al-Turtushi (d. 1126), a scholar from Tortosa who settled in Alexandria.[21] Al-Turtushi included the Pact in his *Siraj al-Muluk* (*The Lamp of Kings*), a treatise on Islamic government rather than a work of jurisprudence, dedicated to the vizier al-Ma'mun al-Bata'ahi (executed in 1125).[22] The Pact is preserved as a *hadith* authenticated by a prefatory note attributing the recorded text to 'Abd al-Rahman ibn Ghanm (d. 697), who served 'Umar as a judge in Syria. Versions of the document preserved by other writers indicate that it was well known by the end of the eighth century, and Milka Levy-Rubin argues that it emerged out of eighth-century discussions on the treatment of *dhimmi*s. The original treaties, though in principle still binding, conceded too much liberty to unbelievers who now lived among Muslims; moreover, cities taken by force or founded by the conquerors (like Fustat) had no treaties.[23] Thus, the Pact of 'Umar was evidently devised as a general document that would override particular agreements and reflect the assertiveness of the Muslim elite from the ninth century. Although it refers explicitly only to Christians, most of its regulations were applied to Jews as well.[24]

The Pact takes the form of a petition said to have been offered to the second caliph by the Christians of Syria, who sought protection (*aman*) for themselves and their religious community (*millah*) in return for accepting a number of conditions. 'Umar allegedly ratified their petition after adding, 'We shall not strike any Muslim.' The petitioners acknowledged that they would forfeit their *dhimmah* and 'become liable to the penalties for contumacy and sedition' if they violated the conditions.[25] Like al-Shafi'i's draft, the petition format seems to reflect the style used for decrees promulgated by Muslim rulers long after the time of 'Umar I in response to petitions. In this case, it had the advantage of 'explaining' the origins of stipulations imposed on *dhimmi*s that could not be traced back to the Qur'an or the words of the Prophet and legitimating their imposition on non-Muslim subjects.[26]

Only a few provisions listed in the Pact seem to reflect the original peace agreements. Christians allegedly promised to offer board and lodging to Muslim travellers for up to three days and not to harbour enemy spies. As al-Shafi'i further specified, *dhimmi*s were not to deceive Muslims or aid their enemies, for example by showing them the weak points in the Muslims' defences; nor were they to fight the Muslims.

Most elements of al-Shafi'i's model and the Pact of 'Umar actually drew upon the discriminatory customs of the Byzantine and Sasanian societies that had preceded the conquests. Restrictions concerning state employment, places of worship, intermarriage, owning slaves belonging to the dominant religion, religious conversion and defaming true religion reflect Byzantine anti-Jewish legislation.[27] The imposition of specific clothing and other distinguishing signs (*ghiyar*) by which *dhimmi*s could be recognised evidently derived from the Sasanian practice of demarcating social classes by their respective dress codes. Now, the social hierarchy was simplified by a basic division between Muslims as the new elite, and non-Muslims as the new commoners.[28]

Conquered Christians could not really have requested to live under a range of restrictions that gave them less liberty than the documented peace settlements, but the Pact became central to Muslims' conceptions of the place of unbelievers within Islamic society. It seems likely that 'Umar II's regulations concerning *dhimmi*s came to be confused with the developed Pact. Later, although 'Umar II was well regarded by subsequent generations, a mistaken attribution of the *ghiyar* and other impositions to the first 'Umar — a Companion of the Prophet and a conqueror — further enhanced their authority.[29] Since it was an Islamic invention, it is not surprising that *dhimmi*s themselves seem to have had no knowledge of the Pact until it was promulgated publicly in the Mamluk period (1250–1517).[30]

Provisions in both documents regulating the clothing of *dhimmi*s and their public comportment indicate an effort to demonstrate the superiority of Islam and Muslims over unbelievers, whether Jewish or Christian. According to al-Shafi'i, *dhimmi*s were not permitted to obstruct Muslims by occupying the middle of the road or seats in the market, and the Pact says that they must surrender their seats. *Dhimmi*s' saddles and mounts had to be distinguished from those of Muslims, and the Pact explains that Christians were not to sit astride saddles or carry swords or other arms. This was not because they posed a security threat but because riding on horseback and bearing arms were marks of power and status. *Dhimmi*s had to have a distinctive mark on their *qalansuwah*s (conical hats) and wear a distinctive girdle or belt, the *zunnar*, on the outside of their clothes. Coloured belts had distinguished the adherents of different religions under Sasanian rule, but under Islamic rule their imposition became a means of stigmatising unbelievers.[31] The Pact added that Christians would wear distinguishing footwear, clip the hair of their foreheads (like freed captives) and avoid parting their hair in the manner of Muslims. Nor would they use seals with Arabic inscriptions (symbols of authority) or imitate the speech of Muslims — though in what way is unclear.[32] A Christian was not to be addressed by a *kunya* in the Arab manner, which showed respect by calling someone the father or mother of their first-born son. Christians were not permitted to build houses taller than those of their Muslim neighbours.

Muslims were to be protected from exposure to other religions. Al-Shafi'i

forbade Christians in Muslim cities from displaying crosses, striking clappers, building new churches or teaching Muslims about their 'polytheistic' beliefs concerning the divinity of Jesus.[33] The Pact required Christians to refrain from public demonstrations of their religion, notably by displaying crosses or scriptures where Muslims would see them or by holding public processions on Palm Sunday or at Easter.[34] They could only summon the faithful to worship using clappers quietly inside churches. Nor could they pray too loudly in church when Muslims were around, or in funeral processions. As al-Shafi'i noted, special provisions applied to sacred places: Christians could travel anywhere in the Dar al-Islam except Mecca and they could only stay a maximum of three days in any city of the Hijaz (the western coastal region of Arabia that includes the holy cities of Mecca and Medina). By preventing Jews and Christians from too openly practising their religions, Muslims could dominate public space and enjoy the reassurance that other religions had been superseded.

Some *dhimmi* regulations were evidently intended to prevent the conversion of Muslims to Judaism or Christianity. Both documents forbade *dhimmi*s from encouraging the conversion of Muslims (which would be a capital crime on the part of the apostate), and the Pact added that Christians must nevertheless allow conversions to Islam. In two manuscripts of the Pact, a letter from 'Umar added that Christians were not to purchase 'anyone made prisoner by the Muslims', presumably a gloss on the provision that Christians would not take slaves allocated to Muslims.[35] Perhaps this was to assert the hierarchy of Muslims over all others, but it could be expected that young slaves in particular, usually war captives, would convert to the religion of their masters. Jewish traders evidently did convert their slaves even though, in theory, only conversion to Islam was permissible.[36]

By comparison with al-Shafi'i's model treaty, the Pact envisages a more integrated society where the interaction of *dhimmi*s and Muslims is inevitable; in consequence, there is more emphasis on constraining the unbelievers to the advantage of Muslims. The restrictions listed by al-Shafi'i did not apply to cities with peace agreements (which could not be overridden) but only to the *amsar al-muslimin*, by which he meant cities conquered by force or built by

Muslims. Christians living in cities where there were no Muslims, according to the *Kitab al-Umm*, were free to build new churches and practise their religion openly.[37] The Pact, by contrast, largely overrides this distinction: the original treaties are ignored, and the restrictions imposed on Christians are applicable throughout the Dar al-Islam.[38] While still assuming a degree of communal separation, the Pact presents Christians as promising not to build new churches, monasteries, convents or monks' cells either in their own cities or in Muslim neighbourhoods. Nor would they repair religious ruins or buildings located in Muslim areas or bury their dead near the graves of Muslims.

In legal affairs not affecting Muslims, *dhimmi*s could be left to themselves even if they belonged to different religious communities, but, al-Shafi'i observed, if either party to a business transaction brought a complaint to a Muslim judge, the latter would adjudicate according to Islamic law. Al-Shafi'i noted that a wedding between a Muslim groom and a *dhimmi* bride had to be conducted before Muslim witnesses in a rite recognised by Islamic law. Marriage between a Muslim woman and a non-Muslim man could not be countenanced since this would invert the God-given order whereby Muslims held authority over non-Muslims. It would also lead to a Muslim woman bearing and raising non-Muslim children (following their father's religion), thereby building up the number of unbelievers at the expense of the believers.[39]

As outlined by al-Shafi'i, the legal protection offered to *dhimmi*s covered their persons and property (as long as it was considered licit under Islamic law) against all wrong-doers, whether Muslim or non-Muslim. Thus, it did not cover food items prohibited (*haram*) to Muslims (notably blood, wine, carrion or pigs). Such things were permissible to non-Muslims but could not be displayed in Muslim cities or given to Muslims.[40] Their sale to Muslims was invalid: the proceeds would be confiscated, the goods destroyed, and the vendor punished. The Pact mentions only selling wine and, in some versions, keeping pigs. Al-Shafi'i's greater emphasis on *haram* foods seems to reflect a danger, or at least a source of irritation, to Muslims that concerned his contemporaries but lessened as Muslims became more dominant and *dhimmi*s more submissive.[41]

In the case of serious crimes listed by al-Shafi'i, the legal status of *dhimmi*s differed little from that of Muslims even if his decision to mention them reflects the anxieties of his time.[42] Al-Shafi'i's template declared that any unbeliever who spoke improperly of the Prophet, the Qur'an, or the religion of Islam would lose his protection: his life and property would be forfeited to the ruler and he would be treated like an enemy inhabitant of the Dar al-Harb. While presumably less likely to commit (or be accused of) blasphemy (*qadhf*, 'slander'), a Muslim judged to be an apostate could be liable for the death penalty. Al-Shafi'i similarly held *dhimmi* fornication with a Muslim as well as brigandage to be capital crimes that forfeited the protection of a *dhimmi*'s life and property. The penalties for Muslims committing the same crimes also included execution. If convicted of manslaughter, a *dhimmi* or his paternal relatives would have to pay the blood price, and a murderer would have to suffer retaliation or pay the blood price immediately — if the victim's heirs were agreeable. A *dhimmi* thief brought before a Muslim judge might have his hand amputated just as a Muslim thief would, and a convicted *dhimmi* slanderer would also suffer the same penalty as a Muslim. *Dhimmi*s would be punished for offences against the property or honour of Muslims and of unbelievers who had a safe-conduct, but so, in principle, would Muslims.

Al-Shafi'i's model treaty includes details about the *jizyah*, payable only by free males (not slaves) who had reached puberty or the age of 15. The rate was one dinar at the beginning of each year; since the poor were not exempt, wealthier members of the community were expected to pay for them. Travelling merchants were to be charged an additional 10 per cent levy on their merchandise. Shorter than al-Shafi'i's draft, the Pact is not a complete statement of the place of Christians under Islamic rule (neither mentions Jews) and makes no reference to the *jizyah*. Different scholars advocated different amounts for the *jizyah*, some preferring a scale of 48, 24 or 12 dirhems (the latter equivalent to one gold dinar), depending on the means of the payer.[43] Most thought the destitute should be exempt, an opinion sometimes attributed to al-Shafi'i himself, though there were different rulings about what actually constituted penury.[44] Since the payment was usually thought to be owed in lieu of military service, it followed that women, children, slaves and the infirm were exempt.

According to ibn Qayyim (d. 1350), author of the first major treatise on *dhimmah*, most Muslim scholars held the *jizyah* to be a penalty, though some viewed it as a payment for the rights of residence and protection it conferred on unbelievers within an Islamic state;[45] that is, for most, in their ancestral lands. The Qur'an (9:29) declares that *jizyah* must be paid *'an yadin wa-hum saghiruna*, which can be rendered 'out of hand, having been brought low'.[46] This may mean that it was originally considered a just recompense to one who spared the lives of those he defeated.[47] Some interpreters, for example ibn Qayyim's contemporary and fellow Hanbali, ibn al-Naqqash (who died in Cairo in 1362), read these words as an instruction to humiliate the one making a payment.[48] It was commonly asserted that the *dhimmi*s should be slapped on the neck; the preservation of several *hadith*s warning against undue humiliation indicates that some felt the *jizyah* collectors were too harsh.

The extent to which the *ghiyar* and other *dhimmi* policies were enforced is a matter of some debate, with Levy-Rubin arguing recently, contrary to previous writers, that Muslim rulers increasingly sought to apply them from the ninth century rather than from the twelfth.[49] Arguably, the repromulgation of regulations like those of al-Mutawakkil shows that they were not consistently enforced since otherwise reasserting them would have been unnecessary. Be that as it may, the renewed enforcement of *dhimmi* rules also indicates that they embodied a legal norm to which Muslim rulers recognised a need to conform, especially when courting popularity or legitimacy.

Juristic theory did have a negative impact on the lives of Egyptian *dhimmi*s. In 1301, for example, the Mamluk government dismissed state-employed *dhimmi* scribes and asserted the provisions of the Pact of 'Umar by imposing distinctive dress codes on Jews and Christians, forbidding them to ride on horses or mules, demolishing houses taller than those of their Muslim neighbours, lowering the floors of *dhimmi*-owned shops below the level of those owned by Muslims, and boarding up churches. According to ibn Naqqash, these measures were taken 'to enhance the religion [of Islam]', and he personally rejected the authorities' opinion that only recently built churches

should be demolished. In some places, Muslim mobs destroyed churches and synagogues they deemed illegal.[50]

Although not mentioned in the Pact, the prohibition against appointing *dhimmi*s to positions of authority over Muslims was effectively linked to it under the Mamluks.[51] Such appointments seemed to conflict with the Qur'an's warning that believers who took Jews or Christians as allies would themselves be reckoned Jews or Christians (5:51; cf. 3:118). Nevertheless, although temporarily dismissed under al-Hakim and Salah al-Din (d. 1193), *dhimmi*s were usually over-represented in the Fatimid (969–1171) and Ayyubid (1171–1250) administrations and continued to be employed under the Mamluks.[52] Jews were also well represented among physicians, some even serving the army in this capacity.[53] Apart from their particular skills, commonly passed on within families in the absence of a secular education system, *dhimmi*s offered rulers another considerable advantage, albeit involuntarily. As occurred in 1301, they could be dismissed at will to appease a mob whose resentment, ostensibly directed at over-powerful unbelievers, was just as likely caused by anger at governmental rapacity.[54]

Perhaps because it is the only Shari'ah provision concerning subject unbelievers legitimated by reference to the Qur'an — or perhaps simply because it justified the collection of revenue — levying *jizyah* was the most consistently enforced *dhimmi* regulation. Beginning as a tribute imposed on a defeated population, it was retained as a lucrative but discriminatory source of revenue. Given charge of Egypt's finances by his father, the governor 'Abd al-'Aziz, al-Asbagh first imposed the *jizyah* on monks in 693. Although monks were often exempted, the matter was subject to debate, not least for fear that some men entered monasteries to avoid the *jizyah*.[55] The Fatimids' most authoritative jurist was Qadi al-Nu'man (d. 974), an Isma'ili Shi'i like themselves, who permitted collecting *jizyah* from the destitute. His policy was evidently maintained by the Ayyubids who favoured the Shafi'i legal school.[56] Even *dhimmi*s facing starvation were required to pay.[57] Defaulters could be imprisoned, and forced to pay the gaoler, who could treat them cruelly and whose duties did not include the provision of food.[58] The *jizyah* (or *jaliyah* as it was sometimes called) could be collected from boys as young as nine, and arrears were collected from a deceased *dhimmi*'s heirs. Even prolonged absences from the country did not justify exemption; travellers had to carry a certificate showing they had paid — and hope it would be accepted at their destination.[59] Jewish and Christian philanthropists as well as monasteries paid the *jizyah* for their impoverished co-religionists.[60] In addition to the *jizyah*, Egyptian rulers often extorted money from Christians, sometimes imprisoning the patriarch while the funds were raised.[61]

There can be no doubt that coercion — mostly fiscal or social — was an important element in the decision of many Christians and Jews to adopt Islam. During a period of political instability, the governor Hafs ibn Walid (741–4) formed his own army in part from converts to Islam to whom he offered release from the *jizyah*: some 24,000 Christians are said to have apostatised.[62] The implementation of al-Mutawakkil's anti-*dhimmi* policies included the destruction of churches, requiring distinctive clothing, affixing 'frightful pictures' to the doors of Christian homes, and the dismissal of non-Muslim state servants. Inevitably, some felt forced to convert, whether out of poverty or to keep their jobs.[63] If the Fatimids are remembered as relatively benign towards *dhimmi*s, the most notorious outbreak of persecution in Egypt was instigated by the Caliph al-Hakim (996–1021). While requiring Jews to wear heavy images of the golden calf and Christians to wear large crosses in the public baths, he destroyed churches and synagogues. After forcing *dhimmi*s to convert to Islam, he unaccountably reversed his policies, permitting some rebuilding and reversion to Judaism and Christianity.[64]

The periodic loss of patronage when Jewish or Christian officials lost their livelihoods and property through purges of the state bureaucracy increased the inducement for poor *dhimmi*s to escape the *jizyah* by adopting Islam.[65] This outcome could sometimes be averted when scribes conformed outwardly and used their positions and income to obtain better conditions for their former co-religionists.[66] In 1354, Sultan al-Malik al-Salih responded to popular pressure by dismissing *dhimmi* scribes and reimposing the *ghiyar* requirements. He went further than most of his predecessors by requiring converted scribes

actually to attend a mosque and by confiscating 25,000 *faddan*s (up to 200,000 hectares) of ecclesiastical land held in trusts. Along with the state's connivance in the destruction of churches by Muslim mobs, these measures led to numerous apparently permanent conversions.[67]

*D*himmis, then, were citizens of a kind: they were guaranteed protection for their lives and property as well as access to justice but, since they were legally subordinate to Muslims and subject to discrimination, their citizenship status is fittingly characterised as 'second-class'.[68] The purpose of the Pact of 'Umar and other *dhimmi* regulations was to keep unbelievers in their proper stations within Islamic society. They were indeed part of that society, for they could live among Muslims, share the public baths with them, and even, despite the admonitions of Muslim scholars, form friendships and business partnerships with them. In the case of Jewish or Christian women, *dhimmi*s could even marry Muslims, and in practice some Jews, Christians and Muslims even participated in each other's religious festivals, such as Epiphany.[69]

While *dhimmi*s lived within the restrictions imposed by law they were usually afforded its protection, but when *dhimmi*s reached positions of power and wealth many Muslims felt their sense of justice violated. Justice (*al-'adl* and its synonyms) was not merely a matter of legality, but also one of proper balance and the right ordering of society.[70] Any exercise of authority by Jews or Christians over Muslims was not only illegal but contrary to the divinely appointed order. The Shari'ah, not just law but the very path prescribed by Allah, placed *dhimmi*s lower in the social hierarchy than Muslims.[71] When they seemed to reach beyond their divinely appointed bounds, they threatened the superiority of Muslims — or at least of those whose own social status was fragile — and could be subjected to prosecution or indeed persecution. Those elite Muslims who not only permitted unbelievers to flourish but also raised them above believers were not themselves threatened by this imbalance but responded to popular anxiety by dismissals, confiscations and repression.

The proper balance was undermined by Napoleon Bonaparte's occupation of Egypt (1798–1801) when the historic *dhimmah* regulations were abolished, but, under the Ottoman governor Muhammad 'Ali (1805–48), they were reinstated in 1817.[72] Al-Jabarti (d. 1825), an historian who witnessed the occupation, welcomed the restoration of traditional restrictions because the French had inverted the traditional order by favouring Copts and other non-Muslims, permitting them to wear fine clothes, carry weapons, and exercise authority over believers.[73] But Muhammad 'Ali was no traditionalist; he conscripted Copts into his army, not out of idealistic egalitarianism but as part of his programme to make Egypt a strong, independent military power. Similarly, the Khedive Sa'id (1854–63) abolished the *jizyah* in 1855 and instituted large-scale conscription of Copts the following year.

These measures must be understood in the context of the Ottoman Tanzimat or 'reorganisation' of the Empire in response to Western diplomatic pressure and the need to modernise the state. Especially significant were the 1839 Noble Rescript of the Rosehouse Garden (Gülhane Hatt-i Sherif, delivered in the grounds of the Topkapi Palace) and the 1856 Imperial Rescript (Hatt-i Hümayun). In principle, all subjects were now equal before the law and liable for taxation based on their wealth rather than their religion. However, the Hamayouni Decree, as it is often called, required a licence from the head of state for any new church building. Reflecting as it does the traditional prohibition of new churches, this requirement, made even more restrictive by amendments dating from 1934, would become especially problematic in the period of Islamisation that began during the presidency of Anwar Sadat (1970–81).[74]

From the later nineteenth century, Muslim apologists became acutely aware of liberal Western criticisms of the Shari'ah and of their own political instability and economic underdevelopment. In response, they sought to show that Islam, being morally superior to the West, endorses values such as religious toleration — even though this is an ideal developed by the Western Enlightenment.[75] Unsurprisingly, therefore, twentieth-century Muslim reformers discussing the status of non-Muslim minorities focused on theories rather than historical evidence. Some writers wished to provide an Islamic basis for the full citizenship of unbelievers, while others more explicitly sought to reassert Islamic hegemony.[76] The two approaches can be illustrated by Abd al-Rahman Azzam (d. 1976) and his younger contemporary Sayyid Qutb (executed in 1966), who represent respectively what are commonly labelled 'modernist' and 'Islamist' perspectives.

In a classic expression of modernist Islamic apologetics, the Egyptian diplomat Abd al-Rahman Azzam (Azzam Pasha), first Secretary-General of the Arab League (1945–52), argued that 'in modern terms' the pledge of protection (*dhimmah*) 'means citizenship'.[77] Islam only permits war to overcome tyranny, for 'Persecution, forced conversion, and the deprivation of religious freedom,' he declared, 'are more distasteful to God than the taking of life.'[78] Consistent with this reinterpretation of *jihad*, Azzam asserted that, in contrast to its attitude towards idolaters, 'The religion of Islam establishes itself as the protector of the Christian Church and honors its own commitments to Jews when peoples of these faiths seek and are granted protection.'[79]

Once thought 'to imply second-class citizenship', *dhimmah* actually 'constituted the greatest possible affirmation of the protected one's right to enjoy complete religious, administrative, and political freedom'. As long as they 'refrain from undertakings which might prejudice the beliefs and security of Muslims' and pay the 'individual poll tax or community tribute' each year, non-Muslims are guaranteed 'security . . . guardianship and protection'. A *dhimmi* is 'juridically . . . entitled to exactly the same justice as is received by the Muslim in Muslim courts' and cannot be oppressed, persecuted, insulted, or deprived of his rights.[80]

Al-Tabari reports that the Muslim general al-Nu'man ibn Muqarrin warned the Persian king Yazdagird that paying *jizyah* was 'a bad thing but not as bad as the alternative; if you refuse [to pay], it will be war'.[81] In Azzam's Panglossian re-evaluation of *jizyah*, however, it was inconceivable that people would renounce their religion just to save the one dinar levied only on laymen who could pay, so converts must simply have found Islam more pleasing than their former religion.[82] Azzam acknowledged there had been exceptional and isolated instances of tyranny against Christians, for example under al-Hakim and some Mamluk sultans, but Muslim subjects had also suffered at such times. Occasionally, Christians had been persecuted because of envy or fear and for political reasons, but not to make them adopt Islam — whereas Christian rulers had indeed persecuted Jews and heretics for religious motives.[83]

Sayyid Qutb, an educationalist and writer who joined the Muslim Brotherhood, scorned the opinion of apologists like Azzam that *jihad* could only be defensive: such thinking reflected a capitulation to Western orientalist criticisms of Islam. In his view, *jihad* was a means of asserting 'God's absolute sovereignty and people's servitude to Him'.[84] Whether initiated by Muslims or by their enemies, war was inevitable whenever an authentically Islamic community came into existence in the midst of *jahiliyyah*, the barbaric ignorance that characterised the time of the Prophet and, Qutb believed, his own time as well. As the divinely ordained system for the whole world, Islam had a right to overcome humanly devised alternatives that, as the Muslim envoys had told Rustam, enslaved people to other human beings. Qutb cited as authentic al-Tabari's account of an Arab envoy explaining to Rustam that Allah had sent the Muslims to free people from servitude to (or worship of, *ibadah*) earthly rulers and make them servants of God.[85] Only Islam really offers freedom of religion, because human rulers usurp the uniquely divine prerogative of making laws and thereby effectively make themselves into false gods who enslave people.[86]

Judaism and Christianity were among the systems that demanded servitude to other human beings, for as the Qur'an says, Jews and Christians have taken their rabbis and monks as lords besides God — and Christians take Jesus as their lord as well. For Qutb, this was 'in total conflict with the principles of the faith of truth which is based on total submission to God alone, who has no partners'.[87] Indeed, the scripture goes on to say that Allah sent his messenger (Muhammad) to ensure that the religion of truth would prevail over all other religions despite the efforts of the unbelievers, including monks and rabbis who devour people's property and deter them from the way of God (9:30–34). Jews and Christians were no longer authentic monotheists and had been at war with Islam since the days of the Prophet. It was therefore an Islamic duty 'to smash the power of those authorities based on false beliefs until they declare their submission and demonstrate this by paying the submission tax'. The *jizyah* contributed to the defence of the state and other costs as well as constituting a promise 'not [to] stand in physical [or better, "material"] opposition to the efforts [of Muslims] advocating the true Divine faith'.⁸⁸

Qutb was emphatic that, under Islamic rule, Jews and Christians would not be forced to become Muslims because 'there is no compulsion in religion' (Qur'an 2:256).⁸⁹ In an Islamic society, 'every person is free to adopt whatever beliefs he or she wants', but this does not mean they can 'choose to remain in servitude to people like them, or that some of them are elevated to the status of lordship over the rest'.⁹⁰ For Qutb, such practices as being paid for hearing confession or raising money for missionary work were examples of how priests devoured wealth.⁹¹ By following laws made by their religious leaders, Jews and Christians recognised them as lords, which was tantamount to worshipping them.⁹²

It is difficult to see how Judaism and Christianity could survive in a society dominated by Islam if the leadership of these religions were undermined in the name of religious freedom while Muslims could proselytise at will. Despite his doublethink concerning religious freedom — possible only because he regarded Islam as a divinely revealed way of life and other religions as little more than disembodied philosophies — Qutb's prescription seems even more likely to extinguish other religions than the traditional practice of *dhimmah*.

The difficulty of reconciling Western-inspired ideals of citizenship with the Shari'ah, traditionally understood as requiring the domination of Muslims and subordination of non-Muslims, remains a problem in Egypt.⁹³ Between 2011 and 2014, two successive presidents were overthrown and a revised constitution ratified before the election of a third. The 2014 constitution of the Arab Republic of Egypt declares the state to be based on citizenship (*muwataniyyah*) and the rule of law (article 1).⁹⁴ Islam is the religion of the state and the principles of the Islamic Shari'ah are the principal source of legislation (art. 2), but all citizens are allegedly equal before the law, and discrimination is prohibited (art. 9, 19 and 53). Even though freedom of belief is said to be absolute, freedom of religious practice is clearly limited: only the revealed religions (Judaism, Christianity and Islam) have the right to establish places of worship (art. 64). The laws of Egyptian Christians and Jews provide the principles for 'regulating their personal status, religious affairs, and selection of spiritual leaders' (art. 3).

Article 235 promised a new law to regulate the construction and repair of churches consistent with freedom of religious practice within the first term of the new House of Representatives. After prolonged and contentious debate, the new law was passed with the approval of the Coptic Church on 30 August 2016.[95] This was certainly a milestone in raising Christians to the status of full citizens. Egypt's Copts, however, are still waiting to receive the protection of the state against violent sectarian conflicts which, echoing the events of 1301, 1354 and other occasions, continue to take place.[96] In Egypt, one still has to be a Muslim to be accorded the status of a full citizen in practice.[97]

ENDNOTES

1. The word 'Copt', from the Greek *aigyptios* via the Arabic *qibt*, originally applied to all Egyptians, but is used here for members of the Coptic Orthodox Church, the principal church of Egypt. As an adjective, 'Coptic' refers to the Copts and their culture; as a noun it refers to their traditional language.
2. Hugh Kennedy, *The Great Arab Conquests* (Philadelphia: Da Capo Press, 2007), 160–1.
3. Robert G. Hoyland, *In God's Path: The Arab Conquests and the Creation of an Islamic Empire* (Oxford: Oxford University Press, 2015), 55–7.
4. Hoyland, *In God's Path*, 63–5. The passage is quoted in al-Tabari, *The History of al-Tabari*, vol. 12, 'The Battle of Al-Qadisiyyah and the Conquest of Syria and Palestine,' trans. Yohanan Friedman (New York: State University of New York Press, 1992), 84 (Arabic edition, I. 2289), which also refers to martial valour and ethnic pride. Some interpreters hold that 'the earth' or 'the land' here refers to paradise (cf. 39:73–4), but other passages make earthly victory even more explicit (7:128–9; 24:55; 40:51). See further Walid A. Saleh, 'The Psalms in the Qur'an and in the Islamic Religious Imagination,' in *The Oxford Handbook of the Psalms*, ed. William P. Brown (Oxford: Oxford University Press, 2014), 281–5.
5. Al-Tabari, vol. 12, 64 (I. 2268).
6. The final *ta marbuta* is often omitted in transliterating Arabic words like *jizya(h)*, *dhimma(h)* and Shari'a(h).
7. Al-Tabari, *The History of al-Tabari*, vol. 13, 'The Conquest of Iraq, Southwestern Persia, and Egypt,' trans. Gautier H. A. Juynboll (New York: State University of New York Press, 1989), 167–8 (Arabic edition, I. 2285–6). Hagar, the mother of Ishmael and thus, with Abraham, an ancestor of the Arabs, was thought to be Egyptian, but the envoys apparently considered this a rather distant relationship.
8. Al-Tabari, vol. 13, 164 (I. 2582).
9. Milka Levy-Rubin, *Non-Muslims in the Early Islamic Empire: From Surrender to Coexistence* (Cambridge: Cambridge University Press, 2011), 56; John of Nikiu, *The Chronicle of John, Bishop of Nikiu*, trans. Robert Henry Charles (London: Williams & Norgate, 1916), CXX, 27. http://www.tertullian.org/fathers/nikiu2_chronicle.htm; accessed August 2016.
10. Kennedy, *Arab Conquests*, 162–3, 165–6.
11. Mark N. Swanson, *The Coptic Papacy in Islamic Egypt, 641–1517* (Cairo: American University in Cairo Press, 2010), 38–40; Michael Brett, 'Egypt,' in *The New Cambridge History of Islam*, vol. 1, ed. Chase F. Robinson (Cambridge: Cambridge University Press, 2010), 550–1.
12. Brett, 'Egypt,' 555–6, 580.
13. Shaun O'Sullivan, 'Coptic Conversion and the Islamization of Egypt,' *Mamluk Studies Review* 10 (2006): 78.
14. Patricia Crone, *God's Rule: Government and Islam* (Columbia: Columbia University Press, 2004), 368–73.

15 Kennedy, *Arab Conquests*, 153–4.
16 Al-Tabari, vol. 13, 170–2 (I. 2588–9); Kennedy, *Islamic Conquests*, 153–4. The treaty seems to concern the city-fortress (*misr*) of Babylon rather than Egypt (Misr) as a whole, which had not yet been conquered.
17 Levy-Rubin, *Non-Muslims*, 51; John of Nikiu, CXX, 17–20.
18 Levy-Rubin, *Non-Muslims*, 89–96, quoting 95; ibn Naqqash in Bat Ye'or, *The Dhimmi: Jews and Christians under Islam* (Rutherford, NJ: Fairleigh Dickinson University Press, 1985), 182.
19 Bernard Lewis, ed. and trans., *Islam: From the Prophet Muhammad to the Capture of Constantinople* (New York: Harper & Row, 1974), vol. 2, 224–6; Lewis, *The Jews*, 47–8; Mark R. Cohen, *Under Crescent and Cross: The Jews in the Middle Ages* (Princeton: Princeton University Press, 1994), 164; Levy-Rubin, *Non-Muslims*, 96, 103–8; al-Tabari in Bat Ye'or, *The Dhimmi*, 185–6.
20 Levy-Rubin, *Non-Muslims*, 173–6. Quotations from al-Shafi'i are from this translation; cf. Lewis, *Islam*, 219–23.
21 Mark R. Cohen, 'What was the Pact of 'Umar? A Literary-Historical Study,' *Jerusalem Studies in Arabic and Islam* 23 (1999): 100–57 reviews the different versions.
22 Cohen, 'Pact of 'Umar,' 104–5.
23 Levy-Rubin, *Non-Muslims*, 60–70.
24 Cohen, *Crescent and Cross*, 57–8.
25 Levy-Rubin, *Non-Muslims*, 171–2. Quotations from the Pact are from this translation, which includes annotations based on other versions; cf. Lewis, *Islam*, 217–9 and Cohen, 'Pact of 'Umar,' *passim*.
26 Cohen, 'Pact of 'Umar,' 120, 124–30.
27 Levy-Rubin, *Non-Muslims*, 6–7, 116–8, 121–5.
28 Levy-Rubin, *Non-Muslims*, 95, 97–8, 127–9, 136–7, 141–3.
29 Levy-Rubin, *Non-Muslims*, 88–9, 127; cf. Lewis, *The Jews*, 47.
30 Cohen, *Crescent and Cross*, 73, 231, n. 132; al-Maqrizi in Lewis, *Islam*, 229–32. *Mamluks* were foreign slaves raised as Muslims, trained for war and then emancipated. Egypt was ruled by *mamluk* sultans from the fall of the Ayyubids to the Ottoman conquest.
31 Cohen, *Crescent and Cross*, 62–3; Levy-Rubin, *Non-Muslims*, 153–7.
32 M. M. Bravmann, *The Spiritual Background of Early Islam: Studies in Ancient Arab Concepts* (Leiden: Brill, 2009), 200–5; Cohen, *Crescent and Cross*, 61.
33 A clapper (*naqus*) is a wooden board struck to make a noise summoning worshippers to church.
34 Levy-Rubin, *Non-Muslims*, 158–62, explains the origins of the restrictions on processions (including shining lights in the market place, forbidden by the Pact) by their association with royal authority, especially in Persia. Beating drums became a caliphal prerogative and raised voices were considered vulgar or pagan, leading to restrictions on the *naqus* and loud worship.
35 Cohen, 'Pact of 'Umar,' 108.

36 Cohen, *Crescent and Cross*, 64–5; Levy-Rubin, *Non-Muslims*, 123.
37 Levy-Rubin, *Non-Muslims*, 65–6, 82–3, 86.
38 Levy-Rubin, *Non-Muslims*, 83–4.
39 Levy-Rubin, *Non-Muslims*, 123–4.
40 Carrion refers to meat not killed by *halal* methods. Of these foods, only wine was permitted under Jewish law.
41 Levy-Rubin, *Non-Muslims*, 81.
42 Levy-Rubin, *Non-Muslims*, 79–81.
43 Cohen, *Crescent and Cross*, 69; Eli Alshech, 'Islamic Law, Practice, and Legal Doctrine: Exempting the Poor from the Jizya under the Ayyubids (1171–1250),' *Islamic Law and Society* 10, no. 3 (2003): 354.
44 Alshech, 'Islamic Law,' 351–8.
45 Cohen, *Crescent and Cross*, 69.
46 Cohen, *Crescent and Cross*, 56, 67–8; 224, n. 26.
47 Bravmann, *The Spiritual Background*, 199–212.
48 Lewis, *The Jews*, 15.
49 Levy-Rubin, *Non-Muslims*, 6, 100.
50 Ibn Naqqash in Bat Ye'or, *The Dhimmi*, 192–4; al-Maqrizi in Lewis, *Islam*, 229–32; D. P. Little, 'Coptic Conversion to Islam under the Bahri Mamluks, 692–755/1293–1354,' *Bulletin of the School of Oriental and African Studies* 39 (1976): 554–8.
51 Al-Maqrizi (1301) and al-Qalqashandi (1354) in Lewis, *Islam*, 231, 234.
52 Goitein and Lassner, *Mediterranean Society*, 160.
53 Goitein and Lassner, *Mediterranean Society*, 180–1.
54 Tamer el-Leithy, 'Sufis, Copts and the Politics of Piety: Moral Regulation in Fourteenth-Century Upper Egypt,' in *The Development of Sufism in Mamluk Egypt*, ed. Richard McGregor and Adam Sabra (Cairo: Institut français d'archéologie orientale, 2006), 97.
55 Swanson, *Coptic Papacy*, 18; Brett, 'Egypt,' 548; el-Leithy, 'Sufis,' 90–2.
56 Alshech, 'Islamic Law,' 350, n. 4.
57 Alshech, 'Islamic Law,' 363–9.
58 Goitein and Lassner, *Mediterranean Society*, 178, 182–3, 186; Alshech, 'Islamic Law,' 365.
59 Goitein and Lassner, *Mediterranean Society*, 181.
60 El-Leithy, 'Sufis,' 93–4.
61 Swanson, *Coptic Papacy*, 29–30, 35, 44, 46, 97–9.
62 Swanson, *Coptic Papacy*, 20.
63 Swanson, *Coptic Papacy*, 33–5.
64 Swanson, *Coptic Papacy*, 54–6; Cohen, *Crescent and Cross*, 74, 164–5, 176, 180 (cf. Exodus 32; Qur'an 2:51–4, 92–4; 4:153; 7:148–52; 20:83–91).
65 Goitein and Lassner, *Mediterranean Society*, 187.
66 Amalia Levanoni, 'The Mamluks in Egypt and Syria,' in *The New Cambridge History of Islam*,

vol. 2, *The Western Islamic World, Eleventh to Eighteenth Centuries*, ed. Maribel Fierro (Cambridge: Cambridge University Press, 2010), 250.

67 Levanoni, 'The Mamluks,' 257; al-Qalqashandi in Lewis, *Islam*, 234–5; Little, 'Coptic Conversion,' 567–8; O'Sullivan, 'Coptic Conversion,' 79.
68 Lewis, *The Jews*, 62.
69 Goitein and Lassner, *Mediterranean Society*, 294–5, 297–300; Cohen, *Crescent and Cross*, 131–6.
70 Lewis, *The Jews*, 53.
71 Much the same perspective is found among modern Islamists; see Gudrun Krämer, 'Dhimmi or Citizen? Muslim–Christian Relations in Egypt,' in *The Christian–Muslim Frontier: Chaos, Clash or Dialogue?*, ed. Jørgen S. Nielsen (London: I.B. Tauris, 1998), 41–2.
72 Nelly van Doorn-Harder in Magdi Guirguis and van Doorn-Harder, *The Emergence of the Modern Coptic Papacy* (Cairo: American University of Cairo Press), 70–1.
73 Lewis, *The Jews*, 64–5.
74 Youssef Sidhom, Chief Editor of *Watani* (Coptic newspaper), interviewed by the author in Cairo, 2 May 2008; Fiona McCallum, 'Muslim–Christian Relations in Egypt: Challenges for the Twenty-first Century,' in *Christian Responses to Islam: Muslim–Christian Relations in the Modern World*, ed. Anthony O'Mahony and Emma Loosley (Manchester: Manchester University Press, 2008), 72–4, 137; Samia Sidhom, in *Watani International*, 24 August 2016, http://en.wataninet.com/coptic-affairs-coptic-affairs/coptic-issues/do-christians-in-egypt-need-a-law-to-build-churches/17204/.
75 Krämer, 'Dhimmi or Citizen?,' 33–4.
76 Krämer, 'Dhimmi or Citizen?,' 39.
77 Abd al-Rahman Azzam, *The Eternal Message of Muhammad*, trans. Caesar E. Farah (New York: Mentor, 1965; Arabic original, 1946), 124.
78 Azzam, *Eternal Message*, 130.
79 Azzam, *Eternal Message*, 56.
80 Azzam, *Eternal Message*, 124.
81 Al-Tabari, vol. 12, 36 (I. 2240); Kennedy, *Arab Conquests*, 51.
82 Azzam, *Eternal Message*, 164.
83 Azzam, *Eternal Message*, 170.
84 Sayyid Qutb, *In the Shade of the Qur'an*, vol. 7, trans. and ed. Adil Salahi (Markfield, Leicestershire: Islamic Foundation, 2003), 22.
85 Al-Tabari, vol. 12, 64, 67 (I. 2268, 2271); Kennedy, *Arab Conquests*, 63, 112.
86 Qutb, *In the Shade*, vol. 7, 18–25.
87 Sayyid Qutb, *In the Shade of the Qur'an*, vol. 8, trans. and ed. Adil Salahi (Markfield, Leicestershire: Islamic Foundation, 2003), 120.
88 Qutb, *In the Shade*, vol. 8, 122–3.
89 Qutb, *In the Shade*, vol, 7, 20, 134; vol. 8, 41, 102, 307.

90 Qutb, *In the Shade*, vol. 7, 11.
91 Qutb, *In the Shade*, vol. 8, 142–4.
92 Qutb, *In the Shade*, vol. 7, 10–1; vol. 8, 136–9.
93 Krämer, 'Dhimmi or Citizen?,' 44.
94 For a translation, see https://www.constituteproject.org/search?lang=en (accessed August 2016).
95 Adel Mounir and Nader Shukry, in *Watani International*, 31 August 2016, http://en.wataninet.com/politics/parliament/finally-law-for-building-churches-passed/17257/.
96 For recent violence and the partisan role of state authorities, see Marina Ihab, in *Watani International*, 1 June 2016, http://en.wataninet.com/coptic-affairs-coptic-affairs/sectarian/sweeping-the-law-aside-2/16545/; Nader Shukry et al., in *Watani International*, 20 July 2016, http://en.wataninet.com/coptic-affairs-coptic-affairs/sectarian/the-copts-painand-bitterness/16916/; Soliman Shafiq, in *Watani International*, 27 July 2016, http://en.wataninet.com/coptic-affairs-coptic-affairs/sectarian/why-minya-3/16967/.
97 For continued discrimination in sport, see Youssef Sidhom, in *Watani International*, 18 September 2016, http://en.wataninet.com/opinion/editorial/outcome-of-a-crisis-era/17392/.

6. CITIZENSHIP, COMMUNITY & DISEASE IN AN EARLY MODERN CITY

Karen Jillings

CITIZENSHIP, COMMUNITY & DISEASE IN AN EARLY MODERN CITY

'Illness is the night-side of life, a more onerous citizenship. Everyone who is born holds dual citizenship, in the kingdom of the well and in the kingdom of the sick. Although we all prefer to use only the good passport, sooner or later each of us is obliged, at least for a spell, to identify ourselves as citizens of that other place.'[1] The cultural analyst Susan Sontag's metaphor has particular resonance in its application to pre-modern communities, for whom both endemic and epidemic disease were unequivocally the result of divine vengeance for individual and communal sin. This interpretation of sickness added a moral dimension to the treatment — literally and figuratively — of those whose transgressions granted them citizenship of the kingdom to which no one wished to belong.

Taking as its case study the affluent port of Aberdeen on Scotland's north-east coast in the period before 1550, this chapter explores the multiple ways in which the experience of disease invariably divided society. After all, from ancient Rome to nineteenth-century New Zealand at least, the concept of the 'ideal citizen' invariably created outsiders within a society, particularly when that society was placed under stress through political upheaval, war or — in early modern Aberdeen's case — sickness. Even at the best of times, as Andrew Brown notes in the Introduction to this volume, citizenship across time and place was likely to be both an inclusive and an exclusive process. Crises exacerbated these tensions, with the result that more often than not communal values proved to be shot through with division.[2]

As this discussion of early modern Aberdeen will show, not only did disease group together individuals in their shared experience of infection, and consequent segregation and forced identification, but it also created scapegoats who were held culpable for the spread of epidemics by virtue of their profession (or lack thereof). In so doing, disease delineated parameters by which social exclusion and inclusion were conceptualised and articulated by civic authorities, thereby creating citizens of various communities constructed by their unifying experiences.

The centrality of faith to pre-modern societies in western Christendom impressed upon believers one absolute certainty about the origin of most diseases, of which plague may be considered the paradigm. As any number of biblical stories made clear, plagues were quite simply the ultimate manifestation of divine anger at, and consequent punishment of, sinful behaviour: 'a scourge and punishment of the most just God', as the Aberdeen physician Gilbert Skene described it in *Ane Breve Descriptioun of the Pest* (1568), the only plague treatise of Scottish origin.[3] Various diseases could be manifested by His wrath whose symptoms might correspond to the particular type of sinful behaviour that had provoked it: leprosy and the Great Pox (commonly identified with modern syphilis) arose from individual acts of sexual immorality, while plague tended to be visited upon a community in response to general sin and was often depicted in contemporary imagery as a shower of poisonous arrows raining down on a given locality.[4]

The most effective way to counter the scourge of disease, therefore, was to appease God; as Skene put it, 'to return to [Him], who is most puissant with an affectionate and ardent will and heart, to implore the support of his Majesty . . . to pacify his wrath against us'.[5] This was manifested in a well-documented variety of spiritual responses in the face of plague in particular, including not only individual acts of repentance such as charitable donations and bequests to the parish church, but also the undertaking of public fasts and the staging of processions and pageants in urban areas. These brought the community together in shared acts of divine appeasement that helped 'to articulate and enact a sense of belonging within multiple, overlapping identities'.[6]

These communal responses — such as the general fasts and humiliations undertaken to eschew plague in 1665 and 1720[7] — could be articulated at the national as well as the local level. In Scotland they were often instigated at

the behest of the ruling Privy Council and implemented within settlements of all sizes by civic councillors and church leaders. The interpretation of plague as the result of sin had as a natural consequence the desire to rid the community of sources of immorality, particularly since these also accorded with medical understandings about the origins of disease causation and transmission. On certain parts of the continent responses to the Black Death of the mid-fourteenth century — the devastating plague pandemic that killed upwards of a quarter of the population — were manifested in the expulsion and execution of Jews as 'unchristian' elements of society.[8] These anti-Semitic actions at the hands of both civic and ecclesiastical authorities, justified by accusations of deliberate plague-spreading as part of a plot to destroy Christian communities, gave way in later decades to the targeting of other minorities — those positioned beyond the margins of acceptability — who were deemed to thwart efforts to appease God when He inflicted disease on society.

The coastal city of Aberdeen dominated the north-east of Scotland as a major player in both national and international affairs, having been recognised in the fourteenth century as one of 'the four great towns of Scotland' by the authorities of Bruges, the foremost commercial centre in northern Europe.[9] By the turn of the sixteenth century it was home to around 5000 residents and boasted a bishopric and university (Scotland's third), both situated in the adjacent burgh of Old Aberdeen. Diplomatic, ecclesiastical, commercial and intellectual interaction entailed the exchange of disease, with sufferers of endemic leprosy banished to a leper house founded in the fourteenth century between the Old and New burghs. Civic concern with the disease, recognised by modern scholars as being in many cases a socially constructed diagnosis applied to a variety of skin complaints,[10] dwindled in line with the numbers of those afflicted.

By the end of the fifteenth century this concern had been almost entirely replaced by legislation to tackle two other distinct diseases, the Great Pox and plague. As with leprosy, both were believed to have been inflicted by divine vengeance and hence both were ascribed moral no less than medical origins. Moreover, albeit to differing extents, the civic treatment of those afflicted with both could unify as well as divide.

Aberdeen's historical experience of disease is remarkable, both in its comparative avoidance of infection and in the innovativeness of its civic legislation. The city is unparalleled in a British context for registering no alarm about plague for a full 98 years after 1401, despite intermittent outbreaks further south in Scotland's central belt. Before plague was once again to threaten the burgh after such a substantial gap, its magistrates had to confront the challenge to both the moral and physical wellbeing of the *common weal* from what was recognised from the outset to be an entirely different and hitherto unknown disease. Continental commentators acknowledged its first appearance in Europe to have been in Italy during the months after 1495, among soldiers fighting for Charles VIII of France in his bid for the kingdom of Naples. Mercenaries who had participated in this shortlived campaign subsequently returned home, spreading the disease as they went. It became described variously as the 'Great Pox' (in contrast to smallpox), the 'disease of Naples', and 'Morbus Gallicus' or the 'French disease', thus showing how the nomenclature of a new disease could scapegoat entire cities or even nations in the identification of its origins.

Modern debate continues about the origins and clinical identification of this malady, particularly over whether it was a form of syphilis that already existed in Europe before the return of explorers from the New World, perhaps evolving as a result of favourable biological and ecological changes. Whatever its precise origins, contemporaries quickly acknowledged the venereal character, high contagiousness and low mortality of this new disease, which differentiated it from plague.[11] Descriptions of symptoms clearly identified it as prevailing through sexual activity, and municipal efforts to curb its spread focused on curtailing the professional activities of prostitutes, a social minority whose presence tended to be a tolerated irritant in urban areas. In April 1497 magistrates in Aberdeen notably became the first civic authority in the British Isles to enact such legislation. Terming the disease 'the infirmity come out of France and strange parts', they ordered 'all light women' to cease their 'vices and sin of venery', and instead to seek lawful employment or face branding and banishment.[12]

Significantly, to the fore in this innovative proclamation is the recognition that prostitutes' professional activities were sinful and hence as much a moral as a medical threat to the community. Despite this, Aberdeen was a major port and the temporary home of many single (and married) men for whom prostitutes provided a popular service, and this might have influenced civic efforts to tackle the spread of the disease through control rather than elimination of those activities which caused it. In seeking only to curb rather than prohibit, the council's orders were less proscriptive than those of other urban governments including that of Paris, who favoured the forcible identification of prostitutes through distinctive clothing or even their expulsion.[13] Medical and moral beliefs about the origins of disease intersected in the civic treatment of those deemed susceptible to the Great Pox through identification of their persons and restriction of their movement, actions which cast them as threats to both the moral and literal health of the social body. This was even more prominent in efforts to tackle those suspected of harbouring and spreading that most feared and intractable of pre-modern diseases: plague.

Between the Black Death pandemic of the mid-fourteenth century and the final, severe outbreak of the 1640s scarcely a decade passed without a visitation of plague occurring somewhere in Scotland, though the city of Aberdeen is notable for its comparative immunity, being stricken with outbreaks on only two occasions — in the 1510s and the 1540s — before that of a century later. As Gilbert Skene's interpretation in his *Breve Descriptioun* made clear, physicians as much as theologians and playwrights held the omnipotence of God as fundamentally dictating the appearance and course of any episode of plague. However, this in no way precluded temporal efforts to tackle the secondary means by which He inflicted the disease.

Medical understandings about plague were based on classical assumptions about disease causation and transmission that were rarely challenged until the later seventeenth century. Skene's explanations of the causes, treatment and cure of the disease, which he termed a 'cruel miserable tyrant and manslayer',[14] were absolutely typical of other writers on plague who came both before and after him.[15] Plague — described in civic records in such flowery terms as 'this violent and contagious sword of pestilence',[16] in addition to the more straightforward 'pest' — was believed to be generated by environmental corruption and to be spread in two interrelated ways: through polluted airborne vapours (miasma) and by contact, both direct and indirect, with sources of infection (contagion).

Skene emphasised that plague was particularly malevolent because it spread through the medium of the air, the one thing that was 'necessary for man's life'. It had a hidden, venomous quality which had 'strength and wickedness above all natural putrefaction'.[17] The airborne plague poison subtly entered the body through the pores, corrupting the four humours (fluids) of which the human body was composed, and putrefying its organs, before attacking the principal organ, the heart. It was particularly dangerous to patients and challenging to physicians because it was so insidious and invasive; 'theiflie' is how Skene described it.[18]

Councillors also recognised, through empirical observation as much as commissioned medical advice, that plague arose in malodorous, polluted environments and that it could spread through the air, breath and sight as well as by direct contact with sources of infection, which encompassed not only humans but also animals and inanimate objects such as cloth. These principles underpinned civic measures in Aberdeen as elsewhere that, with deference to the overarching omnipotence of God, were implemented to prevent the spread of plague within the locality. Just as the identification of the Great Pox with sexual promiscuity had led to proscriptions on prostitutes in 1497, legislation to tackle plague likewise targeted certain categories of people deemed to pose a particular threat to the *common weal* as a result of their susceptibility for moral as well as practical reasons.

Since it was accepted that plague could be carried by people, animals and goods, total bans on the entry or reception of all three of these categories were often imposed during outbreaks, particularly those deemed to have originated in plague-ridden areas. But the perceived threat posed by each of these broad categories was nuanced and there existed certain elements within

each that were considered to be particularly disposed to harbouring infection. Foodstuffs that spoiled quickly such as meat, fish and certain vegetables were deemed especially susceptible, as were porous, absorbent textiles such as linen, wool and hemp, and hence these types of goods were often targeted for confiscation.[19] While all animals were capable of transmitting plague, dogs, cats and pigs were identified as being especially dangerous during outbreaks. The owners of these targeted animals were ordered to keep them tethered and it became lawful to slay any found loose without fear of reprisal.[20]

However, it was within the general category of people that there existed the greatest proscriptions during times of plague, applied both to those seeking entry to the burgh and to those already within it. Consequent civic legislation articulated starkly the categorisation of individuals and groups in accordance with those who were deemed, indeed permitted, to belong to the community and those who were not. In common with other urban authorities, when plague was rumoured or confirmed to have broken out in the vicinity, Aberdeen's council sought initially to prevent sources of infection from entering the city's boundaries through the imposition of a *cordon sanitaire*, which involved primarily the monitoring of official entrances to the burgh (the gates or 'ports' and the harbour) and the vetting of arrivals. Throughout the entire plague period (that is, to ca. 1650) civic officials in Aberdeen were greatly helped in their task by the coastal location of the city and by the inhospitableness of its surrounding topography, which made access difficult whether by road or by sea.

Although in theory, therefore, vetting visitors to the city — whether through the ports, over the rivers or at the harbour — was an achievable precaution in times of plague, tardiness by magistrates in implementing such measures and negligence by those charged with the task meant that interlopers gained access on an alarmingly regular basis during outbreaks, a situation exacerbated by the influx of migrants from the hinterland seeking employment or at least sustenance in such times of economic crisis and dearth of victuals.[21] Successive councils were also hindered in their attempts to regulate visitors by the illicit entry to the town, often 'under silence of night', of those coming in via unguarded access points. In common with most of Scotland's towns at this time, Aberdeen was not walled, and the security of the burgh was to a great extent dependent on the vigilance of those residents whose back walls and gates effectively delineated its external boundaries. Convictions during both of Aberdeen's sixteenth-century epidemics for the illegal scaling of external walls and the unlawful lodging of outsiders show that residents could prioritise the provision of hospitality to family and friends over a concern for health and safety, whether their own or that of the wider community.[22]

Accepting that interlopers might yet gain entry, officials were tasked to patrol the streets of each quarter, making home visitations if necessary, in order to root out illicit visitors and suspected cases of sickness which were also required to be notified to the authorities. For the social theorist Michel Foucault, early modern 'plague management was the political dream', as the powers this gave for civic control over the movements of everyone into and within the town, under the guise of a concern for public health, created what he regarded as 'the utopia of the perfectly governed city'.[23]

It entailed the targeting of those whose presence might be considered socially undesirable for ideological no less than practical reasons. This was evident in the civic approach to tackling both the Great Pox and plague: such diseases were the articulation of divine vengeance, hence the prohibition, removal or limiting of immoral elements within society was rational and justifiable on both medical and moral grounds. An associated concern to suppress disorder is revealed in certain specific civic regulations relating to plague, such as the requirement for officials to search houses both for cases of sickness and for 'all unlawful folks', and the stipulation that those monitoring the ports ought to 'resist incomers and lurdans (miscreants) who would make any demand'.[24]

For governments at the local as well as national level, the greatest threat to the health of the social body in times of plague came from people whose movements were intractable. As with their orders to tether animals

whose liminality (between a life on the streets and domesticity) disposed them to infection, magistrates in Aberdeen sought to prohibit entry to the burgh, and movement within it, of those whose daily means of acquiring a living required them to travel from place to place and from house to house within those settlements. Hence, when plague threatened from the south in 1513, no 'gangerall folkis' arriving from that area were to be permitted to enter without first having been vetted.[25] The targeting of 'gangrels' — a vagabond or, literally, a 'going-about person' — shows that it was what might be termed the social promiscuity of these individuals which most concerned authorities: their unchecked meanderings increased the likelihood of their having picked up infection. The magistrates' concern might not have been entirely unfounded: by the time 'gangrels' were next targeted plague was raging within the city (for the first time in recorded history) and officers were ordered to patrol the streets to round up any they came across who had managed to gain access to the burgh 'of new'.[26] On the next two occasions when plague subsequently threatened, no chapmen — itinerant salesmen — were permitted to 'set forth their packs' in the town and no 'gangralis puirralis' (that is, poor vagabonds) were to be granted entry.[27]

During times of plague, repeated efforts by successive councils to curb social promiscuity focused most particularly on those who survived by begging for alms, including those resident mendicants of the burgh whose alms-seeking had a spiritual impetus. Many beggars presented a particular threat to the health of the community in two ways: their social indiscrimination and their perceived disposition to infection, which was underpinned by both moral and medical suppositions.[28]

As one of the seven works of mercy, providing for the poor was a necessary act of charity when directed towards those individuals who deserved support, having been impoverished through adverse circumstances including old age, infirmity and disability. During times of socio-economic stability in Aberdeen, which was a relatively affluent city, the benevolence of the faithful was generally sufficient to ensure provision not only for those poor who were native to the burgh but also itinerant paupers who survived by peripatetic begging.

Charitable donations were typically solicited by begging from house to house or among the congregation at church services, hence beggars came into contact with a substantial number of people on a regular basis. During times of plague, however, this social indiscrimination severely jeopardised public health. When plague first threatened Aberdeen at the end of the fifteenth century, magistrates ordered all beggars to 'ask their alms' only at the doors of the parish church of St Nicholas rather than enter the building and mix with the congregation, while during the first epidemic they were directed to sit by the walls or doors of the kirk away 'from company of people' to receive this charity.[29]

The threat posed by beggars' indiscriminate social movements was exacerbated by their particular disposition to infection. Plague flourished in dirty and malodorous environments, where contaminated water and rotten foodstuffs prevailed, and these were precisely the kinds of conditions in which the poor were forced to exist. Gilbert Skene, whose *Breve Descriptioun of the Pest* may have been influenced by circumstances in Aberdeen during the second epidemic, wrote of plague that 'we see daily the poor more subject to such calamity because they are constrained by poverty to eat evil and corrupt foods'.[30] Furthermore, while richer inhabitants fled from infection (often on learned medical advice)[31] the destitute could not afford to escape it, which guaranteed their presence within the burgh and further threatened the health of others who remained.

Moreover, plague severely inflated the presence of beggars within the burgh, among both outsiders and those native to it. Aberdeen was by far the largest settlement in the north-east, dominating a substantial hinterland whose occupants migrated to the city in search of support, having had their subsistence livelihoods devastated by the outbreak. In addition, plague created a category of pauper native to the burgh comprised of those from formerly self-sufficient lower-income groups, able typically to eke out a precarious living, who became destitute as a result of the disruption to commercial life. They had homes in which to live, but their means of earning a living were, for the time being at least, severely curtailed: their poverty was 'shameful as well as

unpleasant'.[32] They stood in contrast to those paupers whose poverty resulted from unwillingness (rather than an inability) to work. These individuals, termed 'codderars' (from 'coddroch', an 'idle, low-class person') in Aberdeen, were considered lazy and undeserving of charity, particularly when public resources were stretched during the economic crisis of an epidemic.

As the sixteenth century progressed, European commentators including Juan Luis Vives, Cornelius Agrippa and Thomas More responded to the 'growing dimensions of the problem of the poor'[33] by denouncing the idle poor, whose immorality disposed them to wander 'idly, lasciviously and dissolutely' about, spreading their 'sundry and diverse diseases, contagions and infections' with no regard for the health of those around them.[34] Their immorality made them particularly susceptible to plague: the dual threat that 'coddrochs' posed was articulated by magistrates in Aberdeen who ordered their expulsion not only during the first outbreak but also when a particular type of plague known as the botch subsequently threatened (though was averted).[35] Not only did this enable precious resources to be apportioned to those who deserved them, but also it was a method of divine appeasement: an 'act of propitiation and a gesture of public piety or charity on the part of the state itself'.[36] Licentious idleness made the undeserving poor depraved as well as deprived; as with the treatment of prostitutes in light of the Great Pox, getting rid of them eliminated a literal and figurative source of corruption from the community.[37]

The idle poor may have been distinguishable from the deserving poor in a moral sense, but medically their social indiscrimination and the conditions in which they lived made all paupers equally threatening: hence, the same legislation ordering beggars not to enter the church building could also forbid the poor (presumably those 'shamefaced' paupers who at least had a home) from holding 'open house'.[38] Thus, regardless of the circumstances that had led to their poverty in the first place, the poor were unified through legislative discrimination which in various ways segregated them from the rest of the community.

In addition, civic authorities justified further social control of the poor by the need to audit their numbers within the burgh, which was undertaken for several reasons: to determine their need or eligibility for charity, to assess whether their presence was legitimate, or simply to place checks on their mobility. Officers could be required to apprehend any paupers with no fixed abode who were found on the street, to make house-to-house enquiries to account for those with somewhere to live (or at least to lodge), or to convene all poor in one central location in order to assess their eligibility to receive charity.[39]

Pragmatism according to the city's current financial situation and availability of resources might explain the inconsistency with which eligibility for support was determined: only to the native poor (regardless of whether or not they were considered deserving of it), only to deserving paupers (regardless of whether or not they were native to the burgh), or to all claimants if the relative affluence of the city (in spite of plague) enabled this.[40] It cannot therefore be assumed that native status would take precedence in assessing eligibility to receive charity, even though it has been claimed that 'early modern citizenship was above all a citizenship of towns and cities'.[41] Magistrates were pragmatic first and foremost, and were concerned primarily with preventing the social disorder that a starving minority, fearful of an uncertain future, could provoke. Furthermore, plague was a sign of God's wrath, so repentance through the distribution of charity was as important a step in bringing about the end of an epidemic as was ridding the community of immoral elements.

One way of differentiating a social sub-group is through distinguishing adornments, such as the clothing required of prostitutes in some continental towns. As in many urban areas, those poor who were deemed eligible to receive charity were identified by having affixed to their clothing a token made of lead, with those issued in Aberdeen imprinted with 'the towns arms' and 'ABD'.[42] This certified their belonging to the burgh, of being regarded as *bona fide* members of the community, but at the same time it also marked them out as being different from its other members.

Ineligible claimants were routinely expelled, but this did not always rid the authorities of the financial or administrative burden of these individuals. Orders for banishment were not always easy to enforce, particularly when they were applied to multiple people, and when deficiencies in both the

watch at official entrances and in the security of unmonitored access points meant that new arrivals could not always be prevented. Attempts to expel unlicensed beggars (that is, those not considered eligible according to the criteria then current) required time, money and manpower, all of which added to the administrative burden already caused by the monitoring of the burgh undertaken in order to detect paupers of all categories, interlopers, and cases of sickness.

So far this chapter has discussed the Aberdeen authorities' efforts to monitor the entry to, and movement within, the burgh of categories of people who were deemed particularly to threaten the moral as well as physical health of the wider community: prostitutes, itinerant and local beggars, vagabonds and layabouts. There were additional areas of plague legislation that entailed the civic creation and control of sub-groups of individuals who were either suspected or known to be infected. These policies created miniature communities who were unwillingly bonded together by a shared citizenship in the kingdom of the sick. For example, the enclosure of an entire household reinforced the English puritan William Gouge's description of the family as 'a little commonwealth'.[43]

In enforcing such segregation magistrates had, to guide them, a national legislative framework embodied in the Rule of the Pestilence (1456), which was supplemented by the statutes contained in the form of a letter in the name of King James IV, issued in January 1513. These two ordinances showed that the isolation of both suspected and confirmed cases of plague was a recognised practice. While on several occasions the Aberdeen council impounded or destroyed goods deemed to be harbouring the disease, the vast majority of regulations concerning the isolation of possible sources of plague related to people.[44]

This was implemented initially by shutting up potentially infected individuals within their own homes and enclosing these buildings to minimise any interaction with the community outside. Enclosure within one's own residence could be undertaken for several purposes. It could be imposed to segregate ostensibly healthy people deemed to have come into contact with sources of infection (deliberately or otherwise), who could then be monitored over the duration of their confinement for the development of any symptoms.[45] It could be implemented to isolate an individual either before or after their stay in a quarantine camp outside the burgh, or to contain members of a household among whom a case of sickness had been detected.[46]

This latter purpose filled residents with particular dread, as not only did it bring about the cessation for an indefinite period of normal day-to-day activities such as going to church and market, socialising, and earning a living, but it could also effectively condemn all members of the household to infection and possible death. Governments did not implement the practice of enclosure lightly, since the dispersal throughout the city of infected inhabitants (or those suspected of being so) within numerous separate dwellings created an unwelcome administrative burden.

For those whose citizenship of the kingdom of the sick was detected and confirmed by officers, their passport guaranteed them access to a segregated plague camp outside the town boundaries, where citizens of the kingdom of the well would be as safe as was possible from infection whether transmitted by contagion or miasma. The removal of sufferers from the town to one isolated, purpose-built area where they could be supervised, treated and provided for efficiently became standard practice across much of Europe during the decades after its initial implementation by the Italian city-states in the late fourteenth century.[47] It quickly became standard practice across much of Europe, with Scotland's first plague camp built in Edinburgh's Borough Muir during its epidemic of 1499.

Aberdeen's plague camps were situated to the north-east of the burgh towards the coast, and were *ad hoc* entities designed to cater for the needs of those affected by the particular outbreak.[48] They comprised a number of hastily erected wooden huts (known as 'lugis' or lodges), which were cheap and easy to build. Facilities were basic, perhaps with little more than straw provided for bedding, and conditions harsh. Individuals sent to the site would at least have had their portable belongings with them. Those with sufficient finances

to pay for their own supplies fared better than poorer patients, some of whom benefitted from donations from family members or benevolent individuals, in addition to state support appropriated from a variety of sources.[49]

Throughout Aberdeen's second epidemic, and during earlier outbreaks in burghs for which records survive, those sent to the camp were given firewood for warmth, and bread and ale for sustenance.[50] Healthcare for those in quarantine was practically non-existent. Having the financial means to afford a private nursing companion or to purchase additional supplies would have done little to alleviate the uncomfortable conditions at the camp, which compounded the misery for patients of being forcibly separated from loved ones and of facing the uncertainty of when (or if) they would return home. The plague camp could be regarded as a community in miniature, with those languishing in it unified by the uncomfortable and frightening citizenship of sickness, albeit with none of the familiar resources of urban communal life.

For individuals presumed to be infected and sent to the camp, one of two outcomes awaited: recovery or death. Statistics do not exist to establish the mortality rates for Aberdeen's sixteenth-century outbreaks, and references to the practicalities of dealing with high fatalities (such as the personnel and financial outlay involved in digging graves and transporting bodies) are available only for the final epidemic, in the 1640s. It can be surmised that, as with any substantial outbreak, high mortality added considerable grief and loss to the disruption and misery felt by the community in the throes of plague.

Recovery from infection, on the other hand, was not as unlikely an outcome as might be assumed. During the second of Aberdeen's epidemics in particular, the numbers of individuals returned to the burgh from quarantine in the camp is striking.[51] The belief that recovery was eminently possible is consistent with the views of physicians such as Gilbert Skene, who discussed the treatment and cure of the disease with no hint that such efforts were fruitless. A modern interpretation of the apparent recovery of victims might infer that such individuals had been misdiagnosed in the first place, or that the authorities were mistaken in pronouncing them cured (which, in turn, might have perpetuated the cycle of infection).

Once an individual was fortunate enough to be considered to have recovered from plague, he or she no longer posed a threat to citizens of the kingdom of the well and so could leave the camp and return to the burgh. These individuals were deemed to occupy a liminal existence between the kingdom of the sick and that of the well, however, and could be forced to comply with one or more safeguards put in place to certify their absolute recovery, including a further period of convalescence.[52] It was also possible to have other residents stand as guarantors of the individual's good health, which enabled them to 'becom[e] in effect the agents and regulators of civility'.[53]

In managing the return to the burgh of former sufferers, the most common precaution imposed in Aberdeen was their identification in order that 'the common people may evade them as they think expedient', as the council clerk termed it during the second outbreak.[54] During both epidemics recovered residents invariably were ordered to carry a white stick rather than to affix a white cloth to their clothing, the two means of identification that magistrates acknowledged had been stipulated in James IV's letter.[55]

This forcible identification of recovered plague sufferers echoes the clappers and bell borne by the medieval leper, the distinguishing clothing of the prostitute, and the eligibility token worn by the beggar. Each of these methods sought to mark this minority out within society, to warn others of the moral as well as medical danger each posed and, in so doing, to provide a focus of commonality for individuals who, through the conflation of moral as well as medical suppositions about those deemed susceptible to infection, were otherwise denied the rights and privileges granted by citizenship.

Critical analysis of how citizenship was conceptualised in a given time and place invites engagement with the issue of who might be included in that citizenry. The experience of disease among pre-modern communities highlights the way in which concerns about both the moral and medical pollution of the locality intersected in the expulsion of 'bad citizens' deemed harmful to the spiritual as well as physical health of 'good citizens'. In Aberdeen, as in Bruges and many other European towns, governors could thereby ensure that their city

remained a 'sacred and clean space in a way that the area outside its walls was not'.[56]

Even among 'good citizens', however, the sudden onset of sickness highlights the precarious nature of an individual's citizenship of the kingdom of the well. Moreover, in the early modern world, citizenship 'was not singular but multiple'.[57] God's bestowal on a sinner of citizenship of the kingdom of the sick did not abrogate citizenship of the town or city in which he or she resided, but it could override the rights associated with that status. In this case study, an individual could be recognised as a citizen of early modern Aberdeen — that is, as a 'freeman' with the associated commercial, legal and political rights and responsibilities this conferred — yet at the same time could be excluded from participation in those aspects of communal life by virtue of civic proscriptions imposed due to infection. Segregation through enclosure and quarantine, albeit justified by the protection of the health of the wider community, denied those who were citizens in the legal sense the right to be recognised as social beings, with the agency this could confer through participation and interaction.[58]

Conversely, although tokens were issued to eligible beggars during outbreaks in order to distinguish them — 'that they may be known to others' as Aberdeen's council termed it[59] — they were at the same time tokens 'of belonging, worthiness [and] entitlement'[60] and, by extension, of the bearer's social legitimacy. Likewise, though the practice of isolation necessarily divided a society it nevertheless had the capacity to unite, by 'creat[ing] a sense of a "single community" with a shared fate'. In this way, the experience of disease in pre-modern communities such as Aberdeen has much in common with societies today wrestling with global crises such as climate change,[61] and enables us to trace an historical continuum of notions of citizenship from the pre-modern to the modern age.

ENDNOTES

1. Quoted in Bryon Lee Grigsby, *Pestilence in Medieval and Early Modern English Literature* (London: Routledge, 2004), 1.
2. Andrew Brown, 'The Citizen: From Ancient to Post-Modern', in this volume.
3. Gilbert Skene, *Ane Breve Descriptioun of the Pest, quhair in the causis, signis and sum speciall preseruatioun and cure thairof ar contenit* (Edinburgh, 1568), 3.
4. Christine M. Boeckl, *Images of Plague and Pestilence: Iconography and Iconology* (Kirksville, MO: Truman State University Press, 2000), 55; Jack M. Greenstein, *Mantegna and Painting as Historical Narrative* (Chicago: University of Chicago Press, 1992), 71.
5. Skene, *Breve Descriptioun of the Pest*, 15.
6. Andrew Gordon and Trevor Stack, 'Citizenship Beyond the State: Thinking with Early Modern Citizenship in the Contemporary World,' *Citizenship Studies* 11, no. 2 (2007): 119.
7. Ordered in response to outbreaks in London and Marseilles respectively, in the parish of Aberdeen these took place on 18 September 1665 and 28 November 1720, and were held concurrently in many parishes throughout Scotland: National Archives of Scotland, Kirk Session Registers, CH2/448/9/52 [18 Sept 1665], CH2/448/28/322 [28 Nov 1720].
8. For a comprehensive discussion of these events, see Samuel K. Cohn Jr, 'The Black Death and the Burning of Jews,' *Past and Present* 196, no. 1 (2007): 3–36.
9. *Aberdeen Before 1800: A New History*, ed. E. Patricia Dennison, David Ditchburn, and Michael Lynch (East Linton: Tuckwell Press, 2002), xxvi.
10. Timothy S. Miller and John W. Nesbitt, *Walking Corpses: Leprosy in Byzantium and the Medieval West* (Ithaca and London: Cornell University Press, 2014); Peter Richards, *The Medieval Leper and his Northern Heirs* (Woodbridge: Brewer, 1977); Liora Navon, 'Beggars, Metaphors, and Stigma: A Missing Link in the Social History of Leprosy,' *Society for the Social History of Medicine* 11, no. 1 (1998): 89–105. Significantly, the traditional view that medieval society marginalised lepers in accordance with Christian doctrine has increasingly been questioned: Carole Rawcliffe, *Leprosy in Medieval England* (Woodbridge: Boydell Press, 2006); Timothy S. Miller and Rachel Smith-Savage, 'Medieval Leprosy Reconsidered,' *International Social Science Review* 81, nos. 1–2 (2006): 16–28.
11. Commentators also noted that the disease seemed to have declined in virulence only a few decades after its first appearance in Europe: *Sins of the Flesh: Responding to Sexual Disease in Early Modern Europe*, ed. Kevin Siena (Toronto: Centre for Reformation and Renaissance Studies, 2005); J. Arrizabalaga, J. Henderson, and R. French, *The Great Pox: The French Disease in Renaissance Europe* (New Haven: Yale University Press, 1997); E. Tognotti, 'The Rise and Fall of Syphilis in Renaissance Europe,' *Journal of Medical Humanities* 30, no. 2 (2009): 99–113; A. M. Sefton, 'The Great Pox that was . . . Syphilis,' *Journal of Applied Microbiology* 91 (2001): 592–6.
12. Aberdeen City Archives: Aberdeen Council Registers [hereafter ACR], vol. 7, 797 [24 Apr 1497].
13. Such distinctive clothing served a 'labelling function' and further marginalised prostitutes

on the figurative as well as literal social boundaries: Ruth Mazo Karras, *Common Women: Prostitution and Sexuality in Medieval England* (Oxford: Oxford University Press, 1998), 31, 84; Leah Lydia Otis, *Prostitution in Medieval Society: The History of an Urban Institution in Languedoc* (Chicago: University of Chicago Press, 1985), 200: 'all towns and regions of western Europe seem to have required prostitutes to wear distinguishing signs or clothing...'

14 Skene, *Breve Descriptioun of the Pest*, 6.
15 For a comprehensive discussion of plague writings in early modern English, of which Skene's *Breve Descriptioun* is the sole contemporary equivalent in Scots, see Andrew Wear, *Knowledge and Practice in English Medicine, 1550–1680* (Cambridge: Cambridge University Press, 2000).
16 ACR.9.338 [24 Apr 1514].
17 Skene, *Breve Descriptioun of the Pest*, 4, 2.
18 Skene, *Breve Descriptioun of the Pest*, 2.
19 For example, lint which arrived from Danzig during an outbreak in 1538 was to be confiscated and 'put in lofts and cellars and not be handled until the town is further advised': ACR.15.732 [20 Sept 1538].
20 ACR.16.036 [25 Oct 1538]; ACR.20.310 [16 Oct 1549]. The slaughter of dogs and cats during plague is discussed in Mark S. R. Jenner, 'The Great Dog Massacre,' in *Fear in Early Modern Society*, ed. William G. Naphy and Penny Roberts (Manchester: Manchester University Press, 1997), 44–61.
21 Typical of this was the concern expressed by the council in 1539 about 'the great multitude of strangers that have of new come to this burgh to remain in the same, who have nothing of their own to live upon': ACR.16.358 [13 Oct 1539].
22 ACR.9.403 [29 Jan 1515]; ACR.18.519 [6 Aug 1545]; ACR.19.212 [17 Sept 1546].
23 Sean P. Hier and Josh Greenberg, 'Surveillance, the Nation-State and Social Control: Section Introduction,' in *The Surveillance Studies Reader*, ed. Sean P. Hier and Josh Greenberg (Maidenhead: Open University Press / McGraw-Hill, 2007), 15; *Rethinking Architecture: A Reader in Cultural History*, ed. Neil Leach (London: Routledge, 1997), 359: 'the plague-stricken town... immobilised by the functioning of an extensive power that bears in a distinct way over all individual bodies — that is the utopia of the perfectly governed city', quoting from Foucault's *Discipline and Punish: The Birth of the Prison* (New York: Vintage, 1977).
24 ACR.7.935 [19 Feb 1499]; ACR.9.338 [24 Apr 1514].
25 ACR.9.268 [7 Oct 1513].
26 ACR.9.444 [11 May 1515].
27 ACR.12/2.707 [22 Oct 1529]; ACR.15.219 [6 Oct 1536].
28 Useful discussions of early modern poverty include: John McCallum, 'Charity and Conflict: Poor Relief in Mid-Seventeenth-Century Dundee,' *Scottish Historical Review* 95, no. 1 (2016): 30–56; *Experiences of Poverty in Late Medieval and Early Modern England and France*, ed. Anne M. Scott (Farnham: Ashgate, 2012); Brian Pullan, 'Catholics, Protestants and the Poor in

Early Modern Europe,' *Journal of Interdisciplinary History* 35, no. 3 (2005): 441–56; Margaret Pelling, *The Common Lot: Sickness, Medical Occupations, and the Urban Poor in Early Modern England* (London: Longman, 1988); Robert Jütte, *Poverty and Deviance in Early Modern Europe* (Cambridge: Cambridge University Press, 1994); Brian Pullan, 'Plague and Perceptions of the Poor in Early Modern Italy,' in *Epidemics and Ideas: Essays on the Historical Perception of Pestilence*, ed. Terence Ranger and Paul Slack (Cambridge: Cambridge University Press, 1992), 101–24; Paul Slack, *Poverty and Policy in Tudor and Stuart England* (London: Longman, 1988).

29 ACR.7.936 [19 Feb 1499]; ACR.9.366 [7 Aug 1514]. Likewise, on the second occasion when legislation was passed to restrict the spread of the Great Pox, sufferers of 'this strange sickness of Naples' were instructed to remain in their houses, separate from the 'haill folkis', which could be interpreted as either (or both) the 'whole community' or the 'healthy people': ACR.8.753 [8 Oct 1507].

30 Skene, *Breve Descriptioun of the Pest*, 4–5.

31 Skene, *Breve Descriptioun of the Pest*, 16: 'every one [should] remove themselves from country, town, and air, infected or suspect . . .'

32 Gordon DesBrisay and Elizabeth Ewan with H. Lesley Diack, 'Life in the Two Towns,' in *Aberdeen Before 1800*, ed. Dennison et al., 59.

33 A. L. Beier, *Masterless Men: The Vagrancy Problem in England, 1560–1640* (London: Methuen, 1985), 5.

34 Slack, *Poverty and Policy*, 23. They were accused of behaving deviously, such as 'feign[ing] being crippled or lame': H. C. M. Michielse, 'Policing the Poor: J. L. Vives and the Sixteenth-Century Origins of Modern Social Administration,' *Social Service Review* 64 (1990): 7.

35 ACR.9.364 [7 Aug 1514]; ACR.16.346 [15 Sept 1539].

36 Pullan, 'Plague and Perceptions of the Poor,' 102.

37 Michielse, 'Policing the Poor,' 4, 7, 9, 10; Slack, *Poverty and Policy*, 23, 69.

38 ACR.9.366 [7 Aug 1514].

39 ACR.9.364, 366 [7 Aug 1514]; ACR.12/2.454 [20 Nov 1528]; ACR.15.219 [6 Oct 1536]; ACR.16.346 [15 Sept 1539]; ACR.19.110 [18 May 1546]; ACR.19.180 [6 Aug 1546]; ACR.20.311 [16 Oct 1549].

40 ACR.7.936 [19 Feb 1499]; ACR.15.219 [6 Oct 1536]; ACR.16.346 [15 Sept 1539]; ACR.19.110 [18 May 1546]; ACR.20.311 [16 Oct 1549].

41 Gordon and Stack, 'Citizenship Beyond the State,' 118.

42 ACR.20.311 [16 Oct 1549]; DesBrisay et al., 'Life in the Two Towns,' 60.

43 David Harris Sacks, 'Freedom to, Freedom from, Freedom of: Urban Life and Political Participation in Early Modern England,' *Citizenship Studies* 11, no. 2 (2007): 137.

44 ACR.7.1067 [21 Aug 1500]; ACR.12/2.689 [6 Oct 1529]; ACR.18.575 [14 Dec 1545]; ACR.18.577 [18 Dec 1545]; ACR.15.732 [20 Sept 1538].

45 ACR.7.1067 [21 Aug 1500]; ACR.18.524 [10 Sept 1545]; ACR.19.212 [17 Sept 1546]; ACR.20.310 [16 Oct 1549].

46 ACR.9.365, 367 [7 Aug 1514]; ACR.19.296 [25 Feb 1547]; ACR.19.312 [21 Mar 1547]; ACR.19.394

[19 Sept 1547]; ACR.20.310 [16 Oct 1549]; ACR.20.316 [4 Nov 1549].

47 Jane L. Stevens Crawshaw, *Plague Hospitals: Public Health for the City in Early Modern Venice* (Abingdon: Routledge, 2016); Zlata Blažina Tomić and Vesna Blažina, *Expelling the Plague: The Health Office and the Implementation of Quarantine in Dubrovnik, 1377–1533* (Montreal: McGill-Queen's University Press, 2015); Ann G. Carmichael, *Plague and the Poor in Renaissance Florence* (Cambridge: Cambridge University Press, 1986); Carlo M. Cipolla, *Public Health and the Medical Profession in the Renaissance* (Cambridge: Cambridge University Press, 1976).

48 ACR.9.367 [7 Aug 1514]; ACR.18.558 [5 Nov 1545]; ACR.18.578 [18 Dec 1545]; ACR.19.57 [15 Mar 1546]; ACR.20.310 [16 Oct 1549].

49 In addition to specific taxes, these included the upkeep of the parish church and fines accrued by residents for misdemeanours, including the contravention of plague statutes: ACR.18.524 [10 Sept 1545]; ACR.18.527 [25 Sept 1545]; ACR.18.558 [5 Nov 1545]; ACR.18.565 [20 Nov 1545]; ACR.18.578 [18 Dec 1545]; ACR.18.582 [11 Jan 1546]; ACR.19.56 [15 Mar 1546]; ACR.19.057 [19 Mar 1546]; ACR.19.079 [8 Apr 1546]; ACR.19.228 [11 Oct 1546].

50 The scarcity of victuals during plague led magistrates to appropriate these where they could, including confiscated bread, as well as pigs found wandering freely in the market place: ACR.19.150 [3 Jul 1546]; ACR.20.310 [16 Oct 1549].

51 ACR.18.570–571 [4 Dec 1545]; ACR.18.582 [11 Jan 1546]; ACR.18.595 [22 Jan 1546]; ACR.19.034 [19 Feb 1546]; ACR.19.038 [21 Feb 1546]; ACR.19.060 [19 Mar 1546]; ACR.19.097 [2 May 1546]; ACR.19.101 [14 May 1546]; ACR.19.147 [28 Jun 1546]; ACR.19.252 [19 Nov 1546]; ACR.19.256 [30 Nov 1546]; ACR.19.296 [25 Feb 1547]; ACR.19.324 [22 Apr 1547]; ACR.19.353 [13 Jun 1547]; ACR.19.359 [24 Jun 1547]; ACR.19.385 [19 Aug 1547]; ACR.20.318 [8 Nov 1549].

52 ACR.9.367 [7 Aug 1514]; ACR.18.558 [5 Nov 1545]; ACR.18.570–571 [4 Dec 1545]; ACR.18.582 [11 Jan 1546]; ACR.19.116 [24 May 1546]; ACR.19.147 [28 Jun 1546]; ACR.19.252 [19 Nov 1546]; ACR.20.316 [4 Nov 1549].

53 ACR.19.018 [5 Feb 1546]; ACR.19.034 [19 Feb 1546]; Gordon and Stack, 'Citizenship Beyond the State,' 124.

54 ACR.19.060 [19 Mar 1546].

55 ACR.18.566 [23 Nov 1545]. However, despite the decree in the same legislation for the frontage or doors of formerly infected dwellings also to be adorned with a white cloth, in Aberdeen they were never ordered to be distinguished in any manner.

56 Andrew Brown, 'Medieval Citizenship,' in this volume.

57 Gordon and Stack, 'Citizenship Beyond the State,' 119.

58 Emily Beausoleil, 'Twenty-first-century Citizenship,' in this volume; Geltrude Macrì, 'Citizenship: Participation and Exclusion in Early Modern Europe,' *Journal of Money Laundering Control* 14, no. 2 (2011): 121–2.

59 ACR.15.219 [6 Oct 1536].

60 DesBrisay et al., 'Life in the Two Towns,' 60.

61 Beausoleil, 'Twenty-first-century Citizenship,' in this volume.

7. PERSONAL, LOCAL AND ENDURING:
MASCULINE CITIZENSHIP IN FIRST WORLD WAR BRITAIN

David Littlewood

PERSONAL, LOCAL & ENDURING:
MASCULINE CITIZENSHIP IN FIRST WORLD WAR BRITAIN

On 7 September 1916, in the Yorkshire town of Huddersfield, a widowed mother explained why her son should be exempted from conscription into the British Army. She claimed to be totally dependent on his care and on the wages he brought home each week from labouring. After giving her testimony and answering questions, the woman made one final plea for the members of the local military service tribunal to 'Act as British, not as Germans; act as men. This is the only child I have in this world; if you take my son I shall be left destitute.'[1]

Two months earlier, Frank Percy, a bricklayer, had been the subject of an employer's appeal in the nearby town of Featherstone. He was described as indispensable for maintaining the company's coke ovens, which had to be kept operating at full capacity to meet its existing contracts. In granting Percy a conditional exemption, the chairman of the local tribunal remarked that, 'This man will be 100 times more valuable to the country where he is than he would be in the army.'[2]

Such nuanced articulations of rights and responsibilities have rarely featured in the historiography of British First World War conscription. During her influential analysis of the home front, Nicoletta Gullace argues that, by 1916, the traditional benchmarks of responsible male citizenship had been supplanted by the performance of military service.[3] She cites the shift in popular support away from voluntary recruiting, and towards the previously reviled 'continental' method of conscription, as evidence that 'Britain's "two nations" were no longer the rich and the poor, but the proponents of war and the advocates of peace'.[4]

Gullace's work contains several original insights. However, in maintaining that military service became the litmus test of masculine duty between 1916 and 1918, she echoes a long-standing convention. For decades, conscription was discussed largely by reference to conscientious objectors, with the common assertion that these individuals were abused and ostracised for refusing to defend their nation in its hour of need.[5] While a handful of broader works have since claimed that conceptions of citizenship remained multi-faceted throughout the war, the alleged primacy of a man's willingness to join the army still dominates most accounts.[6]

Investigating the appeals made against being conscripted is an ideal way to test these arguments. The Military Service Acts of January and May 1916 rendered all British males aged between 18 and 41 eligible for call-up. However, the legislation also gave each man, or his employer on his behalf, the right to appeal for exemption on one or more of the following grounds: that his conscription would cause 'serious hardship . . . owing to his exceptional financial or business obligations or domestic position'; that it was in the 'national interests' for him to remain in his current occupation; that he suffered from 'ill-health or infirmity'; or that he held a 'conscientious objection to the undertaking of combatant service'.[7] The burden of proof was placed on the appellants, who had to justify their claims through evidence of the surrounding circumstances.

To determine whether the appeals lodged in its district were sufficient to warrant relief, every local registration authority — the urban and rural district councils, and the borough councils — was required to establish a local tribunal. These bodies could either refuse an appeal, or allow it by granting a temporary, conditional or absolute exemption. Hearings usually took place in open court and were extensively covered by the newspapers.[8] As a result, studying exemption appeals provides a wealth of evidence on whether conscripts, tribunal members and the public did indeed allocate to military service the 'authoritative place in measures of civic worth'.[9]

The implementation of conscription proved to be a major disappointment for its proponents. While official statements emphasised an equality of sacrifice, the main reason for the recourse to compulsion was to guarantee that the army would receive enough soldiers to meet its expanding commitments.

R.—42. **MILITARY SERVICE ACTS, 1916.**

Name of Tribunal _____ *Number of Case* _____

APPLICATION AS TO EXEMPTION.

DUPLICATE.

1. Man in respect of whom application made:—
    (a) Name (*in full*)

    (b) Age last birthday   Date of birthday

    (c) Married or single   If married, date of marriage

    (d) Address (*in full*)

    (e) Address at date of National Registration (15th August, 1915)

    (f) Occupation, profession or business (*Give full and exact details*)

2. Whether engaged in the same or a similar occupation before 15th August, 1915.
    If so engaged, (a) The precise occupation

    (b) How long employed in the occupation before 15th August, 1915

    (c) Name and address of last employer when so employed before that date

3. (a) Name of present employer, if any

    (b) Address (*in full*)...   ...   ...

    (c) Business ...   .

4. Ground on which application is made. [*See footnote on back. It will be sufficient if the letter (a), (b), (c), (d), (e), (f) or (g) (whichever is appropriate), is entered.*]

5. Nature of application. (*A certificate of exemption may be absolute, conditional or temporary. Also, a certificate granted on conscientious grounds may be for exemption from combatant service only, or may be conditional on the applicant being engaged in some work which, in the opinion of the Tribunal, is of national importance.*)

Every man who decided to claim exemption under the Military Services Acts had to fill out one of these forms, which were obtainable from their local tribunal or recruiting office. **THE NATIONAL ARCHIVES, UK, MH 47/142**

Some appeals and exemptions were anticipated, particularly for men employed in essential industries, but most government and military leaders believed the passage of the Military Service Acts would finally cement a consensus that being a responsible male citizen meant being willing to fight for the national cause.[10] What actually transpired came as an unwelcome shock.

Anecdotal accounts from across Britain indicate a vast number of exemption appeals were lodged. Those tribunal members who left records of their experiences invariably maintained that attending hearings was an onerous burden. As mayor of Birmingham and chairman of its local appeal body, Neville Chamberlain wrote that serving on the tribunal had proved to be the 'most tiring' of his two roles, given that it sat 'three days a week from 10.30 to 1.30 & 2.15 till 6 or even 6.30'.[11] Likewise, Harry Cartmell, chairman of the Preston body in Lancashire, suggested the number of appellants had 'considerably exceeded the expectations' of the authorities, and that 'the duties of the Tribunals in busy areas made very heavy demands upon the time of their members'.[12]

This was undoubtedly the case at Leicester, where the local appeal body often sat for 10 hours a day; in the Carmarthen Rural District of Wales, where a member quipped that he had been 'sentenced to twelve months hard labour at the Tribunal'; and in the Metropolitan Borough of Hampstead, where Charles Repington bluntly asserted that he and his colleagues had 'worked like niggers'.[13] This overstretching of the appeal bodies caused consternation at the War Office, where it was believed that an inability to process men fast enough was contributing to the unsatisfactory flow of recruits into the army. A reporter for *The Times* observed the director of recruiting's dismay at the tribunals having become 'encumbered and clogged with work', while the adjutant-general lamented that the appeal bodies 'cannot handle all the material satisfactorily at present'.[14]

Statistical evidence supports the tenor of these observations. There is no source that indicates the overall rate of appealing in Britain for the whole of the conscription period. Nonetheless, combining the available information

PERSONAL, LOCAL & ENDURING

does provide some significant insights. The approximately 1.2 million call-up notices issued between January and July 1916 generated 748,587 appeals.[15] In the month of March, 25,941 men were taken into the army under the Military Service Act. Yet at the same time 58,947 were exempted and another 18,079 had cases outstanding.[16] In other words, fully 74.81 per cent of these men were appellants, alongside the enlistees who had their pleas turned down.

Examining the situation for individual parts of the country yields similar results. As British men were called up by age 'group' or 'class' rather than by ballot, it is difficult to relate the number of appeals to the number of men who were summoned. An alternative is to use the 1911 census to calculate the number of appellants as a proportion of the approximate eligible population. Applying this methodology to some major cities produces an appeal rate for Leeds of 21.76 per cent, Bristol 23.36 per cent and Birmingham 28.51 per cent.[17] The relative figures for the less populous Wiltshire Rural District of Calne and the Yorkshire Urban District of Marsden were 29.14 per cent and 36.54 per cent respectively.[18] Most conspicuous of all is the situation in Huddersfield, where the local tribunal received 12,865 claims in 1916 alone, with the 1911 population of males aged 10 to 44 being only 29,651.[19]

Even these figures greatly understate the likelihood of an appeal being made. The population of most districts did increase between 1911 and the outbreak of war, but this was more than counteracted by the extent of volunteering during 1914 and 1915.[20] In addition, the above statistics only relate to men whose cases came within the purview of the tribunals. Each government department was responsible for issuing exemptions to 'men, or classes or bodies of men' in its employment, and was also permitted to direct that the badge certificates, which accompanied each War Service Badge issued to safeguard employees from recruiters under the voluntary system, should now be treated as certificates of exemption from conscription.[21] Men who were protected by either of these measures did not have to go through the tribunals.[22]

With the pressing need to maintain food and armaments production, and to supply essential goods to soldiers and civilians, organisations like the Ministry of Munitions, the Board of Agriculture and the Board of Trade quickly moved to retain large numbers of their personnel.[23] By 30 April 1917, there were over 1.8 million departmental exemptions, compared to 780,000 in force from the tribunals.[24] These findings leave no doubt that, despite the authorities' efforts, a substantial proportion of conscripts and employers viewed appealing as an acceptable course of action.[25]

If performing military service had become the prerequisite of male citizenship, one would expect most appeals for exemption to have originated from conscientious objectors. Yet this was categorically not the case. James Cranstoun in regard to East Lothian, Mike Fraser in regard to Berwick-upon-Tweed, Keith Grieves in regard to Leek, Christine Housden in regard to Kingston, and Marjorie Levine-Clark in regard to Stourbridge and Dudley have all found that cases based on political or religious sensitivities constituted a tiny fraction of the tribunals' workload.[26]

Objectors made up just 1.8 per cent of all the appellants in Wiltshire and 0.8 per cent of the individuals who applied to the Stratford-upon-Avon body.[27] In Yorkshire, there were only six such men among 377 claimants to the Birstall Tribunal and 16 among 3385 Batley appellants.[28] Even Cyril Pearce, who describes Huddersfield as 'a virtual citadel for the anti-war cause', admits less than 1 per cent of the cases brought before the local tribunal were overtly based on a reluctance to join the army.[29] While opinions differ over exactly how many conscientious objectors there were in Britain, the highest estimate of 23,000 would still constitute less than 0.5 per cent of the total number of men recruited during the war.[30]

Most personal claims were actually lodged on hardship grounds. The concept of the male provider had gained considerable standing in nineteenth-century Britain, and the testimony given during appeal hearings demonstrates its enduring influence.[31] At the Dewsbury Tribunal, Norman Pontefract asserted he was the only one keeping his widowed mother out of the workhouse.[32] Likewise, a shopkeeper told the Preston body he had lost his wife three years previously, and had been looking after their business and five young children without female assistance ever since.[33]

Appellants tended to link these concerns to the responsibilities they had inherited after the enlistment or conscription of their siblings.[34] A 31-year-old painter's labourer from Goole stated he was the last of four brothers at home, which made him essential to the upkeep of their invalid father and mother.[35] The primary concern for most married men was continuing in their 'natural' role as head of the household. Andrew Coult explained his previous failure to volunteer by insisting it would 'have done his wife and children a great injustice', while Leonard Hartley had 'thought it my duty to stick to the obligations to my parents, and to look after my wife and children'.[36] Many other appellants balked at the idea of their spouses having to take on paid employment, arguing this was not a role women could, or should, be expected to fulfil.

Similar views were expressed in business hardship cases. These appellants frequently asserted their enterprise would no longer be financially viable if they were taken, due to a lack of family expertise or suitable outside help. A saddler and harness maker told the Barnsley Borough Tribunal that he had spent his entire life savings on making the concern profitable. It would have to be closed down if he were conscripted, thereby ruining the prospects of his young family.[37] Arthur Slack, who worked as 'secretary, departmental sub manager & classifier of hide skins' for his family's business in Nottinghamshire, detailed similar fears. After a frank discussion with his parents, Slack became convinced that the commercial side of their operation could not be carried on without him. He spent the weeks before his appeal in a constant state of agitation, confiding to his diary that he felt 'pretty gloomy, thinking of poor father if I have to go'.[38]

Enduring ideals of male citizenship were also used to support occupational appeals. The pre-war working class was divided into skilled artisans, semi-skilled labourers and the unskilled, with very little movement, but a great many economic and social distinctions, between these categories.[39] Under conscription, employers from urban areas emphasised that they were willing to carry out their patriotic duty by releasing unskilled or non-essential men, but only if they could keep the indispensables. Textile manufacturers in Yorkshire lodged vast numbers of claims for carders, fettlers and spinners, arguing that output would be drastically curtailed without them.[40] Likewise, thousands of appeals were made for boot and shoe clickers, heelers and machinists in Northamptonshire.[41]

Occupational claims were also common in rural areas, where farmers desperately pleaded for the retention of their experienced personnel. One appellant to the Goole Rural Tribunal insisted that he had exchanged all of his more recent employees for boys or pensioners. As a result, there was no way he could supply enough milk to the nearby towns if any of his leading hands were taken.[42] When the discussion turned to potential compromises, most employers refused to perceive men who were outside the military age as suitable replacements. The director of H. H. Holdsworth & Co. labelled the proposed use of 50-year-olds as roving overlookers 'absurd', while a nurseryman exclaimed that 'he would go short' rather than employ school-leavers.[43]

An even stronger resistance greeted the suggestion of female labour. Taylor Yielding & Co., textile manufacturers, based several claims on the fact that their materials and machines were simply too heavy for women to manage.[44] Similarly, a Northamptonshire farmer stated that women 'won't do for me . . . they want too much looking after', and an umbrella and sunshade manufacturer from London stressed that his company's premises could not be made to comply with the regulations governing separate lavatories.[45]

For these arguments to succeed in gaining exemption, they had to coincide with the tribunals' own understandings of masculine duty. Some of Britain's local registration authorities appointed anti-conscriptionists, or even pacifists, on to their tribunals. But this was exceedingly rare.[46] Most of the chosen individuals were middle-class local councillors who believed victory was essential for protecting the British way of life, and who had been involved in the war effort from the beginning through patriotic or charitable organisations.[47] Given this background, one would expect any conflation of citizenship and military service to be particularly apparent among the tribunals.

Their members did contend that some appeals should never have been made. During the claim of a work's chemist at New Mill, councillor Roebuck questioned why the tribunal was being asked to exempt an unmarried

individual on the grounds that he was indispensable when there were numerous men with families scheduled for hearing.⁴⁸ Using analogous logic, the Goole Urban body informed the employer of a single carter that such men 'were wanted in the Army' and that he would simply have to do his best to find a replacement.⁴⁹

Disapproval was also expressed when the appellant was of a young age. For suggesting that one such individual was worthy of exemption, a solicitor before the Barnsley Borough Tribunal was reminded that 'if the young ones do not go we shall have to take those between 40 and 45'.⁵⁰ At Spenborough, a director's plea that his firm had not appealed for anyone prior to their leather workman was also rejected, with the chairman stating that the tribunal had no intention of relieving men who were only 27 years old.⁵¹

A third factor that tended to provoke ire was that a man had been placed in medical category A: suitable for 'general service'. When a firm requested that one of its employees should be given time to sit for an exam, the chairman of the Pontefract Borough Tribunal heatedly replied that they had sent barely suitable 40-year-olds to the front and could not be expected to exempt those who were in perfect fighting condition.⁵² The same sentiment was voiced by the Spenborough body, which told a painter's employer that 'the first thing we have got to do is to get fit A men for the Army'.⁵³

The tribunal members showed even less sympathy for men from families who were not represented at the front. In these instances, it was invariably argued that the household had not only neglected its responsibilities previously, but that the decision to appeal revealed a continued willingness to let others fight on their behalf. When Mr Arrand appeared before the Hemsworth Rural Tribunal to plead for his 20-year-old son, his case quickly foundered once he admitted that his other four boys were all still at home. Councillor Burns stated that it was a 'positive waste of time discussing the matter further', councillor Beach scathingly remarked that 'You have five sons, and not one serving the country', while Mr Jagger enquired how they might go about getting their hands on the sons who were still at large.⁵⁴ Similarly, after several cases of untouched households had come to the attention of the New

Mill body, councillor Gill vehemently insisted that 'every family with sons of military age ought to be represented in the forces'.[55]

Some employers also received short shrift, especially when the tribunals perceived a reluctance to make sacrifices. The Batley members informed one manufacturer that 'people are discarding their chauffeurs everywhere', while the claim made for a bailiff at Pontefract prompted the allegation that the public departments were 'the last people to realise we are at War'.[56] Employers experienced further difficulties if their work was deemed to be unnecessary for the national interests. A home furnishing company was told that 'carpets and linoleums . . . won't win the war', and a theatre owner was refused on the grounds that 'tens of thousands' of more important concerns had already been shut down.[57] Among the most scornful rebukes was that delivered by the chairman of the Wakefield Tribunal, who told the director of a window-cleaning firm 'we must go with our windows dirty if necessary. We have got to beat the Germans.'[58]

Yet the tribunals did not adopt a one-sided understanding of male citizenship. Indeed, the very nature of their position made it inevitable that they would question, and quite possibly reject, any attempt to establish the performance of military service as a uniform definition of masculine duty. The tribunals were part of a nationwide conscription system, and were constantly bombarded with official instructions that described the refusal of appeals as being in the 'national interest'.[59] However, the primary qualification for appointment to a tribunal was prominence in the local economy and the local community. As businessmen, manufacturers or union leaders, it would have been irrational for the members to reduce trade and productivity by forcing the widespread closure of local enterprises.

Likewise, involvement in charitable and patriotic organisations would have given most members a fulsome appreciation of the difficulties that the war had already caused to many families in their area. Self-interest is also likely to have exercised a degree of influence. Being mostly elected local councillors, the tribunal members needed to retain the goodwill of their district's population. Refusing to send any men to the front would undoubtedly have seen them

THE MILITARY SERVICE ACT, 1916

Applies to Unmarried Men who, on August 15th, 1915, were 18 years of age or over and who will not be 41 years of age on March 2nd, 1916.

ALL MEN, NOT EXCEPTED OR EXEMPTED, between these ages who on November 2nd, 1915, were unmarried or widowers without any child dependent on them will on

THURSDAY, MARCH 2nd, 1916,

Be deemed to be Enlisted for the Period of the War.

THEY WILL BE PLACED IN THE RESERVE UNTIL CALLED UP IN THEIR CLASS.

MEN EXCEPTED :

SOLDIERS, including Territorials who have volunteered for Foreign Service;
MEN serving in the NAVY or ROYAL MARINES;
MEN DISCHARGED FROM ARMY OR NAVY, disabled or ill, or TIME-EXPIRED MEN;
MEN REJECTED for the Army since August 14th, 1915;
CLERGYMEN, PRIESTS and MINISTERS OF RELIGION;
VISITORS from the DOMINIONS.

Men who may be exempted by Local Tribunals :

Men more useful to the Nation in their present employments;
Men in whose case Military Service would cause serious hardship owing to exceptional financial or business obligations or domestic position;
Men who are ill or infirm;
Men who conscientiously object to combatant service. If the Tribunal thinks fit, men may, on this ground, be (a) exempted from combatant service only (not non-combatant service), or (b) exempted on condition that they are engaged in work of National importance.

Up to March 2nd, a man can apply to his Local Tribunal for a certificate of exemption. There is a Right of Appeal. He will not be called up until his case has been dealt with finally.

Certificates of exemption may be absolute, conditional or temporary. Such certificates can be renewed, varied or withdrawn.

Men retain their Civil Rights until called up and are amenable to Civil Courts only.

DO NOT WAIT UNTIL MARCH 2nd.
ENLIST VOLUNTARILY NOW

For fuller particulars of the Act, please apply for Leaflet No. 64 to the nearest Post Office, Police Station, or Recruiting Office.

Published by the Parliamentary Recruiting Committee, London. Poster No. 153. The Abbey Press, Westminster, S.W.

The British conscription system was a bureaucratic and administrative quagmire. Posters like this one were put up in public places to try to inform prospective conscripts of their rights and responsibilities. **IMPERIAL WAR MUSEUM, LONDON, ART.IWM PST 5044** charged with a lack of patriotism, but depriving families of their breadwinners, or local industries of their essential workers, must surely have struck the members as being equally damaging to their political ambitions.

These conflicting imperatives led most tribunals to explicitly promote a nuanced understanding of male citizenship. At Batley, chairman Turner asserted that his body would do its best to supply enough soldiers, but 'without unduly harassing the trade of the town and district'.[60] Equally, Harry Cartmell interpreted the task of the Preston Tribunal as being to 'hold the balance between the claims of the Army on one hand, and of important business undertakings on the other', and councillor Simmonds described the Holmfirth body as a 'sort of escape valve' where military imperatives were weighed up against the circumstances of each appellant.[61]

During hardship cases, many tribunal members adhered to the principles of the male breadwinner ideal. Appearing at Huddersfield in October 1917, a butcher was awarded exemption on the grounds that his mother suffered from mental troubles and would probably be sent to an asylum without his constant care.[62] Two months later, the Wakefield Tribunal was deeply moved by the appeal of a joiner's apprentice, the son of a widow who had already lost two sons in action, had another who was missing, and a fourth who was suffering from gas poisoning. In granting conditional exemption, the chairman said that they were 'bound to let their feelings have a little play' given the 'appalling circumstances'.[63]

Similarly reprieved were men from families who boasted fine records of service. Appearing before the Goole Rural Tribunal, Mrs Cowling divulged that she already had six sons in the firing line, with another currently on his way from Canada. Delighted with this fulsome evidence of sacrifice, the chairman immediately granted conditional exemption to her remaining son, Frank, and announced that 'Mrs. Cowling has done her share', to a resounding chorus of 'hear, hear'.[64] The tribunals also proved amenable to strong cases made on business grounds. The Featherstone body exempted Eric Cooper, the manager of two fruit shops, who pleaded that both of his former assistants, a brother and a brother-in-law, were serving at the front.[65] Similarly, the Goole Urban Tribunal awarded a six-month exemption to G. H. Thompson, ironmonger, arguing that it would be 'a serious matter' to close down his 'well-established' enterprise.[66]

Cases lodged on behalf of skilled and essential workers were also favourably received. The Shepley body granted all the appeals made by a quarry manager who outlined the importance of his operation to the local economy, while substantial praise, and a conditional exemption, was afforded to a contractor claiming for his son, who informed the Normanton Tribunal that three of his other boys, and 35 out of his 86 staff, had already joined the forces.[67]

Most striking of all are those instances where the appeal bodies specifically opposed the idea that all men should join the army. In March 1916, the members of the Golcar Tribunal took exception to Major Tanner's complaint that there had only been one refusal all day, and replied that they had judged each case solely on its merits.[68] Eight months later, the Marsden Tribunal resisted Captain Mallalieu's assertion that 15 claims from a woollen firm should be determined on the basis that all men under 30 were needed at the front. Pointing out that this would cause a drastic reduction in output, the chairman asserted that the appeal bodies' role was 'to keep industries going'.[69]

These nuanced conceptions of male duty were of particular benefit to married appellants. The tribunals unanimously believed men with families had greater domestic responsibilities than single men and that their conscription would cause considerably more hardship.[70] When the first married reservists were called up in April and May 1916, many appeal bodies simply adjourned their hearings until all the single men could be dealt with.[71] If the director of recruiting regarded such actions as 'disquieting' and a threat to the 'national interests', they were symptomatic of the tribunals' approach throughout the conscription period.[72]

Members frequently questioned the need to conscript local married individuals while government departments were protecting so many young singles, with several appeal bodies even going on 'strike' over this issue.[73] Married men also had a much easier time when their cases were heard. In her study of Stourbridge and Dudley, Levine-Clark has found that 'Tribunal members consistently asked single applicants to weigh their circumstances against those of married men' and that 'single men were refused exemptions more than twice as often'.⁷⁴ There is every reason to think this situation represented the rule rather than the exception.

The tribunals' nuanced attitude towards masculine citizenship can best be illustrated by the statistics of their verdicts. If adjourned and withdrawn cases are excluded, then, in Yorkshire, the Marsden Tribunal awarded a temporary, conditional or absolute exemption 85.56 per cent of the time.⁷⁵ Both the Batley and Huddersfield bodies granted exemptions in over three-quarters of the cases they determined, while the Birstall Tribunal was only slightly less favourable to appellants, recording a total of 74.14 per cent positive decisions.⁷⁶ Even the Spenborough members, described by one solicitor as 'the smallest sieve people had to go through', only refused around one-third of all the claims that came before them.⁷⁷ A similar picture emerges elsewhere in Britain. The Stratford-upon-Avon Tribunal reached a negative verdict in just 14.81 per cent of cases, while the relative total for the Calne Tribunal was a meager 9.15 per cent.⁷⁸ If the approaches of the Scottish Haddington Burgh and East Lothian County tribunals, and the Audenshaw Tribunal in Lancashire, were slightly less liberal, they still afforded exemption to 82.76 per cent, 75 per cent and 74.77 per cent of appellants respectively.⁷⁹

Of final significance are the opinions voiced by the military. Far from perceiving the tribunals as partners in a collaborative effort to meet the army's demands, the War Office actually saw their members as overly sentimental obstructionists who did considerably more to hinder the national cause than to advance it. Why would the military hierarchy have felt compelled to meet with the tribunal chairmen in an attempt to stiffen their resolve if the appeal bodies were already dismissing most of the claims that came before them?⁸⁰

As early as March 1916, a correspondent for *The Times* noted that 'exemptions are being freely granted, despite the protests of the representatives at the tribunals of the Military Authorities'.⁸¹ The adjutant-general greeted the overall increase of exemptions during late 1916 with undisguised fury, and the director of recruiting railed against the tribunal members' tendency to base their verdicts 'almost entirely on individual or local considerations'.⁸²

An even greater sense of betrayal is apparent among the army's generals, who portrayed the appeal bodies as working with government departments such as the Ministry of Munitions to 'nullify to a great extent the object of the Military Service Acts'.[83]

There were members of the British public who regarded certain appeals as a failure of masculine citizenship. The belief that the Germans had committed all manner of atrocities in occupied Belgium led some people to assert that only a coward would vacillate over defending his country against the same fate.[84] Such criticism was almost always directed against young single men, or at the employers who were perceived as sheltering them.

One correspondent to a local newspaper wrote that it made her 'blood boil' to think of single appellants still claiming 'the title of Englishmen', while 'A "Stiff" From Huddersfield' described his disgust at seeing so many 'smart young fellows . . . chaffing with girls down Westgate'.[85] Organisations sprang up across Britain to promote the interests of married reservists and to demand that all singles should first be 'combed out' of the protected occupations.[86] Furthermore, tribunals and the military authorities regularly cited the large volume of anonymous letters they had received, most of which complained about 'young men who ought to have joined up long ago'.[87]

The public's attitude towards other hardship and occupational claims was more benign. Given that hearings were usually held in open court, there was ample scope for appellants to be labelled as 'shirkers' within their communities. Yet the local newspapers, many of which deliberately avoided printing names or addresses, rarely took up this opportunity.[88] Their coverage was generally limited to a handful of the more 'interesting' or informative cases from each sitting, while some publications refused to report on the tribunals' activities altogether, so that men who had exercised their legal right to claim exemption would not be 'made the butt of idle and mischievous gossip'.[89] The accessible nature of the exemption system also raised the prospect of appellants being hounded during their hearings, but again there are very few recorded instances of this taking place. On the contrary, many sittings attracted few, or even no, onlookers, and any heckling that did take place was far more likely to be directed at the tribunal members than at the appellants.⁹⁰

This last point can also be applied more widely. Whereas the military authorities tended to lambast the tribunals for granting too many exemptions, almost everyone else argued that they were granting too few.⁹¹ One Member of Parliament likened the appeal bodies to 'recruiting sergeants' and 'the old press gangs', another cited their relentless efforts at 'driving men into the army', while a third lamented the 'very poor' hearings that were being accorded.⁹² Indeed, there was scarcely a sitting of Parliament that did not witness at least some complaints about the tribunals breaking up families and crippling businesses.

Such indictments were also voiced locally. After the first few weeks of sittings, the *Dewsbury Reporter* concluded that the tribunals had decided to operate 'as the tool and instrument of the military'.⁹³ Likewise, the *Huddersfield Examiner* suggested that their members were 'sweeping all kinds of men into the Army', and the Huddersfield Friendly and Trade Societies' Club opined that unless the appeal bodies began to show more consideration then 'there is likely to be a serious shortage of farmers' production'.⁹⁴ For her part, Beatrice Webb described the tribunals as 'a scandalous example of lay prejudice', while George Bernard Shaw branded many of their members 'insolent snobs, impenetrable blockheads, or both'.⁹⁵ It is little wonder the chairman of the Castleford body hastened to reassure his colleagues against the 'flood of abuse' that had been heaped upon them by individuals who apparently believed they were 'lacking in intelligence and full of partiality and prejudice'.⁹⁶

Historians of the First World War have begun to identify similarly nuanced understandings of masculine citizenship across other parts of the 'British World'. In New Zealand, exemption claims were more frequently equated with 'shirking', and this seems to have been a major factor in this country's lower rate of appealing.⁹⁷ Nevertheless, around one-third of balloted New Zealanders lodged claims with the military service boards, primarily on domestic, business and occupational grounds, and stood a better than even chance of gaining exemption when they did so.⁹⁸

The passage of a Military Service Act in Canada prompted an even greater

reaction. Many French Canadians set themselves against being compelled to fight for a monarchy and a government they did not recognise, while the number of exemption appeals throughout the country was immense. Fully 90 per cent of Class 1 men — those who were unmarried and aged 20 to 34 — chose to appeal on the grounds of hardship, occupation, or obvious physical disability.[99] Australian attitudes towards military service were so conflicted that the introduction of conscription was narrowly rejected in two referenda. Moreover, Bart Ziino has found that over three-quarters of respondents to the 1916 Call to Arms Appeal indicated an unwillingness to enlist voluntarily, with family and employment circumstances again dominating the list of reasons.[100]

It might be thought that the implementation of conscription during the First World War has little relevance to present-day debates around citizenship. After all, Britain and its former dominions have not mobilised their whole societies for war in over seventy years, nor do they any longer compel people to serve in the armed forces. Yet there are at least two pertinent lessons that can be drawn from the experiences of 1916 to 1918.

First, although this was a time when the role and power of national governments increased to an exponential degree, and when the necessity of adopting a national outlook was constantly emphasised, understandings of 'good' citizenship were still as dependent on personal and local factors as they were on centrally developed imperatives.[101] Individuals did not simply accept that the introduction of conscription meant the need for soldiers had become all-important, but rather continued to weigh the onus to serve the nation against their own unique concerns. Ultimately, many conscripts and tribunal members determined 'that other responsibilities could prevail over the call to arms'.[102]

Second, despite the unprecedented demands and upheavals occasioned by the world's first 'total war', people continued to base the principles of male citizenship as much on the long-standing paradigms of family, work and community as on the short-term need for a mass army. Tribunal members and large sections of the public consistently held that a man's domestic circumstances, occupation and importance to the locality must play a significant role in determining the precise nature of his rights and duties.

These findings illustrate the limitations of narratives that describe citizenship as becoming a progressively more monolithic and centrally defined concept. Even during the unprecedented national mobilisations that the First World War entailed, many people's understandings of 'good' citizenship remained personal, local and enduring.

ENDNOTES

1 *The Worker*, Huddersfield, 9 September 1916, 3.
2 *Pontefract & Castleford Express* (hereafter *PCE*), 21 July 1916, 5.
3 Nicoletta F. Gullace, *'The Blood of Our Sons': Men, Women, and the Renegotiation of British Citizenship During the Great War* (Houndmills: Palgrave Macmillan, 2002), 101–9.
4 Gullace, 'The Blood of Our Sons,' 111–2.
5 David Boulton, *Objection Overruled* (London: MacGibbon & Kee, 1967), 123–39; W. J. Chamberlain, *Fighting For Peace: The Story of the War Resistance Movement* (London: No More War Movement, 1928), 47–53; John W. Graham, *Conscription and Conscience: A History, 1916–1919* (London: George Allen & Unwin, 1922), 65–89; Denis Hayes, *Challenge of Conscience: The Story of the Conscientious Objectors of 1939–1949* (London: George Allen & Unwin, 1949), 43–4; Thomas C. Kennedy, 'Public Opinion and the Conscientious Objector, 1915–1919,' *Journal of British Studies* 12, no. 2 (1973): 105–19; Arthur Marwick, *The Deluge: British Society and the First World War* (London: Bodley Head, 1965), 80–5; Adrian Stephen, 'The Tribunals,' in *We Did Not Fight: 1914–18 Experiences of War Resisters*, ed. Julian Bell (London: Cobden-Sanderson, 1935), 377–92.
6 Adrian Gregory, *The Last Great War: British Society and the First World War* (Cambridge: Cambridge University Press, 2009), 92–5; Marjorie Levine-Clark, *Unemployment, Welfare, and Masculine Citizenship: 'So Much Honest Poverty' in Britain, 1870–1930* (Houndmills: Palgrave Macmillan, 2015), 124–36; Sascha Auerbach, 'Negotiating Nationalism: Jewish Conscription and Russian Repatriation in London's East End, 1916–1918,' *Journal of British Studies* 46, no. 3 (2007): 594–5; Gerard J. DeGroot, *Blighty: British Society in the Era of the Great War* (London: Longman, 1996), 143–56; Will Ellsworth-Jones, *We Will Not Fight: The Untold Story of the First World War's Conscientious Objectors* (London: Aurum, 2007), 62–78; Caroline Moorhead, *Troublesome People: Enemies of War, 1916–1986* (London: Hamish Hamilton, 1987), 31–4.
7 Military Service Act, 1916, Section 2(1).
8 Local Government Board Circular R. 36, 3 February 1916, MH 47/142, the National Archives, Kew (hereafter TNA).
9 Gullace, 'The Blood of Our Sons,' 3.
10 R. J. Q. Adams and Philip P. Poirier, *The Conscription Controversy in Great Britain, 1900–18* (Columbus: Ohio State University Press, 1987), 147–9.
11 *The Neville Chamberlain Diary Letters, Volume One: The Making of a Politician, 1915–20*, ed. Robert Self (Aldershot: Ashgate, 2000), 110.
12 H. Cartmell, *For Remembrance: An Account of Some Fateful Years* (Preston: George Toulmin & Sons, 1919), 68.
13 F. P. Armitage, *Leicester, 1914–1918: The War-Time Story of a Midland Town* (Leicester: Edgar Backus, 1933), 169; *Carmarthen Journal*, 18 February 1916, 4, quoted in Robin Barlow, 'Military Tribunals in Carmarthenshire, 1916–1917,' in *The Great War: Localities and Regional Identities*,

ed. Nick Mansfield and Craig Horner (Newcastle: Cambridge Scholars, 2014), 12; Lieut.-Col. C. À Court Repington, *The First World War, 1914–1918: Personal Experiences of Lieut.-Col. C. À Court Repington* (London: Constable & Co., 1921), 203, 297.

14 Michael MacDonagh, *In London During the Great War* (London: Eyre & Spottiswoode, 1935), 98–9; Cabinet Committee on the Co-ordination of Military and Financial Effort, 10 April 1916, CAB 27/4, TNA.

15 Brigadier-General Sir James E. Edmonds, *Military Operations: France and Belgium, 1916. Sir Douglas Haig's Command to the 1st July: Battle of the Somme* (London: Macmillan and Co., 1932), 152; A. J. P. Taylor, *Politics in Wartime and Other Essays* (London: Hamilton, 1964), 24.

16 Cabinet Committee on the Co-ordination of Military and Financial Effort: Second Report, 13 April 1916, CAB 27/4, TNA.

17 William Herbert Scott, *Leeds in the Great War, 1914–1918: A Book of Remembrance* (Leeds: Leeds Libraries and Arts Committee, 1923), 316; *Bristol and the Great War, 1914–1919*, ed. George F. Stone and Charles Wells (Bristol: J. W. Arrowsmith, 1920), 116; Reginald H. Brazier and Ernest Sandford, *Birmingham and the Great War, 1914–1919* (Birmingham: Cornish Brothers, 1921), 29; *1911 Census of Great Britain*.

18 Ivor Slocombe, 'Recruitment into the Armed Forces During the First World War: The Work of the Military Tribunals in Wiltshire, 1915–1918,' *The Local Historian* 30, no. 2 (2000): 111; Agendas for Tribunal Sittings, Harris Hoyle Papers, S/NUDBTW/34, Kirklees Archives, Huddersfield (hereafter KA); *1911 Census of Great Britain*.

19 Huddersfield Local Tribunal Minutes, 3 January 1917, KMT 18/12/2/52/1, KA; *1911 Census of Great Britain*.

20 Adrian Gregory, 'Military Service Tribunals: Civil Society in Action, 1916–1918,' in *Civil Society in British History: Ideas, Identities, Institutions*, ed. Jose Harris (Oxford: Oxford University Press, 2003), 184.

21 Military Service Act, 1916, Section 2(2) and (5).

22 Memorandum by the Adjutant-General, 10 January 1917, CAB 17/158, TNA.

23 Rt Hon. Christopher Addison, *Four and a Half Years: A Personal Diary from June 1914 to January 1919*, vol. I (London: Hutchinson & Co., 1934), 161; J. K. Montgomery, *The Maintenance of the Agricultural Labour Supply in England and Wales During the War* (Rome: International Institute of Agriculture, 1922), 7.

24 HMSO, *Statistics of the Military Effort of the British Empire During the Great War, 1914–1920* (London: HMSO, 1922), 367.

25 Gregory, *The Last Great War*, 102.

26 James G. M. Cranstoun, 'The Impact of the Great War on a Local Community: The Case of East Lothian,' PhD thesis, Open University, 1992, 117; Mike Fraser, *'Does My Country Really Need Me?' The Work of the Berwick-upon-Tweed Military Service Tribunal* (Berwick-upon-Tweed: Blue Button, 2015), 47; Keith Grieves, 'Military Tribunal Papers: The Case of Leek Local Tribunal in the First World War,' *Archives: The Journal of the British Record Association* 16,

no. 70 (1983): 146; Christine Housden, 'Researching Kingston's Military Tribunal, 1916–1918,' *Occasional Papers in Local History* 2 (2004): 6; Levine-Clark, *Unemployment, Welfare, and Masculine Citizenship*, 127.

27   Slocombe, 'Recruitment into the Armed Forces,' 111; Philip Spinks, '"The War Courts": The Stratford-upon-Avon Borough Tribunal, 1916–1918,' *The Local Historian* 32, no. 4 (2000): 214.
28   Sitting Agendas, Birstall Local Tribunal Files, RD 21/6/2, KA; Batley Local Tribunal Register of Cases, KMT 1, KA.
29   Cyril Pearce, *Comrades in Conscience: The Story of an English Community's Opposition to the Great War* (London: Francis Boutle, 2001), 21, 161.
30   Pearce, *Comrades in Conscience*, 168–9; John Rae, *Conscience and Politics: The British Government and the Conscientious Objector to Military Service, 1916–1919* (London: Oxford University Press, 1970), 71.
31   Wally Seccombe, 'Patriarchy Stabilized: The Construction of the Male Breadwinner Norm in Nineteenth-Century Britain,' *Social History* 2, no. 1 (1986): 54; John Tosh, *A Man's Place: Masculinity and the Middle-Class Home in Victorian England* (New Haven: Yale University Press, 1999), 1–2.
32   *Batley News* (hereafter *BN*), 19 January 1918, 1.
33   Cartmell, *For Remembrance*, 77.
34   James McDermott, *British Military Service Tribunals, 1916–1918: 'A Very Much Abused Body of Men'* (Manchester: Manchester University Press, 2011), 158.
35   *The Goole Times* (hereafter *GT*), 12 May 1916, 4.
36   *PCE*, 21 July 1916, 5 and 14 July 1916, 3.
37   *Barnsley Chronicle* (hereafter *BC*), 3 June 1916, 6.
38   Diary Entry, 1 February 1916, Private Papers of Arthur Ronald Roy Slack, Documents 18453, Imperial War Museum, London (hereafter IWM).
39   Alan G. V. Simmonds, *Britain and World War One* (Abingdon: Routledge, 2012), 3.
40   *BN*, 15 April 1916, 1.
41   McDermott, *British Military Service Tribunals*, 64–89.
42   *GT*, 15 September 1916, 3.
43   *Wakefield Express* (hereafter *WE*), 5 August 1916, 7; *Huddersfield Examiner* (hereafter *HEx*), 11 January 1917, 3.
44   Yielding to Gray, 28 February 1916, Birstall Local Tribunal Files, RD 21/6/2, KA.
45   *The Northampton Mercury*, 6 October 1916, 4, quoted in McDermott, *British Military Service Tribunals*, 108; Solicitor's Brief for Lionel Edward Ball, Documents 5381, IWM.
46   A. J. Peacock, *York in the Great War: 1914 to 1918* (York: York Settlement Trust, 1993), 382.
47   David Littlewood, '"The Tool and Instrument of the Military"? The Operations of the Military Service Tribunals in the East Central Division of the West Riding of Yorkshire and Those of the Military Service Boards in New Zealand, 1916–1918,' PhD thesis, Massey University, 2015, 79–85; McDermott, *British Military Service Tribunals*, 16–7.

48 *Holmfirth Express* (hereafter *HE*), 16 September 1916, 5.
49 *GT*, 4 August 1916, 4.
50 *BC*, 30 September 1916, 2.
51 *Cleckheaton & Spenborough Guardian* (hereafter *CSG*), 24 November 1916, 6.
52 *PCE*, 4 May 1917, 5.
53 *CSG*, 9 March 1917, 3.
54 *PCE*, 16 June 1916, 3.
55 *HE*, 13 January 1917, 6.
56 *BN*, 19 August 1916, 3; *PCE*, 4 August 1916, 2.
57 *WE*, 13 May 1916, 3; *BN*, 28 April 1917, 3.
58 *WE*, 30 June 1917, 6.
59 Parliamentary Papers Cd. 8697: *Forty-Sixth Annual Report of the Local Government Board, 1916–1917* (London: HMSO, 1917), 21; J. H. Worrall, *The Tribunal Hand-Book* (London: W. H. Smith & Son, 1917), 59–60.
60 *BN*, 21 October 1916, 5.
61 Cartmell, *For Remembrance*, 69; *HE*, 18 March 1916, 8.
62 *HEx*, 1 October 1917, 4.
63 *WE*, 1 December 1917, 7.
64 *GT*, 30 March 1917, 2.
65 *PCE*, 19 April 1916, 3.
66 *GT*, 5 July 1918, 5.
67 *HEx*, 27 June 1917, 4; *WE*, 13 May 1916, 7.
68 *HEx*, 29 February 1916, 4.
69 *HEx*, 23 November 1916, 3.
70 *HEx*, 8 March 1916, 4.
71 *PCE*, 17 March 1916, 6; *HEx*, 15 May 1916, 4 and 17 May 1916, 2.
72 Derby to Long, 27 March 1916, Walter Long Papers, 947/497, Wiltshire and Swindon History Centre, Chippenham (hereafter WSHC).
73 *WE*, 30 September 1916, 6; *HEx*, 10 November 1916, 4; *CSG*, 6 July 1917, 3.
74 Levine-Clark, *Unemployment, Welfare, and Masculine Citizenship*, 128–30.
75 Agendas for Tribunal Sittings, Harris Hoyle Papers, S/NUDBTW/34, KA.
76 Batley Local Tribunal Register of Cases, KMT 1, KA; Huddersfield Local Tribunal Minutes, KMT 18/12/2/52/1, KA; Sitting Agendas and Minutes, Birstall Local Tribunal Files, RD 21/6/2, KA.
77 *CSG*, 30 March 1917, 7; Spenborough Local Tribunal Minutes, KMT 39/1/2/1/1, KA.
78 Calne Local Tribunal Minute Book, G3 119/8, WSHC; Spinks, 'The War Courts,' 214.
79 Cranstoun, 'The Impact of the Great War,' 115–7; Keith Grieves, 'Mobilising Manpower: The Audenshaw Tribunal in the First World War,' *Manchester Region History Review* 3, no. 2 (1989): 28.
80 *BN*, 21 October 1916, 1; *CSG*, 6 June 1917, 3.

81 MacDonagh, *In London*, 99.
82 Memorandum by the Adjutant-General, 10 January 1917, CAB 17/158, TNA; Director of Recruiting, the Theory and Practice of Recruiting, 23 July 1917, CAB 24/20, TNA.
83 Army Council to Secretary of State for War, 28 November 1916, CAB 37/160/25, TNA.
84 Gullace, *'The Blood of Our Sons,'* 113.
85 *County Advertiser*, 18 March 1916, 2, quoted in Levine-Clark, *Unemployment, Poverty, and Masculine Citizenship*, 126; *HEx*, 8 November 1916, 2.
86 *HEx*, 10 April 1916, 4; Trevor Wilson, *The Myriad Faces of War: Britain and the Great War, 1914–1918* (Cambridge: Polity Press, 1986), 400.
87 Cartmell, *For Remembrance*, 84; see also Armitage, *Leicester*, 170.
88 *HEx*, 29 February 1916, 2.
89 *HEx*, 11 January 1917, 3; *CSG*, 14 June 1918, 2; *Colne Valley Guardian*, 3 March 1916, 4.
90 *WE*, 26 February 1916, 6; *PCE*, 10 March 1916, 6; *BN*, 6 May 1916, 8; Auerbach, 'Negotiating Nationalism,' 601.
91 McDermott, *British Military Service Tribunals*, 1.
92 Lough, *House of Commons (Fifth Series)*, vol. 80, col. 951; Glanville, *House of Commons (Fifth Series)*, vol. 81, col. 125; Morrell, *House of Commons (Fifth Series)*, vol. 80, col. 2211.
93 *Dewsbury Reporter*, 4 March 1916, 8.
94 *HEx*, 26 February 1916, 2 and 24 May 1916, 2.
95 *Beatrice Webb's Diaries, Vol. 1: 1912–1924*, ed. Margaret I. Cole (London: Longmans, Green & Co., 1952), 55; George Bernard Shaw, *What I Really Wrote About the War* (London: Constable & Co., 1930), 221.
96 *PCE*, 2 June 1916, 6.
97 David Littlewood, '"Willing and Eager to go in Their Turn"? Appeals for Exemption from Military Service in New Zealand and Great Britain, 1916–18,' *War in History* 21, no. 3 (2014): 351–2.
98 Littlewood, 'The Tool and Instrument,' 197–226.
99 J. L. Granatstein, 'Conscription in the Great War,' in *Canada and the First World War: Essays in Honour of Robert Craig Brown*, ed. David Mackenzie (Toronto: University of Toronto Press, 2005), 68; J. L. Granatstein and J. M. Hitsman, *Broken Promises: A History of Conscription in Canada* (Toronto: Oxford University Press, 1977), 84–5.
100 Bart Ziino, 'Enlistment and Non-Enlistment in Wartime Australia: Responses to the 1916 Call to Arms Appeal,' *Australian Historical Studies* 41, no. 2 (2010): 221–9.
101 Sonya O. Rose, *Which People's War? National Identity and Citizenship in Britain, 1939–1945* (Oxford: Oxford University Press, 2003), 286.
102 Adrian Gregory, 'Gender, Citizenship, and Entitlement: Book Reviews,' *Journal of British Studies* 43, no. 3 (2004): 414–5.

8. SPORT & CITIZENSHIP IN NEW ZEALAND

Geoff Watson

SPORT & CITIZENSHIP IN NEW ZEALAND

Sport has long been linked with citizenship in New Zealand. From the beginning of human settlement, competitive physical activity has been used to transmit social values and to publicly represent the desired characteristics of society. This chapter evaluates the changing ways in which sport has been linked to citizenship in New Zealand and concludes with some observations on sport's future role in promoting social citizenship. The chapter interprets social citizenship in a broad sense, namely attitudes and actions that engender a willing engagement in activities which contribute to the individual and public good and in so doing facilitate the functioning of an orderly and democratic society.

In his study of sport in the Ancient Greek and modern worlds, Paul Christesen links sport and democratisation positively, arguing that mass participation in sport generates trust and creates an environment where people submit to rules without being forced to do so.[1] There are, however, some qualifications that need to be made because sport has reflected both inclusive and exclusive expressions of citizenship. On the one hand, sport has been positively linked to community development because, its advocates argue, it encourages physical fitness and accommodates peoples from all ethnicities, social classes and religions within a common framework. On the other hand, some have perceived sport as a site of exclusion. This has taken both explicit forms, such as the marginalisation of athletes and codes deemed 'professional', and implicit forms, where those who do not participate in or support sporting activities are criticised for weakening social bonds and not living up to their obligations as citizens.

There are many ways in which citizenship could be evaluated with reference to sport; this chapter focuses on four. These are sport and personal citizenship: the ways in which sport has been held to contribute to the development of the individual; sport and physical citizenship: the ways in which sport is held to contribute to the physical development of individuals and, by extension, the communities to which they belong; sport and international citizenship: the ways in which sport is used by nations to promote themselves as good international citizens; and sport and bicultural/multicultural citizenship: the ways in which sport purportedly engenders a shared sense of citizenship both within and between communities.

In evaluating the relationship between sport and personal citizenship in New Zealand it is important to acknowledge some distinctions between sport in Māori and European society. First, the notion of sport as a distinct activity requires qualification. In European societies sport has been generally interpreted as rule-bound physical activities, but Robin McConnell has observed that there was not a Māori word for 'sport' as such because physical activities were incorporated into everyday life and were not seen as a discrete category.[2] Despite these differences some broad parallels can be drawn. Both McConnell and Brendan Hokowhitu argue that activities which Europeans regarded simply as games, such as teka (darts) or tops, served the deeper purposes — related to citizenship — of imparting knowledge about tribal history and culture, including elements of tikanga and whakapapa, to young people. Other activities, such as martial arts training, related to life skills.[3]

When New Zealand became a British colony in 1840, a sporting revolution was under way in Britain which would see sport become firmly linked with citizenship by the end of the nineteenth century. While previously sport had been seen primarily as an amusement, nineteenth-century educational reformers saw it as a means of maintaining order through self-government by pupils, and associated games with developing good citizens: that is, something through which young people learned physical courage, unselfish striving towards a team cause and the unquestioning acceptance of authority.

It was also through the public schools that sport became linked to spiritual citizenship, namely 'muscular Christianity', which extolled the virtues of sport

as a means of instilling morals and appropriate physical development among young men. Muscular Christianity gave sport moral legitimacy, elevating it from a mere pastime to an activity through which Christian morals could be publicly demonstrated and transmitted.[4] Charles Kingsley, who popularised the notion of muscular Christianity, nominated George Selwyn, Bishop of New Zealand between 1841 and 1868 and an expert rower in his youth, as an exemplar of the vigorous, practical Christian.[5] From its base in public schools and universities, sport expanded its constituency to encompass the emerging middle classes and, particularly during the last quarter of the nineteenth century, the male working classes.[6]

It must be acknowledged that in the Victorian era the relationship between sport and citizenship was primarily conceived in relation to developing male character. The place of women in sport was problematic for many people during that era. Concerns over whether it was physically and culturally appropriate for women to participate in sport meant that it was introduced only to a limited degree in some university colleges and female public schools, and to an even more limited degree in some workplaces.[7] Nevertheless, by the end of the nineteenth century, many games mistresses had been trained to take exercise classes in both public and state schools.[8]

Another significant development in sport during the Victorian era was the emergence of national sporting organisations which developed a standardised set of rules for their respective codes. This allowed for national and, with the dissemination of sport by British expatriates, international competition. As we shall see, one consequence of this was the linking of sport to notions of national identity and, by extension, national citizenship. The privileging of amateur sport was the other significant legacy of the Victorian era. Although the nineteenth century saw the emergence of professional sporting competitions in their modern form, control of the leading team sports and the Olympic movement remained vested in the hands of amateur administrators.

While amateurism was often framed in terms of whether those who participated in sport ought to receive payment for doing so, in practice many so-called amateurs received generous reimbursement for 'expenses'. As

Richard Holt has observed, amateur regulations and ideals were the means by which the middle and upper classes limited the working classes' access to sport. The amateur athlete, who pursued sport for its own sake, was upheld as the exemplary sporting citizen, whereas professional athletes were viewed with suspicion on the grounds that they might be vulnerable to inducements to fix games. There were also concerns that professional athletes would be more likely to engage in violent play and fritter away their earnings on alcohol and gambling.[9]

It is no coincidence that sports were among the Anglo-Saxon cultural traits transplanted to British colonies, especially white settler colonies such as New Zealand, Australia and South Africa. The act of playing sport demonstrated that the best characteristics of British society could be exported and replicated in its colonies.[10] European sports soon came to New Zealand. Cricket was played at least as early as 1835, and sports were a common feature of the early provincial anniversary celebrations.[11] By the end of the nineteenth century at least a dozen national sports organisations had been formed and New Zealand teams had participated at international level in athletics, bowls, cricket and rugby union.

Why did sport become so firmly established in New Zealand? First and foremost, people wanted to play. Second, there were people with the time, means and willingness to organise sport. In Canterbury, for example, 16 years after the Christchurch settlement was founded, the *Southern Provinces Almanack* of 1866 listed at least ten associations devoted to sport, including a boating club, a chess club, cricket clubs, the Christchurch Football Club, a debating club, the Gymnasium Association, a jockey club, the Lyttelton Regatta and Boating Club, the Regatta Club, and the Heathcote and Railway Rowing Club. (The 1867 census gave the population of Canterbury Province as 53,843.)[12] Although it is not comprehensive, the list of associations does give some idea of the variety of sports available to New Zealanders from the earliest stages of colonisation.

Moreover, participation in sport extended across all classes, with the middle, working and upper classes involved in sport from the outset, making

sport a site of democratisation. Arguably, because of the absence of established social hierarchies, class distinctions were suspended, although not entirely absent, in the formative years of New Zealand sport. Christchurch's Hagley Park, the Auckland Domain and Wellington's Basin Reserve are examples of recreational grounds established with the express intention of being available to all members of the public.[13]

The third reason sport became so firmly established was that, for the most part, it evolved in the absence of any concerted opposition. Indeed, it was supported by the religious, educational, political and tribal establishments. There was a relative lack of sectarianism in New Zealand sport, and the ethos of muscular Christianity was evident in the development of both male and female sport. Illustrative of this is hockey, where the Reverend H. H. Mathias of Kaiapoi played an important role in developing the men's game in Christchurch during the 1890s.[14] The Young Women's Christian Association was similarly important in legitimating and facilitating the development of women's sports in Auckland.[15]

If muscular Christianity linked sport to spiritual citizenship in New Zealand, it was the educational establishment which, as in Britain, linked sport and personal citizenship. In particular, during the nineteenth century New Zealand's few secondary schools exercised an influence in the development of sport that was disproportionate to their number. In the case of rugby union, for example, it was through schools such as Nelson College that the game was initially developed and, thanks to a cadre of committed proselytisers who wanted to keep playing sport after they left school, it expanded from this base to the urban middle and upper classes.[16] Inter-provincial matches quickly became important expressions of community identity and provincial representatives were expected to train diligently in order that they 'uphold the honour of the province'.[17]

Māori engagement in introduced sports was evident from the outset (Charles Darwin records seeing Māori playing cricket in 1835) and was endorsed by both European and Māori leaders.[18] Montague Hawtrey linked the introduction of European sports to 'civilising' Māori in a letter to intending colonists published in 1840: 'Another instrument of civilization and good fellowship, will be the introduction among them of the manly games of England, and, indeed, of any manly exercises requiring skill and bodily discipline, and carried on with temperance and decorum.'[19]

In this way, sport was part of a wider ideology of racial amalgamation in New Zealand; that is, the notion that by intermarriage and acculturation Māori would ultimately adopt European values and lifestyles and over time traditional Māori culture would accordingly be superseded.[20] This, many believed, was in the best interests of Māori as it was through the adoption of European ways that they would obtain the full benefits of citizenship.[21] Scholars such as Harko Brown and Brendan Hokowhitu have argued that it was for these reasons (as well as underlying religious motivations) that missionaries encouraged Māori to turn away from their traditional games in favour of the 'manly games' to which Hawtrey alluded.[22]

The selection of a predominantly Māori New Zealand Native team to tour Britain in 1888–9, and the early inclusion of Māori in national teams, symbolised the widely held belief that New Zealand enjoyed exceptional race relations and granted its indigenous peoples their full rights of citizenship.[23] This view was embodied by the presence of players such as Thomas Rangiwahia Ellison. A qualified lawyer of Ngāi Tahu and Te Āti Awa descent, it was he who suggested the national team play in a black jersey with a silver fern, and he captained the first New Zealand rugby team selected under the auspices of the New Zealand Rugby Football Union (NZRFU) in 1893.[24]

Politicians at local and national level aligned themselves with sport, as did the commercial sector and media. Richard Seddon, Premier of New Zealand between 1893 and 1906, consciously associated himself with the so-called 'Originals' All Blacks team of 1905, personally welcoming the team on their return.[25] This was but one example among many of politicians seeking to ingratiate themselves with successful sporting teams. Many in the commercial sector, especially publicans, were enthusiastic promoters of sport, seeing value in offering their premises to sports teams for after-match functions.

Historically, as Jock Phillips has noted, there was a tension between

The All Blacks were the epitome of physical citizenship in New Zealand. Here the 1905 team — which only lost one of its 35 matches on its tour of the UK, France and North America — win a lineout against the Midland Counties. **ALEXANDER TURNBULL LIBRARY MNZ-1012-1/4-F**

the 'official' and 'unofficial' culture of rugby union. The 'official' culture saw prominent public figures and administrators positively linking sport to the development of moral character. The 'unofficial' culture of sport linked it to binge-drinking and 'mateship'. Although framed with reference to rugby union, Phillips' observations are broadly applicable to other sports. If the 'official' culture connected sport to the dominant narratives of citizenship in public discourse, the 'unofficial' culture offered participants a form of social citizenship in which they gained identity and a sense of belonging in exchange for taking part in team rituals.[26]

The power of sport in formulating public opinion was further reinforced by the press. By the end of the nineteenth century sports reporting was well established in New Zealand, both in the sports section of major newspapers and in dedicated publications like Christchurch's *New Zealand Referee*. The collective support for sport from the political, religious, commercial, tribal and media establishments saw it linked both explicitly and implicitly to citizenship.

In addition to being closely linked to the development of personal and moral citizenship, sport was also associated with physical citizenship. The rise of organised sport coincided with theories of racial classification and social Darwinism. During the colonial period, moral conclusions about the qualities of peoples, indigenous peoples in particular, and their perceived place in the racial hierarchy were, in part, drawn from their physical appearance and perceived physical aptitude. Unsurprisingly, peoples of European ancestry were usually ranked highest in intellectual and physical attainments in such classifications.[27]

There was a strong link between the physical and moral aspects of citizenship because sport was held to develop morality; through attaining fitness individuals were able to physically fulfil their obligations as citizens. Participation in sport also served another function. For all its outward self-confidence, the presumed racial superiority of white settler society rested on an insecure foundation. During the last quarter of the nineteenth century concerns about racial degeneracy among Europeans were voiced, and these

endured well into the twentieth century. Success in sport was one means of demonstrating that standards of physical fitness were not deteriorating. Indeed, one of the boasts made about the 1905 All Blacks, who won 34 out of their 35 matches on their tour of Britain, France and the United States, was that their success was testament to the way New Zealand's environment produced healthy and active citizens.[28]

The perceived physical qualities of New Zealanders were an important part of their self-proclaimed status as 'Better Britons'. Physical citizenship, for New Zealanders, was closely linked to imperial citizenship because it enabled New Zealand to support the British Empire through its armed forces. At a practical level, this was manifested in the education system with the provision of drill for boys.[29] As Keith Sinclair observed, there was great pride in the physical condition and resourcefulness of the more than 6000 volunteer New Zealand soldiers who served in the Boer War between 1899 and 1902.[30] The inclusion of Māori in the armed forces during both the New Zealand Wars and the First World War was especially significant because it simultaneously advertised the survival of the Māori people (whose demise had been widely predicted during the nineteenth century) and their loyalty as British subjects.[31]

Sport, it was widely argued, performed an important role in preparing New Zealanders for war. A 1916 article in the *Evening Post* on the civic reception held for Captain Hardham on his return from Gallipoli epitomises the connection between sport and citizenship: 'They welcomed him as the personification of all that was best and purest in sport and citizenship. If it had not been for the spirit which was fostered by sport, the desire to excel, and the feeling of comradeship, New Zealand's response in the hour of danger would not have been what it was.'[32]

Because sport in New Zealand was interlinked with essentially masculine forms of citizenship, particularly capacity in warfare and physical strength, it is easy to overlook the ways in which it shaped female citizenship in New Zealand. Like many parts of the British world, the opportunities for New Zealand women to take part in organised sport were limited until the last quarter of the nineteenth century. Women's labour was, however, very important in the colonisation of New Zealand. Raewyn Dalziel argued that colonisation was premised on the unpaid labour of women and children, and that the lack of domestic servants meant that colonial women had to perform many physically demanding tasks that their British counterparts did not need to undertake.[33]

The gradual admission of women into sport in Victorian Britain was also evident in New Zealand. By 1914 women's sport was well established in New Zealand, with hockey and netball the principal team sports for women, and tennis, golf and croquet prominent among individual sports. Women's participation in sport was sanctioned on the basis that it would ensure women were fit and that female sport would be conducted in a decorous way that was not injurious to their health. Accordingly, contact sports, such as the football codes, were deemed unsuitable but games such as netball — which clearly prescribed physical movement — were acceptable.[34] The rise of netball, which became the dominant team sport for women during the interwar period, is often attributed to its endorsement by the medical and educational establishments on the grounds that it was a non-contact sport which could be played in a limited space and was accordingly suitable for urban women.[35]

The state became increasingly involved in physical citizenship during the twentieth century. As previously noted, government support for sport during the nineteenth century was primarily rhetorical, although local government was increasingly expected to provide sporting facilities for its citizens. As the twentieth century progressed, however, the government became increasingly involved in the provision of sport, which was seen as a means of addressing social issues. The Physical Welfare and Recreation Act of 1937, which established a National Council of Physical Welfare and Recreation and provided for the establishment of district committees, represented the first attempt by the state to become a provider of sport. Its focus was on promoting community sport in general and on increasing fitness, rather than impinging on the authority of national sports organisations, who were wary of government intervention in sport. Arguably, state involvement in sport was also resisted because it challenged the belief that New Zealanders were a naturally active people.

Concerns about declining participation in sport would later lead to the

formation of the Hillary Commission in 1987 and its successor organisation Sport New Zealand in 2002.[36] One of the most influential documents in this regard was the 2001 *Report of the Sport, Fitness and Leisure Ministerial Taskforce*, better known as the Graham Report, which recommended a greatly increased investment in community and high-performance sport.[37] It identified four key areas, all implicitly related to citizenship, in which sport was a public good; namely, a 'healthier society, social cohesion, an enhanced sense of identity and image' and 'crime prevention'.[38] The unstated implication was that an unhealthy citizen is a potential burden on the state, and that those who pay attention to their physical welfare enhance both their own lives and the lives of New Zealanders collectively.

As previously noted, sport has been an agent through which New Zealand has promoted itself as a good international citizen. One of the earliest examples of sporting diplomacy occurred in 1905, when Richard Seddon funded the All Blacks to visit North America on their return home from Britain.[39] In the colonial era, New Zealand used sport to promote itself as a good imperial citizen; sport reinforced imperial ties to Britain, as much if not more than it generated nationalism. When an English cricket team toured New Zealand in 1864, the first time an English sports team had visited New Zealand, a Dunedin administrator asserted the New Zealanders were 'humble imitators' of their British counterparts, and newspaper reports of the tour emphasised the common bonds between the two countries.[40]

New Zealand's successes in rugby union meant it was more assertive in that area. As early as 1884, New Zealand newspapers approvingly cited reports in Australian newspapers on the prowess of the New Zealand rugby team during its undefeated tour of Australia. Scott Crawford has noted that in an age where classification and hierarchies were prominent, sporting achievements were one of the few areas, along with agriculture, in which New Zealand could claim a high place in the hierarchies of empire.[40A] When Jack Lovelock won the gold medal at the 1936 Olympic Games in Berlin, his achievement was represented as both a British and a New Zealand triumph. In its report on the final *The Times* noted that, in the absence of the Englishman Wooderson, who was eliminated from the race, 'Lovelock carried the main weight of British hopes and fears'.[41]

New Zealand's commitment to amateur sport was another way in which it demonstrated that it was a good imperial citizen. When the NZRFU was considering how it would respond to the introduction of rugby league into New Zealand in 1908, it was faced with a dispute between those who wanted to adopt rule variations which made the game more free-flowing and allow compensation to representative players who had to take time off work to play, and those who argued it was important to adhere to the amateur regulations of the Rugby Football Union (RFU) in England. Ultimately, the fact that New Zealand was financially reliant on tours to and from Britain and the desire to remain part of an imperial network meant the NZRFU remained aligned with the RFU.[42]

Because New Zealand simply did not have the infrastructure to support professional sport, outside of occasional athletics and cycling competitions, the amateur status of New Zealand athletes was largely unquestioned. When A. E. Dome, manager of the Chinese Universities soccer team who toured New Zealand in 1924, declared New Zealand was the 'most amateur country in the world', it is likely that this statement would have been received approvingly.[43] In some respects, amateurism worked to the advantage of New Zealand sport because most New Zealanders had access to sport both domestically and, courtesy of their integration into the networks of the 'British World', international competition.

A self-proclaimed narrative emerged of New Zealand as the humble, amateur sporting underdog who, then and now, 'punched above their weight' on the world stage. Although featuring in different eras, a common characteristic attributed to athletes as diverse as Jack Lovelock, Yvette Williams, Peter Snell, Murray Halberg and the Evers-Swindell twins was a strong work ethic and an innate humility and honesty. These qualities, which exemplified the ideal of the amateur athlete, were also seen as typical of the citizens of the nation to which they belonged.

As New Zealand's formal (but not emotional) connection with the British

Empire faded, sport became a means by which the country asserted itself as a good international citizen. This has been particularly evident in New Zealand's hosting of major sporting events. The 1974 Commonwealth Games in Christchurch were celebrated as the 'friendly games', epitomising the qualities of amateur sport and its capacity to enhance relations between different nationalities.[44] More recently, there has been the hosting of the 2011 Rugby World Cup, in which New Zealand consciously promoted itself as a vibrant, sophisticated and multicultural society capable of welcoming the world to a large-scale commercial sporting event.[45]

Historically, the most severe challenge to New Zealand's self-image as a good international citizen in sport was sporting contact with South Africa. The exclusion of Māori players from All Black teams that toured South Africa in 1928, 1949 and 1960 challenged the widely promoted argument that Māori and Pākehā enjoyed equality of citizenship. By 1960 sporting contacts with South Africa were beginning to have a serious impact on New Zealand's international reputation. The exclusion of Māori players from the 1960 tour appeared discriminatory and reactionary at a time when the 'winds of change' were facilitating decolonisation in Africa and Asia and the civil rights movement was coming to the fore in the United States.

The NZRFU's decision received considerable criticism in a diverse range of overseas newspapers including the *Manchester Guardian*, the *Times of India*, the *Sydney Sun*, New York's *Schenectady Gazette* and Canada's *Windsor Star*.[46] It also generated considerable protest in New Zealand, with approximately 150,000 New Zealanders signing a petition against the exclusion of Māori from the tour. These criticisms intensified during the 1970s and 1980s; to some degree, they reflected a change of focus in the international protest movement against South Africa. The initial basis for the exclusion of South Africa from the Olympic movement and other sporting organisations was the exclusion of non-white athletes from their representative teams, but by the 1970s the anti-apartheid movement was arguing that sporting contact with South Africa was immoral as long as apartheid remained in place.[47]

Māori and Polynesian players were included in All Black teams that toured South Africa in 1970 and 1976 but the changing focus of the protest movement meant that New Zealand was singled out as a nation that supported apartheid. Rugby union was the national game of both New Zealand and South Africa, and in the pre-World Cup era games between the two nations were often portrayed as battles for the world championship of rugby.[48] The clash between the anti-apartheid movement and the New Zealand government came to a head during the 1976 Olympic Games in Montreal, when more than twenty African and Asian nations boycotted the games as a result of the All Black tour of South Africa that year. Although rugby was not an Olympic sport, many African nations argued the New Zealand team ought to be banned from the Olympic Games because they believed the New Zealand government, led by Prime Minister Robert Muldoon, had not actively opposed the tour.

In some respects, the clash reflected different perspectives of individual and international citizenship. The governing National Party, and many of those who wanted sporting contacts to continue, argued that individual liberty meant that New Zealand sporting teams were entitled to play against opponents of their own choosing. The anti-apartheid movement, on the other hand, argued that the collective right of non-white South Africans to be free of racial discrimination outweighed individual rights of freedom of association.[49] Norman Kirk, who had led the Labour Party to victory in the 1972 election (during which time he had pledged to uphold the principle of government non-interference in sport) incurred the wrath of the electorate when he ordered the rugby union to withdraw its invitation to the South African rugby team to tour in 1973, citing security concerns.

During the 1975 election campaign, the National Party indicated that it would not interfere with the decisions of sporting organisations, a policy which was widely viewed as tacit support for continuing sporting contacts with South Africa. These differing perceptions of the obligations of individual and international citizenship were evident again in the lead-up to the 1981 South African tour of New Zealand. In 1977, Commonwealth leaders, concerned at the prospect of a boycott of the 1978 Commonwealth Games, formulated the Gleneagles agreement, which bound its members to 'discourage' sporting

contact with South Africa. For the majority of signatories, this meant taking practical measures such as withholding visas from South African sports teams that may have intended to tour Commonwealth nations. The New Zealand government took a different view, arguing that voicing its opposition to the tour met its obligation to 'discourage' sporting contact with South Africa.

The 1981 South African tour provoked an unprecedented level of violence in relation to a sporting event in New Zealand; over 100,000 New Zealanders took part in demonstrations against the tour. The international criticism of New Zealand was exacerbated by the combative defiance of Robert Muldoon, prime minister between 1975 and 1984, who repeatedly criticised anti-apartheid activists both within New Zealand and overseas.[50] The opprobrium heaped upon New Zealand for its sporting contacts with South Africa might have been expected to cause a much greater degree of long-term damage to New Zealand's international reputation than eventuated. It may be, however, that New Zealand's reputation was ameliorated by the anti-tour movement, perhaps New Zealand's largest peace-time mobilisation of a citizens' coalition. Retrospective narratives imply that its activism restored New Zealand's reputation as a progressive society, by demonstrating that a majority of New Zealanders opposed apartheid, belatedly convincing a blinkered NZRFU to abandon sporting ties with South Africa.

In some respects there is a parallel here with the way in which the Waitangi Tribunal and the settlement of historical Māori grievances have been invoked in support of New Zealand's 'good race relations' narrative; they purportedly demonstrate a progressive New Zealand society addressing, albeit belatedly, the legacy of the New Zealand Wars and the subsequent confiscation of Māori land.

Sport has played a significant role as a symbol of bicultural and multi-cultural citizenship in New Zealand. Historically, sport has been a way in which many New Zealanders have associated with people from different ethnic backgrounds whom they might not otherwise have met in their professional and personal lives. As previously noted, one of the distinguishing features of the development of sport in New Zealand is the involvement from a very early stage of Māori. There is an element of historical irony in these narratives. Greg Ryan has shown that Māori who became prominent in sport were most likely to come from schools like Te Aute, which were established in part to fulfil assimilationist goals, that is producing Māori leaders who would embody European values and disseminate them among their people.[51]

The inclusion of Māori in national teams formed part of a narrative of New Zealand as an inclusive, equal-opportunity society that was by and large accepted in New Zealand and overseas until the 1960s. New Zealand's Asian communities also used sport as a means of simultaneously promoting their collective identity while engaging with the dominant culture. Indian sports clubs were established in Wellington in 1935 and in Christchurch and Auckland in 1936, following tours by Indian hockey teams in 1926 and 1935 (another would tour in 1938).[52] Participating in sport was seen as a way of learning European ways while maintaining a community's ethnic identity.

When the Chinese Universities soccer team toured New Zealand in 1924, a number of local Chinese communities donated cups to be used in local competitions, thereby making a physical contribution as citizens of the wider New Zealand community.[53] The symbolism of this was important at a time when New Zealand's Asian communities (and other non-European and non-Māori peoples) were actively excluded from full citizenship, being openly referred to as 'race aliens' in government literature and subject to restrictive immigration policies and discrimination.[54] Although small in number — as recently as 1981 New Zealand's Asian communities comprised approximately 1 per cent of the population — their participation in sport, particularly through the education system, was a means through which Asian communities could demonstrate that they were taking part in the same activities as other citizens. In recent times, the successes of Danny Lee and Lydia Ko, who became the number one ranked women's golfer in the world in 2015, have boosted the profile of Asian sportspeople in New Zealand.

Since the 1990s, New Zealand's sports teams, especially the All Blacks, have been represented as the embodiment of multiculturalism in New

Zealand. This is partly a reflection of the increasing prominence of Māori and Pacific peoples in elite sport since the 1980s. By 2001 Māori and Pasifika players comprised just over 50 per cent of players in the Super 12 rugby competition at a time when Māori and Pasifika accounted for about 20 per cent of New Zealand's population.[55] They were also increasingly represented in the Silver Ferns, New Zealand's national netball team, and in New Zealand's Olympic and Commonwealth games teams.

Biculturalism and multiculturalism were also evident in the symbolism of New Zealand sports teams, particularly the haka.[56] Although haka had been performed by New Zealand sporting teams since at least as far back as the New Zealand Native team which toured Australia and Britain in 1888–9, they were often performed badly, especially by teams of predominantly (and sometimes wholly) Pākehā players. From the 1980s, however, at the instigation of Wayne 'Buck' Shelford, who captained the All Blacks between 1988 and 1990, and Hika Reid, the team placed a much greater emphasis on performing the haka in a culturally appropriate manner, something which subsequent teams have continued. The Kapa o Pango version of the haka, first performed in 2005, deliberately incorporates references to New Zealanders of all ethnic backgrounds.[57] The 1999 Rugby World Cup saw another symbolic link between sport and biculturalism when Hinewehi Mohi sang the New Zealand national anthem in te reo Māori, following which it became standard practice to sing both the Māori and English versions of the anthem at public events.[58]

The visibility of Māori and Pacific peoples in national teams is also commonly cited as evidence that New Zealand is a multicultural society where all enjoy equal rights of citizenship. Yet arguably the physical embodiment of multiculturalism apparently represented by national teams masks the continuing existence of racial prejudice. Brendan Hokowhitu has argued that Māori and Pasifika peoples have achieved only limited gains through sporting participation because their sporting achievements are often attributed to genetic factors and an alleged natural ability, and the education system still tends to steer Māori towards sports rather than academic subjects.[59] In addition, participation in sport by peoples of Māori, Pasifika and Asian ancestry has not eclipsed racial tropes. When teams predominantly comprised of Māori and Pasifika athletes, such as the Warriors rugby league team, experience a losing streak, racial explanations are often advanced.

The effect of ongoing discourses of racism is to deny full citizenship to non-white peoples by attributing their successes to genetic factors and asserting they lack capacity in the tactical and intellectual aspects of sport. Moreover, the increased representation of Māori, Pacific and Asian peoples has not necessarily resulted in a more positive response to political aspirations. The increasing adoption of Māori symbolism in sport has not, for example, resulted in wider support for Māori political aspirations in areas such as customary rights, exemplified by the foreshore and seabed dispute, or Māori rights to water. Indeed, some have expressed concern about Māori culture becoming commodified and decontextualised as a result of its use in sports advertising.[60] Overall, then, sport has had at best a mixed record in promoting multicultural citizenship. On one level it has considerable symbolic power, but in practice it has also been linked to ongoing expressions of racism.

Despite its limitations, sport today is arguably more important than ever to governments because of its potential to embody, in microcosm, the multicultural society they wish to see in the community at large. Sporting moments have a capacity to create a shared national identity in the way other activities, with the possible exception of Anzac Day commemorations, cannot. This was seen during the 2011 Rugby World Cup, when New Zealand presented itself as a 'stadium of four million', implying universal support for the tournament.[61]

At a local level, sport has been used to build relationships between the police and newly arrived immigrants, who may have come from places where contact with police is feared. Since 2009 the Palmerston North City Council and the police, have supported the 'ethkick' soccer tournament to break down barriers between immigrant communities and the police by building positive relationships through sport, a direct example of sport being used to promote citizenship.[62] At a generic level, asserting one's support for New Zealand sporting teams, especially the All Blacks, is one of the core symbols of

'Kiwi' identity, Kiwi being a pan-ethnic term which transcends boundaries of ethnicity, religion, class or gender. As New Zealand becomes more ethnically diverse, and with many of the newly arrived immigrants being first-generation New Zealanders, sport will likely become even more important to governments due to its capacity to generate collective stories and engender shared, albeit ephemeral, moments of national unity.

ENDNOTES

1. Paul Christesen, *Sport and Democracy in the Ancient and Modern Worlds* (Cambridge: Cambridge University Press, 2012), see especially 64–98.
2. Robin McConnell, 'Maori, The Treaty of Waitangi and Sport: A Critical Analysis,' in *Sport in New Zealand Society*, ed. Chris Collins, 227–39 (Palmerston North: Dunmore Press, 2000), 228.
3. McConnell, 'Maori, The Treaty of Waitangi and Sport,' 228–32; Brendan Hokowhitu, 'Maori Sport: Pre-Colonisation to Today,' in *Sport in Aotearoa/New Zealand*, ed. Chris Collins and Steve Jackson, 78–95 (Albany: Thomson, 2007), 80.
4. Tony Collins, *Sport in Capitalist Society: A Short History* (London: Routledge, 2013), 29–31.
5. Allan Davidson, 'Useful Industry and Muscular Christianity: George Augustus Selwyn and his Early Years as Bishop of New Zealand,' in *The Use and Abuse of Time in Christian History*, ed. R. N. Swanson, 289–304 (Woodbridge: Boydell, 2002), 289.
6. See, for example, Richard Holt, *Sport and the British* (Oxford: Clarendon Press, 1989), 74–202.
7. Holt, *Sport and the British*, 117–34. See also Kathleen McCrone, *Sport and the Physical Emancipation of English Women, 1870–1914* (London: Routledge, 1988); Catriona Parratt, *More than Mere Amusement: Working Class Women's Leisure in England, 1750–1914* (Boston: Northeastern University Press, 2001), 188–219.
8. Jennifer Hargreaves, *Sporting Females: Critical Issues in the History of Sociology of Women's Sports* (London: Routledge, 1994), 63–87.
9. Holt, *Sport and the British*, 98–117; Collins, *Sport in Capitalist Society*, 31–7; Peter Greenhalgh, '"The Work and Play Principle": The Professional Regulations of the Northern Rugby Football Union 1898–1905,' *International Journal of the History of Sport* 9, no. 3 (1992): 356–77.
10. See, for example, Richard Cashman, *Paradise of Sport: The Rise of Organised Sport in Australia* (Melbourne: Oxford University Press, 1995), 22, 33, 105; Holt, *Sport and the British*, 203–79.
11. Charles Darwin, *Journal of Researches into the Geology and Natural History of the Various Countries Visited by H.M.S. Beagle* (1839, reprinted Brussels: Editions Culture et Civilisation, 1969), 509; *New Zealand Gazette and Wellington Spectator*, 26 January 1842, 2.
12. Mrs Charles Thomson, *12 Years in Canterbury New Zealand* (London: Sampson Low, ca. 1867), 20–1. The population figures for the 1867 census appear in 'Abstracts of Certain Principal Results of a Census of New Zealand taken in December 1867,' *Appendix to the Journals of the House of Representatives of New Zealand*, 1868, D1, 9.
13. See, for example, Greg Ryan, 'Sport in Christchurch,' in *Southern Capital: Christchurch. Towards a City Biography 1850–2000*, ed. John Cookson and Graeme Dunstall (Christchurch: Canterbury University Press, 2000), 325–52; Caroline Daley, 'A Gendered Domain: Leisure in Auckland, 1890–1940,' in *The Gendered Kiwi*, ed. Caroline Daley and Deborah Montgomerie (Auckland: Auckland University Press, 1999), 87–111, at 90–1; Redmer Yska, *Wellington: Biography of a City* (Auckland: Reed, 2006), 33.
14. Geoff Watson and Wilf Haskell, *Seasons of Honour: A Centenary History of New Zealand*

     Hockey 1902–2002 (Palmerston North: Dunmore, 2002), 16–9, 27.

15 Sandra Coney, *Every Girl: A Social History of Women and the YWCA in Auckland 1885–1985* (Auckland: Auckland YWCA, 1986), 160–91.

16 Jock Phillips, *A Man's Country? The Image of the Pakeha Male: A History* (Auckland: Penguin, 1987), 89–91.

17 Geoff Vincent, '"To Uphold the Honour of the Province": Football in Canterbury c. 1854–c. 1890,' in *Tackling Rugby Myths: Rugby and New Zealand Society 1854–2004*, ed. Greg Ryan (Dunedin: Otago University Press, 2005), 13–30.

18 Darwin, *Journal of Researches into the Geology and Natural History of the Various Countries Visited by H.M.S. Beagle*, 509.

19 Montague Hawtrey, *An Earnest Address to New Zealand Colonists, with Reference to their Intercourse with the Native Inhabitants* (London: John W. Parker, 1840), 35.

20 M. P. K. Sorrenson, 'Maori and Pakeha,' in *The Oxford History of New Zealand*, 2nd edition, ed. Geoffrey W. Rice (Auckland: Oxford University Press, 1992), 141–66; Hawtrey, *An Earnest Address*, 93–9.

21 See, for example, Peter Meihana, 'The Paradox of Maori Privilege: Historical Constructions of Maori Privilege c. 1769 to 1940,' PhD thesis, Massey University, 2015, 109, 117–8, 120–46.

22 Harko Brown, *Ngā Taonga Takaro: Māori Sports and Games* (Auckland: Penguin, 2008), 9; Brendan Hokowhitu, 'Authenticating Māori Physicality: Translations of "Games" and "Pastimes" by Early Travellers and Missionaries to New Zealand,' *International Journal of the History of Sport* 25, no. 10 (2008): 1361–4.

23 Greg Ryan, *Forerunners of the All Blacks: The 1888–89 Native Team in Britain, Australia and New Zealand* (Christchurch: Canterbury University Press, 1993), 43–56.

24 Denis Dwyer, *Black Jersey Silver Fern: Tom Ellison — First Maori to Captain the All Blacks* (Wellington: Grantham House, 2015).

25 Greg Ryan, *The Contest for Rugby Supremacy: Accounting for the 1905 All Blacks* (Christchurch: Canterbury University Press, 2005), 141–59.

26 Phillips, *A Man's Country*, 82–130.

27 See, for example, Geoff Watson, 'Representations of Central Asian Ethnicities in British Literature c. 1830–1914,' *Asian Ethnicity* 3, no. 2 (2002): 137–51.

28 Ryan, *The Contest for Rugby Supremacy*, 85–100.

29 James Belich, *Paradise Reforged: A History of the New Zealanders from the 1880s to the Year 2000* (Auckland: Allen Lane, 2001), 76–86.

30 Keith Sinclair, *A Destiny Apart: New Zealand's Search for National Identity* (Wellington: Allen & Unwin, 1986), 127–42.

31 A number of Māori soldiers also served in the Boer War: Michael King, *Penguin History of New Zealand* (Auckland: Penguin, 2003), 283–303.

32 *Evening Post*, 29 February 1916, 3.

33 Raewyn Dalziel, 'The Colonial Helpmeet: Women's Role and the Vote in Nineteenth-Century

New Zealand,' *New Zealand Journal of History* 11, no. 2 (1977): 112–23.
34   See, for example, Barbara Cox, 'The Rise and Fall of the "Girl Footballer" in New Zealand During 1921,' *International Journal of the History of Sport* 29, no. 3 (2012): 444–71.
35   John Nauright, 'Netball, Media Representation of Women and Crisis of Male Hegemony in New Zealand,' in *Sport, Power and Society in New Zealand: Historical and Contemporary Perspectives*, ed. John Nauright (Sydney: Australian Society for Sports History, 1999), 50–7.
36   Chris Collins, 'Politics, Government and Sport in Aotearoa/New Zealand,' in *Sport in Aotearoa/New Zealand Society*, ed. Chris Collins and Steve Jackson (Albany: Thomson: 2007), 208–29.
37   *Report of the Sport, Fitness and Leisure Ministerial Taskforce*, 2001, 97–117.
38   *Report of the Sport, Fitness and Leisure Ministerial Taskforce*, 37.
39   Ryan, *The Contest for Rugby Supremacy*, 149–57.
40   *Otago Witness*, 6 February 1864, 7.
40A Scott Crawford, '"Muscles and Character are There the First Object of Necessity": An Overview of Sport and Recreation in a Colonial Setting — Otago Province, New Zealand,' *British Journal of Sports History* 2, no. 2 (1985): 109–26.
41   *The Times*, 7 August 1936, 4, cited in Terry Maddaford, '1936 Jack Lovelock's Berlin Gold,' in *Memorable Moments in New Zealand Sport*, ed. Don Cameron (Auckland: Moa, 1979), 20.
42   Geoff Vincent and Toby Harfield, 'Repression and Reform: Responses within New Zealand to the Arrival of the "Northern Game", 1907–8,' *New Zealand Journal of History* 31, no. 2 (1997): 234–50.
43   *Evening Post*, 17 July 1924, 13.
44   Harry Morton, *Which Way New Zealand?* (Dunedin: John McIndoe, 1975), 235.
45   Martin Snedden, *A Stadium of 4 Million* (Auckland: Hodder Moa, 2012).
46   Linda Johnson, 'Maori Activism Across Borders, 1950s–1980s,' PhD thesis, Massey University, 2015, 88–100.
47   Malcolm Templeton, *Human Rights and Sporting Contacts: New Zealand's Attitudes to Race Relations in South Africa 1921–94* (Auckland: Auckland University Press, 1998), 116–40.
48   See, for example, Terry McLean, *The Battle for the Rugby Crown* (Wellington: A. H. & A. W. Reed, 1956).
49   See, for example, Morton, *Which Way New Zealand?*, 239–40.
50   Templeton, *Human Rights and Sporting Contacts*, 98–203.
51   Greg Ryan, 'The Paradox of Maori Rugby 1870–1914,' in *Tackling Rugby Myths: Rugby and New Zealand Society 1854–2004*, ed. Greg Ryan (Dunedin: Otago University Press, 2005), 92–7.
52   Geoff Watson, *Sporting Foundations of New Zealand Indians: A Fifty Year History of the New Zealand Indian Sports Association* (Wellington: New Zealand Indian Sports Association, 2012), 7–20.
53   Geoff Watson, 'Gentlemen Both On and Off the Field: The 1924 Chinese Universities Soccer Team in New Zealand,' *New Zealand Journal of Asian Studies* 13, no. 2 (2011): 15–6.

54 See, for example, *New Zealand Census, 1921,* Part VI, 'Race Aliens' (Wellington: Government Printer, 1925), 1. See also Manying Ip and Jacqueline Leckie, '"Chinamen" and "Hindoos": Beyond Stereotypes to Kiwi Asians,' in *Localizing Asia in Aotearoa,* ed. Paola Voci and Jacqueline Leckie (Wellington: Dunmore, 2011), 159–86.
55 John Matheson, 'So What's the White Answer?' *New Zealand Rugby World* 47 (2001): 20–38.
56 See, for example, Bevan Erueti and Farah Rangikoepa Palmer, 'Te Whariki Tuakiri (the identity mat): Māori Elite Athletes and the Expression of Ethno-Cultural Identity in Global Sport,' *Sport in Society* 17, no. 8 (2014): 1061–75.
57 Tom Johnson, Andy Martin, Geoff Watson, and Margot Butcher, eds., *Legends in Black: New Zealand Rugby Greats on Why We Win* (Auckland: Penguin, 2014), 135, 192–4, 217, 269–73.
58 Ministry for Culture and Heritage, 'New Zealand's National Anthems,' http://www.nzhistory.net.nz/media/video/new-zealands-national-anthems, updated 15-Oct-2014, accessed 28 April 2016.
59 Brendan Hokowhitu, 'Physical Beings: Stereotypes, Sport and the "Physical Education" of New Zealand Maori,' *Sport in Society* 6, nos. 2–3 (2003): 192–218; Brendan Hokowhitu, 'Tackling Maori Masculinity: A Colonial Genealogy of Savagery and Sport,' *The Contemporary Pacific* 16, no. 2 (2004), 259–84.
60 Steven Jackson and Brendan Hokowhitu, 'Sport, Tribes and Technology: The New Zealand All Blacks *Haka* and the Politics of Identity,' *Journal of Sport and Social Issues* 26, no. 2 (2002): 125–39.
61 Snedden, *A Stadium of 4 Million,* 110–8. For a critique of this argument see Toni Bruce, '(Not) a Stadium of Four Million: Speaking back to Dominant Discourses of the Rugby World Cup in New Zealand,' *Sport in Society* 16, no. 7 (2013): 899–911.
62 Richard Mays, 'Footing it for the finals,' *The Guardian,* 5 November 2009, 1.

9. THE FORMATION OF THE 'GOOD CITIZEN': USING HISTORY TO BUILD A FUTURE IN MID-TWENTIETH-CENTURY NEW ZEALAND

Rachael Bell

THE FORMATION OF THE 'GOOD CITIZEN': USING HISTORY TO BUILD A FUTURE IN MID-TWENTIETH-CENTURY NEW ZEALAND

The concept of citizenship has 'constantly evolved' within Western societies, drawing on current issues and challenges but also past histories and inherited beliefs.[1] In this chapter I look at the concept of citizenship as it emerged in the 1930s, 1940s and 1950s here in New Zealand, and link it to ideas about history and its role in New Zealand society at the time. I suggest that our understanding of history both shaped and was shaped by expanding notions of citizenship over this period.

I take my framework from a series of essays by the Victoria University historian J. C. Beaglehole, written between 1940 and 1954. Well known as an academic but also as one who, after a conscious consideration of citizenship, fought for many years to advance civic causes, Beaglehole believed that historical knowledge was fundamental to national development and to making New Zealand a 'better and more fulfilling place to live'.[2] In articulating a role for history in the making of a good citizen he shows us not only what a 'good citizen' was believed to be in the interwar and post-war years but also the relationship required between oneself and the past in order to sit comfortably within society and to contribute to it.

Beaglehole was one of the very few New Zealanders following the First World War to have been privileged with an international university education. After leaving on a travelling scholarship to London as a young man, he returned in 1929 to a country slipping into economic depression and with a grimness to national life 'not exactly encouraging to the free human spirit'.[3] Prevented at first by this discouraging situation and by his own academic snobbery from seeing the worth of his native country, Beaglehole's transformation into a conscious New Zealander — that is, one versed, as he described it, in European heritage but alert also to the lifeways and traditions of New Zealand — was

J. C. Beaglehole had a strong vision for history's role in the future of modern New Zealand. **ALEXANDER TURNBULL LIBRARY 1/1-018598-F**

THE FORMATION OF THE 'GOOD CITIZEN'

a 'slow and awkward' one.[4] But it was a transformation that he also believed mirrored that of the nation as a whole as it moved from colonial dependence and the 'ready-made' ideologies of imperialism[5] to new forms of political, artistic, literary and cultural independence. In recording this transformation in a series of essays — 'The New Zealand Mind' (1940), 'History and the New Zealander' (1946), 'Thoughts on New Zealand's Social History' (1952) and 'The New Zealand Scholar' (1954)[6] — he has provided us with a remarkable view of mid-century Pākehā consciousness from which to consider issues of citizenship and the role of history.[7]

This chapter addresses Beaglehole's model for history and citizenship in four steps. The first examines the political impetus that gave rise to an expanded view of citizenship in the interwar and early post-war periods. The second gives consideration to the place Beaglehole saw for history in this new national schema. The third offers examples of this relationship in practice through an examination of state-sponsored history projects over these years and some of their outcomes. The fourth concludes the chapter with a reflection on the implications of this model for the role of history in society today. If, as Beaglehole suggests, history informs not only our relationships but also our morality — morality in its 'widest sense', as 'a system of *mores*, of habits and ways of thinking and assumptions and institutions that cover the whole of life'[8] — what place might history take today in a globalised and rapidly changing world?

Expectations of the role of the state in New Zealand have always been high. From the demands of struggling New Zealand Company settlers to the beginning of individual state-funded benefits with the Old Age Pension in 1898, state spending in nineteenth-century New Zealand was locked in a perpetual tussle: on one side were the requirements for infrastructure and development that would realise the economic potential of the colony, while on the other were the welfare needs of its citizens.

While infrastructure and development claimed the central role through extensive public works programmes, fears within government of moral degeneracy among the poor and of fostering dependency upon the state kept welfare spending to a minimum. Paid only in kind, and with strong distinctions between the deserving and the undeserving, those reliant on welfare led a precarious existence, dependent on the vagaries and opinions of visiting welfare officers and required to demonstrate good moral conduct in order to qualify for assistance.[9] Even the Old Age Pension, however ground-breaking it may have been in terms of legislation, was miserly in its provision and left a large proportion of those who might nowadays be considered eligible outside its criteria. By way of balance, however, the raft of labour legislation brought in by the Liberal government in the 1890s reinforced the notion of New Zealand as a land of opportunity and the expectation of self-reliance. State assistance in the form of improved conditions for workers rather than benefits for the unemployed implied that security and advancement were within the reach of all if they were prepared to work for them, and that good citizens were those who helped themselves.

Those critical of the Old Age Pension as opening the door to higher expectations of state assistance may well have been justified. Although hardly a flood, the incremental expansion of welfare payments, which by 1926 had come to include invalid miners, widows, the blind, and those qualifying for a means-tested family benefit, indicated an increased willingness by the bureaucracy of state to accept financial responsibility for those in need. Reforms in youth justice and education and the establishment of a host of child-orientated community organisations in the 1900s, 1910s and 1920s also showed a greater recognition of, and interest in, children as the future of the nation,[10] to be valued as social capital rather than for their labour and contribution to the family economy. Collectively, these initiatives and similar measures marked a fundamental shift in the relationship between the state and the citizens of New Zealand as the rhetoric of individual self-reliance that had underwritten the priorities and spending of earlier governments gave way to the collectivist and modernist zeitgeist of the mid-twentieth century.

Two events in particular in the early 1900s hastened and confirmed an expanded notion of citizenship and its relation to the state. These were the First

World War and the Great Depression. As New Zealand's first mass mobilisation of the citizen soldier, and its first instance of conscription to enforce it, the First World World War was an unprecedented enactment of a citizen's responsibility to the state, played out in homes across the nation. With war came other experiences also: the filth, horror, maiming and slaughter that were to leave a generation of men and their families changed forever.

Understandably, expectations of assistance and reward for those returning home were based on notions of a reciprocal commitment: that having required soldiers to lay down their lives for their country, the state would ensure those who survived returned to a 'land fit for heroes'. This was to include a rehabilitation scheme generous enough to re-establish them in society and ameliorate, to a certain extent at least, the economic effects of the years lost in service. While the success of the First World War rehabilitation scheme has been the subject of considerable historical debate,[11] there can be no doubt that it raised public expectations of government provision and responsibility and, like other aspects of wartime administration, brought the tolerance for state involvement in the private lives of New Zealand citizens to a new level.

In the case of the Great Depression of the 1930s, the demand for increased state intervention came not from the government but from the citizens themselves. As the global financial markets fell and New Zealand's export earnings plummeted, the initially conservative responses of government through cost-cutting and retrenchment seemed only to increase the already rising unemployment levels. As foreclosures, evictions, soup kitchens and swaggers became the public face of economic hardship, calls for more constructive measures to be provided by the government grew. However unpopular the new 'work for dole' schemes were, with their seemingly make-work projects in urban centres and camps that took single men off to remote and frigid locations in the countryside, they were considerable innovations in their time. It is ironic, however, that the impacts of perhaps the most effective measures of them all — the devaluation of the New Zealand pound and the establishment of the Reserve Bank, which are now credited with New Zealand's quick end to the Depression and its rapid recovery[12] — were attributed not to the by now deeply unpopular United/Reform coalition government that instigated them, but to its successor, the Labour Party. For it was within the misery and general insecurity of the Great Depression that a new political vision for the economy and for citizenship began to take hold.

Formed in 1916, and with some measure of success over its early years, the New Zealand Labour Party — once the preserve of the staunchly working class and party faithful — began during the Depression to garner the support of middle New Zealand. This was partly the result of moderating its strongly left-wing policies and the new leadership and quiet charisma of Michael Joseph Savage,[13] but due also to a greater tolerance by the public of the high level of state intervention around which the Labour manifesto was based. This included a breaking down of the stigma of state assistance and welfare, moving it from a recourse of last resort to a universal right of citizenship.

In a series of reforms following its 1935 election victory, Labour began to restructure not only work and welfare legislation but also the very notion of what it meant to be a citizen in New Zealand. Along with massive public works programmes and innovations such as the 40-hour week, compulsory unionism, a more inclusive benefit structure and the family wage came a new concern for the intellectual and cultural life of the nation. This included especially a belief that those elements of higher education, literature and performing arts that were once the preserve of the social elite should, through the assistance and support of government, be within the reach of all. It is to this cultural and intellectual aspect of national life — the development of a critical, engaged citizenship and of 'culture organising'[14] — that our attention now turns.

A common characteristic of the leadership of the new Labour government was an impoverished upbringing and the valuing of education as a result. Of the principal triumvirate, the new Prime Minister, Michael Joseph Savage, had left primary school after only five years and had begun his socialist education as a ditch digger on an outback station in Australia; the Deputy Prime Minister, Peter Fraser, had also left school early to contribute to the household income; and the family of Walter Nash, Minister of Finance, had

been so poor that he was unable to pursue the educational scholarship he had won at the age of 11, resulting in him leaving school to begin his working life as an office boy.[15] All had honed their political views through avid reading as adults.

Central to the restructuring of the state under Labour, therefore, were educational reforms that abolished the proficiency exam and enabled all children to acquire secondary education irrespective of achievement, and a series of initiatives to encourage the development of an 'educated democracy' among the existing adult population. These included a significant expansion of the cultural and intellectual 'infrastructure' of national life,[16] through projects as diverse as the country library service and the national orchestra.[17] All of these projects were based on the dual assumptions that cultural and intellectual activities were an important and legitimate part of New Zealand citizenship and that the state was the most appropriate institution to get them up and running. That this move coincided with the emergence of a group of left-leaning, nationalistic academics and public intellectuals centred around Victoria University College, as it was known at this time, fuelled the flames and provided both the impetus and the empirical basis for this expansion.

As part of this group, Beaglehole teamed up with Joe Heenan, the undersecretary of the Department of Internal Affairs, to put some of these ideas into practice. In an often quoted description of Heenan's contradictory qualities — including romance, pig-headedness, sentimentality, scepticism, tolerance and prejudice[18] — Beaglehole captured some of the idiosyncrasy, energy and limitations of the 'catch all' department he ran and which approved and funded a wide array of cultural initiatives. Between them, Beaglehole and Heenan's shared love of history and their belief in its importance in forming an intellectual base for national development saw many historical projects included in the department's portfolio. Before we look at some examples of these and the way in which history was used to encourage a more engaged public, I would like to explore Beaglehole's own views of history to show the relationship as it was seen between historical knowledge and the New Zealand citizen.

Overall, Beaglehole believed that New Zealanders in the first half of the twentieth century were inclined to be critically weak and historically uninformed. The colonial tendency to 'idealise alike what is past and what is far away' had led to both a nostalgic yearning for Britain and what Beaglehole termed the 'Victorian myth of New Zealand history'.[19] Through this myth, elements such as the working-class and lower-middle-class origins of New Zealand settlers and the 'dishonest and disastrous' conduct of the New Zealand Company,[20] for example, had been elevated to levels of respectability quite unwarranted by fact. Despite new levels of archival research, there was a deep unwillingness to question the existing dogma or to forego such flattering 'exercise[s] of imagination',[21] as Beaglehole's colleague Professor Fred Wood (another eloquent champion of history) termed them, in order to acknowledge the less favourable aspects of settler behaviour and the 'sly and indecent dealings' in land.[22] Such unwillingness, to Beaglehole, resulted in a fundamental national weakness: a sort of perennial immaturity which would, ultimately, hold the nation back.

The ideas and techniques of empirical research that Beaglehole, Wood and others were introducing in their history courses, and which students at the university colleges were applying to New Zealand history topics in increasing numbers, were part of a conscious attempt to turn the flow of historical interpretation: to put aside the swashbuckling narratives and popular frontier yarns of journalists turned historians such as James Cowan and T. Lindsay Buick in favour of more measured, critical and closely researched appraisals. Let our history be the product, Beaglehole wrote, of 'firmly controlled imagination'[23] and 'fine disinterested critical integrity',[24] even if such practices seemed at first to be pedantic. 'I have suffered too much from an amiable lack of pedantry,' he claimed, '. . . to be afraid of a good healthy layer of it over New Zealand.'[25] Let these research methods and the newly established archives in which to practise them lead to a more balanced understanding of the past. Let New Zealand's new national history be rich, let it be varied but, most of all, let it be honest: let us 'not glide lightly over our failures', he wrote.[26]

To merely determine facts, however, was not enough. Equally important, in Beaglehole's mind, was the ability to convey historical knowledge to the

general public and in ways that would integrate it into the fabric — the felt tradition, as he termed it — of national life. In explaining events of the past, the historian could provide both a 'preliminary to improvement'[27] in areas where conduct had been lacking and help to develop a 'sense of the age'[28] in the present day. Both in, of, and yet outside of the tradition, the historian's role was to mediate between scholarly knowledge and the citizenry. As the historian 'disentangles our tradition', Beaglehole argued, 'as he makes us conscious of ourselves, he gives us ourselves'.[29] It was time, he believed, for the existing notions of New Zealand history to be taken apart; to be reworked, rewritten and rewoven with fresh strands of empirical knowledge so that it might form an 'ampler and more adequate' basis to national life.[30]

The historical projects carried out through the Department of Internal Affairs were just such undertakings, the first steps in bringing the new findings of history out of the academy and into the ken of everyday New Zealanders. In this way, through a more honest interpretation of history, New Zealand citizens might better know themselves — their strengths and their weaknesses — and, by relating experiences here back to the broader ontological traditions of Western thought, know also their place in the world. In the excesses of nationalism that had led up to the Second World War and in the complex and shifting allegiances that followed it, this call for a critical, balanced appraisal was all the more poignant.

So in what ways were these new emphases on empiricism and criticism in New Zealand history made available to the public? Three historical projects undertaken by the government during the interwar and post-war periods offer examples of the relationship between history and citizenship in action. The first was the publication schedule to celebrate the New Zealand Centennial in 1940, the second, the official history series produced by Internal Affairs immediately following the Second World War, and the third, the Education Department's social studies and history bulletins written to incorporate New Zealand material into the new school curriculum in the post-war period. Each of these projects shows a conscious attempt to set a national narrative around history that was both balanced and based on in-depth archival research —

history that would, through its official or government status, help to overwrite less critical, popular accounts. Although meeting with varying measures of success, perhaps, each demonstrates an implied connection between sound historical knowledge, the formation of a 'good citizen', and the willingness of the government to intervene to this end.

The Centennial celebrations, although considered by Beaglehole at first to be a 'series of fatuities, all of them depraved',[31] were, he came to concede, a turning point for history in New Zealand. The publications that arose from them were the essence of this historical transformation in action. In the enthusiasm of the staff for the projects, and in the new history graduates particularly, he saw a belief in the worth of New Zealand history and the range of critical and archival skills to put the new vision in place. An ambitious publication programme was planned. Aside from a great number of local histories, which were the concern of provincial committees, Heenan's department produced a fortnightly pictorial magazine aimed at schoolchildren and a family readership, began work on a planned historical atlas, completed a dictionary of New Zealand biography, already partly written, and published a series of 11 substantial volumes — the Centennial Historical Surveys. The most prestigious of the Centennial publications, these Surveys were 'authoritative yet designed to appeal to the general reader',[32] and aimed at covering the 'whole field' of national life.[33]

Of the Centennial publications, the Surveys also offered the clearest challenge to the historical canon. In their fresh, critical assessments they were deliberately intended to destroy 'old fallacies' in favour of a new, 'well-proportioned view' of New Zealand history,[34] and to reflect the advanced and well-educated nation that New Zealand perceived itself as becoming. 'Not only is the modern interest in social conditions of the past being served,' enthused David Hall, the Centennial publicist, 'but the whole of New Zealand's past is by implication being completely rewritten.'[35] Beaglehole, Wood and other academics joined a list of authors from governmental and technical fields to produce volumes on topics as diverse as exploration and

THE FORMATION OF THE 'GOOD CITIZEN'

discovery, women, foreign affairs and 'letters and arts'.

In the sweep of topics, and print runs of several thousand, there was clearly the anticipation of an engaged and critical readership who, like the self-educated men in government, were keen to advance their knowledge of New Zealand history and its shaping of their life as citizens. Such a view was also supported by their media reception, in which an interest in the Centennial and its history was linked to 'public spiritedness'[36] and the knowledge imparted in the course of the programme seen as being of 'incalculable value'.[37] 'People had been made richer for the knowledge gained of the history and progress of their nation,' the Christchurch *Press* maintained, suggesting this demonstrated a 'faith' also in an independent future for the country[38] or, as the *Evening Post* termed it, the ability of New Zealand to live a 'life of her own'.[39]

Although the success of the volumes in imparting a full and objective view of the nation's history varied across the series — some contentious material concerning the 1860s land wars was removed from James Cowan's volume, *Settlers and Pioneers*,[40] for example, while volumes on religion and, in the end, Māori history and also welfare were omitted entirely [41] — the links between their production and the creation of historically informed citizenship were clear.

This concept of citizenship and an independent national life for New Zealand was also the driving force behind the official war histories, the enormous scale of which was encouraged, in part, by the success of the Centennial volumes. The coinciding of the planning for New Zealand's 1940 Centennial with the course of global politics and the relentless slide towards war meant that the celebrations, when they did occur, were often tempered by the farewells of departing troops.[42] Preparations for recording what was to be New Zealand's second major conflict in just 25 years began almost as soon as war was declared, and the official war history project, as it evolved, rode very much on the coat-tails of the Centennial histories. There was the same call for a national stocktake and honest evaluation of national endeavour, the same underlying justification of an authoritative record to counter the excesses of popular journalism and sensationalist accounts of the war.[43] The memos outlining the programme were prepared, even, by the same Centennial staff, but this time there was a moral imperative that made the scale of the project, and the government funding to achieve it, almost impossible to refuse.

New Zealand had again called her citizens to war, and the wish to capture honestly their experiences — all that we 'suffered, escaped and endured and accomplished',[44] as Major General Sir Howard Kippenberger, the editor-in-chief, termed it — both for their own and future generations, turned New Zealand's official history series into one of the most comprehensive of all the Commonwealth allies. At 48 volumes covering the participation of only 140,000 combatants and a national population of 1.7 million, the series contained a level of detail and individual recognition that countries such as Britain and Canada, with approximately 5 million and 1.1 million combatants apiece, could never hope to achieve.

The appointment of Kippenberger, New Zealand's most popular and experienced citizen soldier, gave weight and legitimacy to the project in the eyes of the public. It also avoided censorship, with Kippenberger taking the position of editor-in-chief only on the assurance that, other than in matters of ongoing security, there would be no military vetting or interference with the volumes.[45] Like the Centennial Surveys, the official histories were intended to provide an authoritative yet accessible foundation to a collective understanding. The employment of a raft of qualified researchers working 'without fear or favour . . . malice or concealment', as Kippenberger described it,[46] to provide the factual basis of the volumes aligns closely with Beaglehole's goal of a rational empirical footing to the felt tradition of national life.

Even though they comprised only an 'infinitesimal'[47] part of the cost of the war they recorded, the official histories were an extravagant series for their time, with high quality, finely bound volumes and well-produced battalion histories provided free to each member, or to their families if a soldier had been killed. While this was promoted as a gesture of thanks from the government for their participation, the principle behind the expense was, again, that of a discerning citizenry, one that expected a detailed explanation of the war and New Zealand's part in it. '[O]ne of the main functions of the official history',

the initial planning document stated, 'will be its explanation of facts that, in the nature of things, cannot be revealed in a time of war . . . [A]s educated members of a democracy, New Zealanders have the right ultimately to learn the underlying reasons, and they should be able to find them in the pages of the official history.'[48]

But while detailed and informative, as national histories they were also to remain accessible and popular. 'Now many will say, "When you have produced all this",' Kippenberger stated in one of his early radio addresses, '"who will read it?" I hope and expect that a great many people will. We have a great story to tell. There is no need for an Official History to be dull . . . We are not going to produce a dull history, the subject matter makes that almost impossible.'[49]

Belying the image of official war histories as dusty tomes, unread and remaindered in their thousands, New Zealand's Second World War history project was another ambitious, and largely successful, attempt to put the new forms of 'citizen-based' history into action.[50] Empirically informed, nationally focused, eagerly anticipated and going in some cases to a number of reprints, the volumes were read and appreciated by a broad slice of New Zealand society. Although, understandably, across a series of 48 volumes, 37 authors, two editors and several decades, the appeal of the volumes and their topics varied — with the history of the army dental service, for example, proving rather less than a bestseller — media reviews that praised the gentle humour and fine description present in some volumes,[51] or the ability to engage 'men and women with no background of interest in war' and to explain to families the combat experiences of their loved ones,[52] suggest that in many regards these broad historical goals were met.

The war history project was thus linked closely to notions of citizenship as they had developed in New Zealand in the interwar and post-war periods. The new views of citizenship that emphasised a well-informed engagement with contemporary issues as well as recognising the abilities and contributions of everyday New Zealanders linked with empirical history to provide a detailed, citizen-based account of a defining global event, positing it as a source of national cohesion and strength and claiming for New Zealand a unique part in its outcome. Indeed, the official war history series remains one of the foremost sources on the Second World War in New Zealand today, for historians and the general public alike.

While the level of history may have been simpler, in our third example, the citizenship imperative, in the sense of moulding a national future, was stronger. The growth of the School Publications Branch as the result of a civics-based and New Zealand-focused education programme began in relation to primary schools as early as 1939,[53] and in high schools following the release of the 'Thomas Report' in 1944.[54] Major curricular changes were put in place to address the 'challenge of relevancy'[55] in the largely British-based teaching materials used in New Zealand schools and to replace the 'utilitarian, standardised view' of education with a more humanistic and 'genuinely democratic' system that reflected New Zealand's egalitarian aspirations.[56]

With 'less emphasis on the rote learning of names and dates' and 'more effort to make students understand the society in which they lived',[57] the new subjects of social studies and civics required the rapid production of 'well-prepared and up-to-date books' on New Zealand topics at an 'economical price'.[58] Rather than waiting for full textbooks, bulletins proved a more practical solution. So began, over the 1940s and 1950s, a close relationship between historians and the School Publications Branch that simultaneously exposed an entire generation to the new style of history aspired to by the earlier government projects. It was an opportunity not to be missed. Not only did Beaglehole and Wood contribute bulletins, but so also did a raft of other historians and writers, including Antony Alpers, Eric McCormick, Monte Holcroft, Michael Turnbull, Dan Davin, W. B. Sutch, Roderick Finlayson, James K. Baxter, W. H. Oliver and Keith Sinclair. Indeed, with its determination to 'seek out and commission'[59] writers and artists of the highest quality, the School Publications Branch has served, as Gregory O'Brien suggests, as a major supporter of emerging talent over many years.[60]

At primary-school level the merging of history with geography to form social studies, which took place in 1947,[61] gave a real impetus to New Zealand history. Under the editorship of Michael Turnbull, particularly, a more

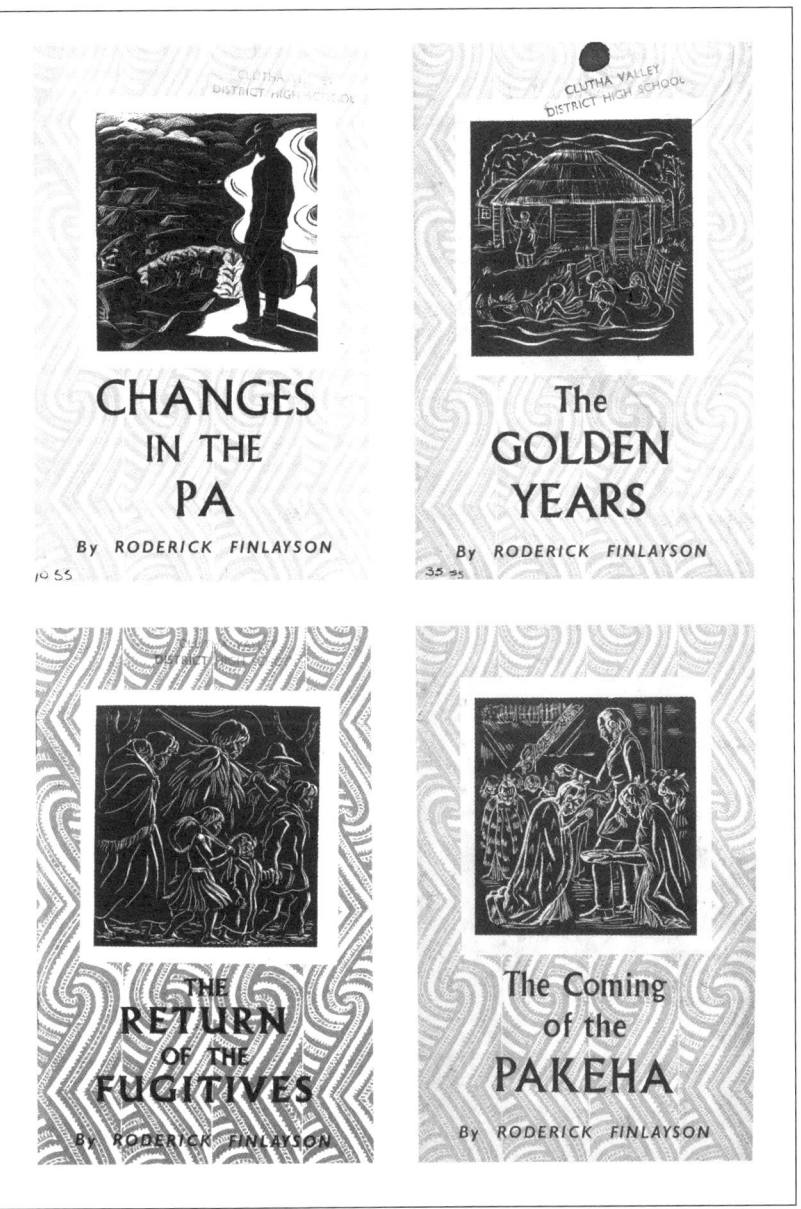

The School Publications bulletins were an opportunity to challenge and rewrite some enduring historical assumptions. **AUTHOR'S COLLECTION**

balanced and critical version of colonisation and settler life was presented. In the mid-1950s a series of bulletins by Roderick Finlayson on Māori life from migration to Aotearoa up to the present provided a counter-narrative to Pākehā settlement and, especially in *The Return of the Fugitives*,[62] was openly critical of the 1860s land wars and their devastating impact on Māori society. In acknowledging the searing and destroying of once fruitful lands, for example, or the bayonetting of Māori women and children at Ōrākau,[63] there was official recognition of the kind censored out of James Cowan's volume in the Centennial histories.

Other bulletins by Ruth Ross and Turnbull himself dealt with Treaty signings and aspects of early settler life in a similarly critical manner. While not always successful in terms of teaching material, perhaps,[64] perspectives were recorded in the bulletins' stories that were not yet acceptable in mainstream Pākehā society, and which encouraged children to critically assess historical narratives and challenge received wisdom.[65]

While at high-school level the emphasis was more on historiography than the historical narratives presented in the primary-school bulletins, the principal themes of critical evaluation, described there by Beaglehole as 'the careful examination and estimation of worth',[66] and the citizenship model of rights and obligations in relation to knowledge remained the same. 'If you are reading a piece of history I have written,' Beaglehole explained about footnotes, for example, 'you have the right to follow the whole of my work of collection and criticism and interpretation . . . I have the duty of providing you with all the means of following me.'[67]

A focus on establishing wherever possible the 'distinctions' between 'the things that happened, and the way men think or say they happened'[68] was repeatedly emphasised. Extended also were the revisionist themes of the primary-school bulletins. A large proportion of Turnbull's post-primary bulletin *Writing in New Zealand: Historical Writing*, for example, was given over to the issue of Māori history and 'the errors which have arisen from insufficient attention being given to the Maori side of New Zealand history'.[69] 'The task of clearing away the misunderstanding of early New Zealand history

THE FORMATION OF THE 'GOOD CITIZEN'

that has arisen from the tendency to push the Maori side of the story into the background,' he noted, 'will be a long one.'[70]

In the rhetoric of the 1930s, 1940s and 1950s, extended access to education became synonymous with ideals of 'civilised living'[71] and with preparing the schoolchild, in the words of the Thomas Report, 'for an active place in our New Zealand society as worker, neighbour, home-maker and citizen'.[72] Shifts in the focus of historical material from British examples to the children's own nation and communities reflected the growing 'significance of the local'[73] in early twentieth-century New Zealand education. Where the focus on Pākehā narratives of progress and achievement had meant that such New Zealand history material as had been available in schools had, like Beaglehole's Victorian myth generally, 'segued into congratulation',[74] the counter-narratives supplied in the School Publications bulletins offered critical, inclusive and decidedly challenging histories that paved the way for later bicultural imperatives. While social studies and history could be 'bitterly criticised'[75] by some for a lack of obvious application in the rising worlds of science and commerce, the ability to make a stand on matters based on the assessment of evidence and 'what seems right to you'[76] remained a crucial civil skill. History was intrinsically linked to critical evaluation and the search for truth. And 'the truth', Beaglehole maintained, 'belonged to all men'.[77]

As these three case studies show, the concept of a 'good citizen' under the expanded view of mid-twentieth-century New Zealand included, among the rights and benefits of an egalitarian and democratic state, a concern for the intellectual and cultural life of the nation. This emphasised access to a sound historical framework on which to base one's sense of place in society and to participate in it. As noted in the Introduction to this volume, the ability to question present norms, values and identities still demands of citizens today the same critical perspective on the histories of their own political communities and those of others.[78]

Coming to terms with our past in New Zealand has been at times a fraught and contested process as many of the reassessments and interpretations instigated under the type of historical practice advocated by Beaglehole have worked their way into mainstream Pākehā society and government institutions. Recognition of the misappropriation of land, for example, and challenges to the myth of a benign colonisation have absorbed the energies of multiple generations of Māori and Pākehā alike, both through protest and in terms of redress through claims to the Waitangi Tribunal — an institution in which historians have, indeed, as Beaglehole envisaged, been one of the key interfaces between scholarly and institutional knowledge and public understanding.[79]

Since the presentation of Beaglehole's model in the 1940s and 1950s, notions by which British tradition and British settler practices in New Zealand could be neatly disassociated from a parallel and distant Māori historical experience have long since been disposed of, while in an increasingly globalised and media-saturated world the need for intellectual integrity and the ability to critically assess information from both one's own and others' perspectives have come ever more to the fore. By approaching history, as Beaglehole described it, not so much as a 'collection of facts' but rather as 'a process of thought',[80] good historical practice can and should equate to history in the public good. History represents now, as much as it did in the middle of last century, a 'continuity' outside of which no citizen can stand.[81] It forms for us a collective notion of who we are and where we are going through the understanding of where we have been. It shapes, as Beaglehole maintained, 'the outlines of our hope'.[82]

THE FORMATION OF THE 'GOOD CITIZEN'

ENDNOTES

1. Andrew Brown, 'The Citizen: From Ancient to Post-Modern,' in this volume.
2. Doug Munro, *J. C. Beaglehole: Public Intellectual, Critical Conscience* (Wellington: Steele Roberts, 2013), 10, 11.
3. J. C. Beaglehole, 'The New Zealand Scholar: Margaret Condliffe Memorial Lecture, Canterbury University College, 21 April 1954,' in *The Feel of Truth: Essays in New Zealand and Pacific History, Presented to F.L.W. Wood and J.C. Beaglehole on the Occasion of their Retirement*, ed. Peter Munz (Wellington: A. H.& A. W. Reed for The Victoria University of Wellington, 1969), 237–52, at 243; for discussion on this period of Beaglehole's life, see Tim Beaglehole, *A Life of JC Beaglehole: New Zealand Scholar* (Wellington: Victoria University Press, 2006), 151–87.
4. Beaglehole, 'The New Zealand Scholar,' 245.
5. E. P. Malone, 'New Zealand School Journal and the Imperial Ideology,' *New Zealand Journal of History* 7, no. 1 (1973): 26.
6. J. C. Beaglehole, 'The New Zealand Mind,' *Australian Quarterly* 12, no. 4 (1940): 40–50; J. C. Beaglehole, 'History and the New Zealander,' in *The University and the Community: Essays in Honour of Thomas Alexander Hunter*, ed. Ernest Beaglehole (Wellington: Whitcombe & Tombs for Wellington University College, 1946), 98–124; J. C. Beaglehole, 'Thoughts on New Zealand's Social History: Victorian Heritage,' *Political Science* 4, no. 29 (1952): 29–37; J. C. Beaglehole, 'The New Zealand Scholar: Margaret Condliffe Memorial Lecture, Canterbury University College, 21 April 1954,' 237–52.
7. While Beaglehole has at times been criticised for the absence of Māori from his model for New Zealand's historical tradition, a wide reading of his historiographical essays shows that this is not so. What can be said, however, is that he perceived two parallel streams for tradition and that, while the two streams may meet and 'in certain matters . . . merge', the continuing of Māori tradition was for Māori to do. The issues he perceived with engagement in history were problems of Pākehā origin. If anything, Māori engagement with tradition could be seen as a model for resolving these issues (Beaglehole, 'The New Zealand Mind,' 50).
8. Beaglehole, 'Thoughts on New Zealand's Social History,' 29.
9. The work of Professor Margaret Tennant has been a leading influence in the field of New Zealand welfare history. For a discussion of charitable aid, see particularly *Paupers and Providers: Charitable Aid in New Zealand* (Wellington: Allen & Unwin in association with the Historical Branch, Department of Internal Affairs, 1989).
10. See, for example, Helen Dollery, '"Making Happy, Healthy, Helpful Citizens": The New Zealand Scouting and Guiding Movements as Promulgators of Active Citizenship, c. 1908–1980,' PhD thesis, Massey University, 2012.
11. Ashley Gould, 'Proof of Gratitude? Soldier Land Settlement in New Zealand after World War One,' PhD thesis, Massey University, 1992; Mike Roche, 'Soldier Settlement in New Zealand after WWI: Two Case Studies,' *New Zealand Geographer* 58, no. 1 (2002): 24–32; Michael

Wynd, '"So the End has Come . . . I Shall See You All Again": Demobilising the New Zealand Expeditionary Force, November 1918–September 1919,' MA thesis, Massey University, 2006; Mike Roche, 'Failure Deconstructed: Histories and Geographies of Soldier Settlement in New Zealand 1917–39,' *New Zealand Geographer* 64 (2008): 46–56.
12 David Greasley and Les Oxley, 'Regime Shift and Fast Recovery on the Periphery: New Zealand in the 1930s,' *Economic History Review* 55, no. 4 (2002): 697–720.
13 For the most recent analysis of the Labour Party over this period, see Peter Franks and Jim McAloon, *Labour: The New Zealand Labour Party, 1916–2016* (Wellington: Victoria University Press, 2016).
14 Rachel Barrowman, '"Culture Organising": Joe Heenan and the Beginning of State Patronage of the Arts,' *New Zealand Studies* 6, no. 2 (1996): 3–10.
15 Barry Gustafson, 'Savage, Michael Joseph,' from the Dictionary of New Zealand Biography. Te Ara — the Encyclopedia of New Zealand, updated 29-Jan-2014; URL: http://www.TeAra.govt.nz/en/biographies/4s9/savage-michael-joseph; Tim Beaglehole, 'Fraser, Peter,' from the Dictionary of New Zealand Biography. Te Ara — the Encyclopedia of New Zealand, updated 25-Sep-2013; URL: http://www.TeAra.govt.nz/en/biographies/4f22/fraser-peter; Barry Gustafson, 'Nash, Walter,' from the Dictionary of New Zealand Biography. Te Ara — the Encyclopedia of New Zealand, updated 4-Dec-2013; URL: http://www.TeAra.govt.nz/en/biographies/4n2/nash-walter.
16 Rachel Barrowman, *A Popular Vision: The Arts and the Left in New Zealand 1930–1950* (Wellington: Victoria University Press, 1991), 4.
17 http://natlib.govt.nz/about-us/our-history accessed 14/9/2016; established first as the Centennial orchestra, the National Orchestra of the New Zealand Broadcasting Service (now the New Zealand Symphony Orchestra) was formalised under Labour in 1947: Munro, *J.C. Beaglehole: Public Intellectual*, 38–45.
18 Beaglehole, 'New Zealand Scholar,' 245.
19 Beaglehole, 'Thoughts on New Zealand's Social History,' 32, 30.
20 Beaglehole, 'Thoughts on New Zealand's Social History,' 36.
21 F. L. W. Wood, 'The Historian in the Modern Community: George Arnold Wood Memorial Lecture, Sydney University, 19 September 1949,' in *The Feel of Truth: Essays in New Zealand and Pacific History, Presented to F.L.W. Wood and J.C. Beaglehole on the Occasion of their Retirement*, ed. Peter Munz (Wellington: A. H. & A. W. Reed for The Victoria University of Wellington, 1969), 255–72, at 256.
22 Beaglehole, 'History and the New Zealander,' 117.
23 Beaglehole, 'The New Zealand Scholar,' 250.
24 Beaglehole, 'History and the New Zealander,' 124.
25 Beaglehole, 'The New Zealand Scholar,' 251.
26 Beaglehole, 'History and the New Zealander,' 113.
27 Beaglehole, 'History and the New Zealander,' 108.
28 Beaglehole, 'The New Zealand Scholar,' 250.

29 Beaglehole, 'The New Zealand Scholar,' 250.
30 Beaglehole, 'The New Zealand Scholar,' 250; 'History and the New Zealander,' 107.
31 Beaglehole, 'The New Zealand Scholar,' 245.
32 Eric McCormick, 'Centennial,' in *An Absurd Ambition: Autobiographical Writings of Eric McCormick*, ed. Denis McEldowney (Auckland: Auckland University Press, 1996), 134–51, at 139.
33 Memo, D. O. W. Hall to Heenan, 17 February 1939, IA 1, 62/8/1, II, NA (Archives New Zealand).
34 D. O. W. Hall, 'New Zealand Centennial History,' *Historical Studies Australia and New Zealand* 1, no. 1 (1940): 21–30, at 21.
35 Hall, 'New Zealand Centennial History,' 21.
36 'Centennial Year Ends: Minister Reviews Celebrations, Country Thanked for Response,' *Press*, 16 November 1940.
37 'The Centennial Effort Reviewed by Mr Parry: Part Played by Government,' *Press*, 27 April 1940.
38 'Centennial Year Ends: Minister Reviews Celebrations, Country Thanked for Response,' *Press*, 16 November 1940.
39 'Centennial Surveys: Women of New Zealand,' *Evening Post*, 30 November 1940.
40 James Cowan, *Settlers and Pioneers* (Wellington: Whitcombe & Tombs for Department of Internal Affairs, 1940).
41 For more extended coverage of the Centennial Surveys see Rachel Barrowman, 'History and Romance: The Making of the Centennial Historical Surveys,' in *Creating a National Spirit: Celebrating New Zealand's Centennial*, ed. William Renwick (Wellington: Victoria University Press, 2004), 161–77.
42 Memo, Eric McCormick, 'Official History of New Zealand in the War of 1939 — Provisional Scheme,' October 1944, IA1 181/5/1, NA.
43 Memo, Eric McCormick to Joseph Heenan, Undersecretary to the Department of Internal Affairs, 'Provisional War History Scheme,' 2 February 1945, IA1 181/5/1, NA.
44 Major General Sir Howard Kippenberger, Radio Address, 'The History of New Zealand at War 1939–1945,' 19 August 1946, IA1 181/5/1, NA.
45 Memo, Kippenberger to Prime Minister Peter Fraser, 19 August 1946, IA1 181/5/1, NA.
46 Kippenberger, Radio Address, 'The History of New Zealand at War 1939–1945'.
47 Memo, Heenan to Mackintosh, Prime Minister's Department, 13 February 1945, IA1 181/5/1, NA.
48 Memo, McCormick, 'Official History of New Zealand in the War of 1939'.
49 Kippenberger, Radio Address, 'The History of New Zealand at War 1939–1945'.
50 For an extended analysis of the official war history project, see Rachael Bell, 'Memory, History, Nation, War: The Official Histories of New Zealand in the Second World War 1939–45', PhD thesis, Massey University, 2012.
51 F. M. Mason, 'Broadcast Review of *Journey towards Christmas*,' 2YA, 22 December 1949, IA1 181/7/29B, NA.
52 Angus Ross, 'Review of *Crete* by Dan Davin,' *Historical Studies Australia and New Zealand* 6

(1954): 348–50, at 348; J. W. Robertson, 'Vivid Narrative and Critical Judgement on Crete,' *Southland Times*, 2 November 1953.

53   C. E. Beeby, *The Biography of an Idea: Beeby on Education* (Wellington: New Zealand Council for Educational Research, 1992), 145.
54   Phil Trapp, 'The Post-Primary School Bulletin,' *Education* 5, no. 3 (1956): 37–41, at 37.
55   Thomas Prebble, 'Strategies of Change: A Study of Some Aspects of NZ Education during the First Half of the Directorship of Dr C.E. Beeby, 1940–1949', MA thesis, Massey University, 1970, 14.
56   Phoebe Meikle, *School and Nation: Post Primary Education since the War* (Wellington: New Zealand Council for Educational Research, 1961), 36, 7.
57   Beeby, *The Biography of an Idea*, 144–5.
58   Prebble, 'Strategies of Change,' 68.
59   Prebble, 'Strategies of Change,' 75.
60   Gregory O'Brien, *A Nest of Singing Birds: 100 Years of the New Zealand School Journal* (Wellington: Learning Media, 2007), 152.
61   Prebble, 'Strategies of Change,' 74.
62   Roderick Finlayson, *The Return of the Fugitives* (Wellington: School Publications Branch, Department of Education, 1957).
63   Finlayson, *The Return of the Fugitives*, 2, 3.
64   For a discussion of these bulletins and their efficacy see Rachael Bell, 'A Window for Revisionism: Presenting te Tiriti in the Primary School Bulletins, 1957,' *New Zealand Journal of History* 48, no. 2 (2014), 119–35.
65   'New Zealand Topics in History and Geography, Use of School Journal,' *Education: A Magazine for Teachers* 1, no. 1 (1948), 17.
66   J. C. Beaglehole, *How History is Written*, Post-Primary School Bulletin 1, no. 8 (Wellington: School Publications Branch, 1947) 124.
67   Beaglehole, *How History is Written*, 128.
68   Beaglehole, *How History is Written*, 114; see also Michael Turnbull, *Writing in New Zealand: Historical Writing*, Post-Primary School Bulletin 11, no. 2 (Wellington: School Publications Branch, 1957).
69   Turnbull, *Writing in New Zealand*, 7.
70   Turnbull, *Writing in New Zealand*, 10.
71   Prebble, 'Strategies of Change,' 15.
72   Phil Trapp, 'The Post-Primary School Bulletin,' *Education* 5, no. 3 (1956): 37–41, at 37.
73   Rachel Patrick, '"An Antidote to Bookishness": Local History, Educational Practices and Colonialism in New Zealand Primary Schools 1900–1940,' *New Zealand Journal of History* 45, no. 2 (2011): 192–208, at 192.
74   Chris Hilliard, 'A Prehistory of Public History: Monuments, Explanations and Promotions, 1900–1970,' in *Going Public: The Changing Face of New Zealand History*, eds. Bronwyn Dalley and Jock Phillips (Auckland: Auckland University Press, 2001), 30–54, at 38.

75 Meikle, *School and Nation*, 9.
76 Turnbull, *Writing in New Zealand*, 10.
77 Beaglehole, *How History is Written*, 128.
78 Andrew Brown, 'The Citizen: From Ancient to Post-Modern,' in this volume.
79 For one of the most recent assessments of this process, see *The Treaty on the Ground: Where We Are Headed, and Why It Matters*, eds. Rachael Bell, Margaret Kawharu, Kerry Taylor, Michael Belgrave, and Peter Meihana (Auckland: Massey University Press, 2017).
80 Beaglehole, 'History and the New Zealander,' 107.
81 Beaglehole, 'History and the New Zealander,' 99.
82 Beaglehole, 'History and the New Zealander,' 99.

10. ALL THE RIGHTS & PRIVILEGES OF BRITISH SUBJECTS:
MĀORI & CITIZENSHIP, TAKING THE LONG VIEW

Michael Belgrave

ALL THE RIGHTS & PRIVILEGES OF BRITISH SUBJECTS: MĀORI & CITIZENSHIP, TAKING THE LONG VIEW

Over the last three decades, the work of the Waitangi Tribunal has led to an ongoing debate about the role and place of Māori as New Zealand's indigenous people. Throughout the debate, most of the attention has been focused on the promises of Article 2 of the Treaty, which confirmed Māori rights: rights to property, rights to maintain control over resources and to manage them in ways that Māori consider appropriate. Article 2 confirmed existing Māori rights, acknowledging not only Māori customary ownership of the resources but, to a substantial extent, also recognising tikanga in managing these resources.[1] In contrast, Article 3 has received sparse attention, yet this article introduced something radically new to Māori, the idea of being subjects of Her Majesty and therefore citizens of the British Empire.[2]

Article 3 has become popular with those in New Zealand who would consign indigenous rights to an historical footnote, believing that Māori left their cultural practices behind and were absorbed into New Zealand's constitutional democracy. This perspective, while dressing itself in the cloak of democratic principles, is dedicated to the racially specific objective of excluding Māori from any legal or constitutional recognition other than that guaranteed by one person, one vote.[3]

What this chapter demonstrates is the long-term significance of Article 3 rights in the debate between Māori and the Crown since 1840. Arguments that Māori are inappropriately privileged in New Zealand's constitution are far from new: they are as old as the Treaty of Waitangi.[4] But stripped of their high-minded appeals to constitutional principles, claims that Māori need to be treated the same as everyone else have always been about resisting attempts by Māori to use the constitution to protect Māori rights guaranteed under the Treaty of Waitangi. When Māori were the majority, the last thing these constitution purists were advocating was one man, one vote. When Māori ceased to be a majority, the arguments were reversed. Either way, the objective of what has been presented over the last 175 years as high-minded principle has been to marginalise Māori political influence.

Article 3 was as contested as Article 2, but in 1840 there was no suggestion that Māori were joining a democratic and egalitarian society. In 1840, two of the most significant constitutional changes of the nineteenth century in Britain were very recent memories. In 1829, Catholic emancipation had opened citizenship to a significant religious minority, substantially amending the Protestant ascendancy which had for generations denied Roman Catholics the right to be elected to Parliament.[5] Secondly, the Great Reform Act of 1832 began what became a century-long process of making the British Parliament more representative of the population.[6] But in 1840, the idea that these reforms would lead to universal suffrage, including all men and all women, was almost completely unanticipated, except within the radical rhetoric of the Chartists, who demanded the reform of Parliament be taken much further. In effect, it would take until 1928 before the British Parliament could be considered completely democratic, with a fully universal suffrage.

A further significant change occurred when finally, in 1833, after half a century of campaigning, slavery was abolished within the British Empire. All of these three measures were statements of rights yet, ironically, the least dramatic was the Great Reform Act, because its full consequences lay well into the future. However, all three constitutional measures involved highly fraught debates about citizenship. It was therefore no random or serendipitous act to include in Article 3 of the Treaty of Waitangi a provision that gave Māori complete rights of citizenship within the British Empire.[7]

Article 3 rights in 1840 are very different from those of the twenty-first century. Some of these rights, and in particular equality before the law, had significantly developed in the century before 1840. Juries had wrested a degree of independence from the Crown. The right to own property, slaves now excluded, was fundamental to the idea of citizenship. Early Victorian liberalism was increasingly reflecting the dynamism of an emerging middle class fed

on industry and capitalism. Individualism was far more important than equality. Ancient collective rights, such as communal rights to land and other resources, were being replaced by individual property rights. Communitarian rights, such as those of guilds to regulate work, to exclude those without long apprenticeships and to protect the interests of their members, were under attack. British citizenship in the 1840s did not include the right to join a trade union.

In contrast with the sixteenth century, when constitutional change was accompanied by revolution, in the nineteenth century equally dramatic constitutional changes occurred, but they happened gradually. Māori became part of a debate in full flood over political rights, individualism, representation and self-government.

Neither Māori nor British societies were egalitarian. Both were hierarchical. On one side, an elite exercised chiefly authority, reinforced by whakapapa. On the other, wealth and rank gave political status, with the governor at the apex. Judges, military officers and government officials carried the status of the Crown, as did to some extent the Anglican Bishop, Bishop Selwyn. Although generally not from the social elite, missionaries wore God's mantle.

We should be cautious of also imposing the concept of individualism too heavily onto this political system. Simply dichotomising the collective interests of Māori with the individualism of Britons fails to acknowledge the extent to which much of the theoretical justification for the limited number of people with political rights lay in a form of communitarianism, in the belief that the aristocracy and gentry represented their communities, and spoke for everyone. It was not simply that they had the money and money said everything, but that they saw themselves as the inheritors of the common good, whose incomes gave them independence to truly represent the interests of their wider non-electing community.

In such a society, Māori elites could negotiate with European elites; questions of status, of mana, would be fundamental to this relationship.[8] Making Māori subjects of Her Majesty was always expected to have different consequences for chiefs than for everyone else. Chiefs would become gentry, so take their part in the new society. Even the New Zealand Company argued this, because in the humanitarian climate of the 1830s it was strategically essential to do so. The missionaries, vehemently opposed to the New Zealand Company, understood the importance of rangatira in completing their project of Christianising and civilising Māori.[9] But they thought it would take much more time before Māori had developed the skills to exercise their rangatira rights in a modern constitution. In the meantime, a settler Parliament was something they treated with ambivalence. It would be the governor's responsibility to protect Māori in any constitutional system to be adopted in New Zealand.

Until 1854, governors had almost autocratic powers under the direction only of the colonial secretary half the world away on a sailing ship. Personal relationships between the governor and rangatira continued to give the impression that Māori were participants in decision-making. Despite the constitutional authority given to the governor, and the practical advantage he had in being so far away from his political masters, Māori military, economic and political power was also an effective check on his actions. Rather than the governor, many chiefs may well have dealt with the offices of the protectorate appointed by William Hobson to manage relationships between tribes and the government. But even here settler opposition to the protectorate in the New Zealand Company settlements further reinforced the idea that the government and Māori had a special relationship and worked together.[10]

This does not mean that there were not crises, such as those leading to the northern war in the middle of the 1840s, or around the land claims of the New Zealand Company, which also led to armed conflict in 1843, and more general warfare in 1846 and 1847. In Auckland, the close proximity of Waikato leaders, such as Te Wherowhero, gave the governor's relationship with Māori added weight. This was particularly true while George Grey was governor between 1845 and 1853. Grey enjoyed being part of the Māori world, was fluent in te reo and, despite a high degree of duplicity in his character, managed his relationships with chiefs well. His increasing political and military power enhanced rather than diminished these relationships.

However, in 1854, the change to self-government in New Zealand altered

everything, because self-government was unashamedly self-government by settlers and for settlers.[11] Self-government had been one of the primary objectives of the New Zealand Company settlers from long before 1840. They had unsuccessfully campaigned for a Royal Charter in the mid-1830s. Once New Zealand became a British colony, settlers resisted Crown Colony government, seeing the governor, based at Kororāreka and then Auckland, as distant, unsympathetic and, while New Zealand was attached to New South Wales, imposing an administration designed to rule convicts rather than free Britons.[12] The opposition of the New Zealand Company settlers to the new governor bordered on the revolutionary.

The idea of self-government was fundamental for British citizens overseas and they had considerable sympathy, even among humanitarians such as James Stephen, the secretary of the Colonial Office. Once Lord Melbourne's administration fell in August 1841, the influence of the humanitarians, whose views had created the principles behind the Treaty of Waitangi, declined, while the political influence of the New Zealand Company rose.

In 1844, a select committee of the House of Commons demanded that New Zealand be given self-government and that land used by Māori for hunting and gathering be claimed as wasteland of the Crown.[13] These two objectives were bundled together in instructions to Grey in December 1846. Grey was well aware that this was not the time to give settlers control over the colony.[14] They were still bristling over the debacle at the Wairau in 1843, where a posse of company settlers had been killed trying to arrest Te Rauparaha illegally, and over Governor Robert FitzRoy's refusal to implement land commissioner William Spain's recommendation that 60,000 acres of Taranaki land be awarded to the company. Grey realised that to create self-government at this time was to invite war. When, in 1852, the Imperial Parliament passed legislation granting New Zealand a new constitution, Grey conveniently departed before the implementation of this measure of self-government.

There was nothing in the legislation that denied Māori a vote, but everything in its conception of representation that excluded them. Representation was not for everybody in 1852, limited as it was to men of property. Māori could vote and enter the legislature, but only if they owned or leased property where a Crown grant had been issued. Some Māori attempted and a few succeeded in getting on to electoral rolls in the 1850s, but the message was clear. Rangatira would be entitled to vote only when they gave up customary tenure of land and adopted English systems of title-holding. While European settlers had no intention of being outvoted by Māori, the barriers put in place for Māori inclusion were not racial, but cultural. It was not *all* Māori who were being excluded, but rangatira, whose status in the Māori world was not determined by ownership of land.

The conceit that had operated effectively since 1840, that rangatira access to governors gave them a real say in the new colony and its decision-making, was sorely challenged and exposed for the deception it was. Māori influence was determined not by constitutional structures but by military power. Yet the idea that Māori might openly and actively resist the imposition of this new constitution appears to have been rarely debated, and certainly never used as a direct threat.

The governor still retained reserved powers over native affairs and Governor Sir George Grey had placed £7000 found in a civil list, which the legislature had to supply, for the support of native affairs.[15] This allowed the governor a personal relationship with rangatira and at least some resources, independent of the decision-making of the legislature, to deal with Māori needs and to spread patronage, which recognised the mana of individual rangatira. Someone of Grey's skills could possibly have carried this off, maintaining chiefly relationships while talking down the authority of Parliament, but the flaws in Grey's approach to native policy, and in particular his personal duplicity, were becoming increasingly evident as time went on.[16] His successor, Thomas Gore Browne, was more distant, even imperious, and in his dealings with Māori relied extensively on his proxy and principal adviser, Donald McLean, although he was more active in Māori affairs than once believed.[17]

Māori attempts to become enrolled as electors, often at the encouragement of European candidates for office, brought attention to the disenfranchise-

ment of Māori, and the question was discussed in some detail throughout the 1850s. There was a provision in section 71 of the New Zealand Constitution Act, never implemented, which allowed for the governor to establish self-governing Māori districts. Wiremu Tamihana (Tarapipipi Te Waharoa) of Ngāti Haua had through his commitment to Anglican Christianity become an articulate and considered commentator on constitutional issues. Concerned about the exclusion of Māori from the new constitution, he went to Auckland in ca. 1857 to see the governor.[18] His request was for a Māori Parliament. The demand for separate constitutional recognition was not an attempt to implement section 71, and Tamihana's preference was probably to have Māori fully represented in the New Zealand Parliament, rather than to have two separate institutions. But since Europeans had made this impossible, then a Māori Parliament it had to be.

Not only did Tamihana fail to see the governor, but he was also treated with contempt, forced to sit to one side and wait for two days while Europeans came and went. This was no way to treat a rangatira. In disgust, he walked back to Waharoa, brushing the governor and his constitutional arrangements like the dust from his feet. He would become the evangelist for what became known as the Kīngitanga, the Māori King movement, autonomous, drawing from both the European and Māori worlds, and determined to protect Māori land and chiefly authority. For Tamihana, it was a question of the treatment of chiefs. If rangatira were not to be respected, if their status was not acknowledged as in the terms of the Treaty of Waitangi, there was no future inside the European constitutional structure. Given that the Europeans had wrested self-government for themselves, Māori needed a constitutional structure to take responsibility for their own futures.

The idea of a Māori king was not new; it had been popularised by Tāmihana Te Rauparaha of Ngāti Toa after he visited Britain in 1859 and met Queen Victoria.[19] Te Rauparaha did not join the Kīngitanga, but Wiremu Tamihana borrowed much of his vision for a Māori king.[20] If the French had their king and the English their queen, then Māori could have their own king; there was support for the idea from scripture as well. The Kīngitanga remained unsure of how this relationship between the queen and the king would work. Some thought the king no threat to the queen: the king on one side, the governor on the other, joined in love under the queen. For others, the queen was at best irrelevant, distant, European, and of little relevance to Māori, given that her government seemed primarily committed to settlers rather than Māori.

Europeans tended to dismiss the increasingly intense debates about the need for a Māori king as little more than a childish imitation of the European world.[21] This it certainly was not. Some of this lack of European appreciation of the Māori King movement's significance was due to the intensity of Māori debate. This included most of the iwi of the central North Island as they discussed the impact of this very European institution on tikanga, considering who should take on the new office, whether or not to pledge allegiance to him and what would be the relationship between rangatira and the new sovereign. In the end, Te Wherowhero of Ngāti Mahuta was elected the first Māori King and installed at Ngāruawāhia in 1858, despite his long history of working with governors.[22]

Māori demands for inclusion in the new constitutional arrangements went beyond simply those for a Māori Parliament. Ironically, at the very time when Māori were bridling at the increasing imposition of European power, they were asking for greater access to an impartial judicial system. This was interpreted by the governors, and particularly Grey after he returned in late 1861, as a demand for courts and magistrates. But those Māori who were calling for more access to te ture (the law) were demanding inclusion, not submission to European courts.[23] Te ture was based on biblical understanding of justice, which would ensure Māori access to law in a way that did not privilege Europeans.

The Kīngitanga established its own courts, its own government administration, and its own newspaper, filling a vacuum which had never been filled by the government's administration.[24] Far from recognising these developments, Grey, newly returned from South Africa as governor, established a rival resident magistracy and school in the Waikato, with its own newspaper, and the two systems competed for legitimacy.[25] In the end, Māori lost tolerance

with Grey's magistrate and he was ejected from the Waikato.

The governor had argued unashamedly that his institutions were aimed at undermining the King until he fell. Grey invaded the Waikato in July 1863, initiating a war which left an embittered but intact Kīngitanga controlling an independent territory which became known as Te Rohe Pōtae. This state within a state comprised a substantial part of the central North Island, despite significant losses of land through confiscation. The Kīngitanga exercised a parallel system of government and administration of justice to that of the colonial government. This system relied more on tikanga than on the European-style courts used by the Kīngitanga before the war.

Outside of the Rohe Pōtae, Māori engagement and participation with the colonial constitution increased substantially.[26] In 1867, four Māori political seats were established, recognising the substantial role that Māori were playing in the world, including fighting for the Queen, and following the creation of seats for miners, also electors without property.[27] At this time, despite the increasing ratio of Europeans to Māori, the four seats provided were a limited and containing franchise. Māori were becoming widely incorporated in the constitutional structures of the state. Māori were appointed to quasi-judicial roles, beginning a long tradition of petitioning government, and were soon entwined in the complex judicial and administrative structure of the Native Land Court, as litigants and assessors.[28]

From the late 1860s and through the 1870s those Māori who did not fight against the Crown were briefly given a sense of participation as citizens in the administration of Māori land. This was very shortlived. Even by the late 1860s it was clear that the Native Land Court was responsible for a massive decline in Māori land ownership. By the 1880s, the workings of the Native Land Court and growing demographic marginalisation increasingly convinced those tribes whose loyalty had at least protected them from confiscation in the 1860s that this loyalty had only delayed their experiences of land loss. The tribes of the Kīngitanga, protected by the Rohe Pōtae, had been much more successful in retaining land. Loyalist iwi then joined with the Kīngitanga in seeking a constitutional settlement which would give Māori control over Māori lands and prevent the predations of the government's land court.

Just when Māori had developed a kind of constitutional consensus about their relationship with the New Zealand state, asserting their loyalty to Queen Victoria, but denying the legitimacy of the New Zealand Parliament, everything changed once again. The weaknesses of the Māori position became increasingly obvious. Creating a Māori Parliament was all very well, but while the government simply ignored them, the work of the Native Land Court continued to undermine chiefly authority and Māori land ownership. By the 1890s a new generation of Māori, educated in European schools, and even by that time in university colleges, was coming of age. Some, like John Ormsby of Ngāti Maniapoto and James Carroll of Ngāti Kahungunu, combined Māori and European heritages.[29] But others, such as Āpirana Ngata, Maui Pomare and Peter Buck, were Māori products of an Anglican boarding school, Te Aute College.[30]

In dramatic contrast to indigenous boarding schools in North America and Australia and their 'stolen generations', Māori boarding schools attracted Māori leaders, provided a European education, but still promoted Māori tribal identity and maintained links with Māori communities. Their young graduates were fluent in both cultures and were able to overcome many of the limitations of Māori representation in Parliament; until that time, Māori were isolated by lack of skills in English, delays in translating bills, and lack of experience in legal and parliamentary procedure. But the new generation of Māori leaders brought considerable personal skills, chiefly mana and knowledge of the intricacies of European government into their roles of leadership. By the beginning of the twentieth century, and in particular following Carroll's lead, they shifted substantial areas of Māori opinion into a commitment to participating, from within the existing constitutional structures, forming what became known as the Young Maori Party.

Throughout the nineteenth century, Māori often complained about the impact of government policy on chiefly authority. While the franchise was linked to property ownership, individualisation of landowning was presented

as the only path available to full constitutional integration. The four Māori seats still failed to represent Māori adequately on the basis of population. Individual ownership of land — breaking down collective tribal ownership — was seen as a constitutional as much as an economic policy, as it had been in the 1850s, when a debate over the individualisation of Māori land was described as a debate over enfranchisement.[31] Rangatira complained that the native land laws gave all tribal members a say in tribal land, over and above the views of chiefs, who rightly represented the collective interests of the owners.[32]

By the late nineteenth century, the New Zealand Parliament, including the Māori seats, was elected on the universal franchise, burying the principle that votes represented collective interests, at least in the lower house, where by 1893 political power was concentrated. The Young Maori Party members were acutely aware of this transformation, and while they supported government structures over Māori land which recognised who could be subverted to recognise chiefly authority and collective rights, they were also prepared to work within a constitutional arrangement that was far more democratic and individualistic than had been the case in the 1850s.

Māori took grievances to the courts, but these new Māori leaders would argue that none of this was of any value if there was no direct access to the executive. Ngata, in particular, would become one of the most effective politicians of the twentieth century, able to influence government, even when in opposition. These Māori politicians, a number of whom achieved Cabinet rank, forged what could be described as a social contract between Māori and the state. While they accepted that the non-Māori majority would always win in a conflict that divided European and Māori, where Māori issues were concerned they demanded a say. Māori would be consulted and, if there was significant Māori opposition to a measure, the government did not persist. This form of the social contract was sufficiently broad to include the Ratana political party and the Labour Party after their emergence in the 1920s.[33] Not until 1967 would government again act unilaterally, ignoring united Māori opinion, in reforming the Māori land laws.

The idea that any constitutional concession was temporary had been an integral part of the 1867 establishment of the four Māori seats and it remained a government assumption about all the so-called special measures for Māori. Once Māori were sufficiently integrated into New Zealand society as a whole, then these measures could be abolished. This issue came to a head in the early 1960s, when the idea of any separate provision on the basis of race had echoes in the European world of apartheid, and the Jim Crow laws of the southern United States. Government sought to ensure that Māori could take an equal place in New Zealand society, and one of the tests of equality was the abolition of separate provision. Native schools, the semi-judicial functions of tribal committees, and many of the social welfare, housing and health functions of the Department of Maori Affairs were over time mainstreamed.

In a practical sense, this recognised that Māori were now urban dwellers and genuinely needed the same access to the welfare state as their non-Māori neighbours.[34] Government pursued the idea of modernity, something shared by all developed societies, a shared colour-blind future. Yet, from the late 1960s, Māori would resist these institutional reforms, work to ensure that Māori land continued to be administered by the Māori Land Court, and opposed the abolition of the court. By the 1980s, Māori were promoting the re-emergence of Māori schooling under Māori control, the revitalisation of Māori language and the recognition of iwi authorities in the delivery of government services in health, welfare and education.

In 1967, the National Government pushed through legislation aimed at transferring substantial areas of Māori land out of the jurisdiction of the Māori Land Court, designating it as European land. The proposal had been one of the recommendations of an inquiry into Māori policy undertaken by Jack Hunn and released in 1960.[35] Between 1960 and 1967 the government campaigned in favour of Hunn's recommendation to Europeanise Māori land, despite an increasing opposition from almost all areas of Māori opinion.

The connection between Ratana and Labour had little impact on policy-making during the 17 years of the 1950s and 1960s when National was in power. National created the Maori Council in 1962 in an attempt to provide a consultative body more receptive to the National Party, but the Maori

Council refused to support the proposed reforms. By pushing through the legislation, the government broke with the unofficial social contract forged at the beginning of the twentieth century. Relationships between Māori and the state entered a period of crisis that lasted for several decades. There were many reasons for this, but much was centred on an attempt by Māori to realign their constitutional relationship with the state, in response to increasing Māori disaffection with government.[36]

From the 1970s, New Zealand faced a crisis in its constitutional legitimacy that went well beyond Māori concerns about institutional racism and Māori sovereignty. Māori concern about the domination of the New Zealand Parliament by those of European heritage was only one of the issues fuelling a wave of discontent into the 1980s. New Zealand's freewheeling constitution, where dictatorial power rested in Cabinet, without the moderating influence of an upper house or written constitution, was increasingly seen as a risk to the country's democracy.[37] A three-year electoral cycle and the press were two of the few brakes on executive power. These concerns only intensified when between 1984 and 1993 both Labour and National governments initiated dramatic reforms of the New Zealand state with little in the way of an electoral mandate.[38]

With the establishment of the Waitangi Tribunal and its increasing authority by the late 1980s, the Treaty of Waitangi was used by Māori to demand a greater say in New Zealand's constitution. Under the banner of Māori sovereignty, many Māori denied the legitimacy of the New Zealand state, arguing that the Treaty of Waitangi did not convey the sovereignty of Aotearoa to the British Crown; rather, it confirmed the Māori sovereignty originally recognised in He Whakaputanga o te Rangatiratanga o Nu Tirene (the 1835 Declaration of Independence).[39]

Despite the uncompromising language about sovereignty, which challenged the Crown's very legitimacy, a new social contract did emerge by the early 1990s. Māori set aside demands for the recognition of sovereign independence (although how this could ever have been achieved remains unclear). In return, the government agreed to consult with Māori over everything that related to them, and accepted the need to fund Māori organisations delivering health, educational and social services, while ensuring that mainstream government activities acknowledged the distinct needs and preferences of Māori as tangata whenua. Alongside these conventions was the incorporation of the Treaty of Waitangi into domestic law, despite this incorporation falling far short of Māori expectations.[40]

The social contract has provided a general framework for relationships between Māori and the state, but not without some major crises along the way. The most significant of these were the imposition of the fiscal envelope, developed without any Māori consultation, to resolve Treaty grievances; the government's determination to extinguish Māori rights to the foreshore and seabed, on the untested premise that these did not exist; and finally, the recent establishment of a marine reserve around the Kermadec Islands. In all of these crises, government decided to act unilaterally, just as it had done in 1967. Both the social contracts, of the early twentieth century and of the 1990s, fall far short of being constitutional conventions. In the end, while they governed day-to-day behaviour, the government's ability to ignore them remained.

At the same time, more formal moves to enshrine individual human rights, to promote a Bill of Rights as a constraint on the executive, and eventually for electoral reform, testified to a widespread unease about the health of New Zealand's democratic institutions. A Royal Commission on the Electoral System recommended proportional representation and in its deliberations reviewed the history of Māori representation and involvement in the New Zealand constitution.[41] The Royal Commission recommended Mixed Member Proportional (MMP) representation, which would give significantly greater weight to the interests of minorities.

In the Commission's view, and it considered the issue in depth, separate Māori representation was fundamentally flawed and would be no longer necessary in an MMP-elected Parliament, although it did recommend that Māori parties should not need to gain 5 per cent of the party vote to gain a share of seats when the party had not gained a constituency seat. However, largely as a result of strong Māori opposition to the abolition of the Māori seats, they were

retained when MMP was adopted in 1996. At the same time, provisions were put in place to allow the number of Māori seats to rise to reflect those still wishing to be on a Māori roll.

MMP would free Māori parliamentary politics from its more than half-a-century embrace of the Labour Party, first in an ill-fated marriage with Winston Peters' New Zealand First Party, between 1996 and 1998, and then following controversy over the Labour-led government's proposal to extinguish Māori rights to the foreshore and seabed, with the establishment of the Māori and then Mana parties.[42] While the Māori Party has maintained a strong association with National in government, it is not so embedded in National to preclude forming alliances elsewhere. To that extent the expectations of the Royal Commission have been met. The controversy over whether the compromises of working within government as a minority partner are worth it will continue, as it did through the Young Maori Party and Ratana's relationships with government throughout the twentieth century. When Hone Harawira left the Māori Party in 2011, he argued that Māori could not be advanced with National, but in this he was following in the footsteps of Matiu Rata who had come to a similar parting with the Labour Party in 1980.[43]

Many of these constitutional developments have been overshadowed by the attempts to resolve Treaty of Waitangi claims, through the protracted enquiries of the Waitangi Tribunal, with their hearings, substantial collection of evidence and detailed reports.[44] Since the middle of the 1990s, the government has developed processes to settle these historical claims, which have increasingly occupied iwi. There has been a broad consensus in favour of these settlements among the major political parties. Opposition, in Parliament, is concentrated more on the detail than on the principle of settlement and reconciliation.

In 2004, Don Brash, then leader of the National Party, launched a campaign against what he decried as 'race-based' policies, which he claimed were dividing New Zealand, but he still expressed support for the ongoing settlement of Treaty of Waitangi historical grievances. He renewed the campaign in 2016.

As in 2004, Brash's 2016 attack on what he sees as the privileging of Māori in contemporary society shows that the electoral representation of Māori in local and central government remains extremely contentious, as it has always been. At a local level, where councils sit side by side with tribal authorities, there has been some hesitant recognition of Māori voices. Local authorities have been given substantial responsibility to engage with Māori as well as specific obligations to Māori in managing the Resource Management Act 1991.[45]

In 2001 the Bay of Plenty Regional Council established Māori seats on Environment Waikato, and this led to a move to allow councils to establish Māori wards.[46] When the latter was put to a referendum in New Plymouth in 2015 it was emphatically defeated, despite being sponsored by the mayor, Andrew Judd.

In Auckland, Māori representation in decision-making, through the Independent Māori Statutory Board, emerged largely by accident. Local body amalgamation leading to the creation of Auckland City did create a debate over how Māori should be represented.[47] In the end, and to the surprise of the legislation's authors, the statutory board was created, representing Māori interests in Tāmaki Makarau. While there are representatives on the Auckland board of pan-Māori groups (matāwaka), the board's strength is its ability to acknowledge the complexity of interests among those who have customary relationships with the city (mana whenua).

In 2015 the Rotorua District Council established the Te Arawa Partnership Board. While similar to the Māori Statutory Board, it acknowledges the specific role of Te Arawa in the creation of Rotorua through the 1880 agreement between the tribe and Francis Dart Fenton, which clearly recognised Te Arawa's continuing role in the soon-to-be-established tourist town.

There are critics aplenty, and often the members of the statutory board are referred to as unelected, undermining its legitimacy.[48] While there has been litigation about the process of election, these members are elected, seven of them by mana whenua iwi and two (matāwaka) seats by Māori generally. The most important aspect of this form of representation is that it is largely based on tribes rather than individuals, in this case tribes with customary interests

within Auckland City. The Auckland model works because it represents iwi, not an ethnic minority, even one asserting indigenous rights. Any constitutional arrangement which accepts that Māori need separate representation can only provide a wedge to the representation of other ethnic minorities. If Māori are entitled to their own members, in local government or in the House of Representatives, then why should other ethnic groups, Pacific, Chinese, Korean or Indian migrants or Indian New Zealanders, not also be represented?

Yet, drawing a distinction between Article 2 and Article 3 interests is in the end artificial. In the same way, making distinctions between historical claims and contemporary claims is equally arbitrary. In settling historical claims, the Crown is providing for the first time constitutional recognition of tribal governments; not a Māori Parliament, but of a substantial network of tribal authorities, each created by its own piece of legislation, each with responsibilities to represent its communities, and each with a commitment from the Crown to consult, to work together and to ensure that further grievances are avoided. In 2016, the failure of government to negotiate and consult with Māori over the establishment of the marine reserve around the Kermadec Islands had the potential to undermine the government's policy on establishing the reserve because it discounted Māori fishing rights, recognised by the 1992 Sealord agreement.[49] Government needs a constitutional ability to work with Māori, not just on interests particular to Māori themselves, but also on interests important to the country as a whole. Ironically, the network of tribal governments, recognised by the Crown, is but one step away from a Māori Parliament.

Advocates for New Zealand adopting a written constitution hope that most of these issues would be resolved through some form of constitutional consensus. Both Matthew and Geoffrey Palmer have argued that a constitution could include and define Māori rights under the Treaty of Waitangi.[50] Geoffrey Palmer had originally intended to include the Treaty of Waitangi in his 1990 Bill of Rights Act, but Māori showed no enthusiasm and largely campaigned to have the Treaty of Waitangi left out of the legislation, even before Palmer's bid to make the Bill of Rights Act supreme law was derailed. Former Labour MP Shane Jones, who worked with Palmer on Māori environmental issues, later regretted this opposition.[51]

At the time, Māori feared that once the Treaty had become incorporated into domestic law it could be revised and watered down. This was not an unrealistic fear, for until the 1980s the exclusion of the Treaty of Waitangi from domestic law had quarantined it from judicial interpretation, allowing Māori to define the Treaty according to tribal political agendas. Once within the legal canon of New Zealand, its interpretation would be subject to the interpretation of Pākehā judges. However, given widespread non-Māori opposition to any form of Māori representation, it is an open question whether any constitutional debate can come to a consensus on how rights under the Treaty of Waitangi should be protected, let alone on the nature of Māori representation in central and local government. While this debate may be possible some time in the future, this review of past debate shows how deep-rooted and enduring is non-Māori distrust of Māori being constitutionally recognised.

This chapter has shown the extensive and ongoing relationship between Māori and the New Zealand constitution as it has evolved, continuing to maintain at least some recognition of tribal collective interests, despite increasing emphasis on individual rights and individual representation. The protection of individual rights, such as the Human Rights Act 1993 prohibition of discrimination on the basis of ethnicity or race, has immediate benefits to Māori. However, the increased recognition of the Treaty of Waitangi from the 1980s has acknowledged the importance of collective rights held by iwi and hapū. Despite recognising these rights through its Treaty settlements, the Crown in New Zealand remains unclear about the constitutional implications of these agreements.

Like most of the constitutional reform that has occurred in New Zealand since the 1840s, recognition of Māori rights is partly based on intent and partly on unintended consequences and responses to crises. However muddled this may seem, it is a constitution that displays opportunity and flexibility and can adjust to changing social values and attitudes. Whatever the hopes of those who would relegate Māori to an anachronism, a romantic past no longer relevant in the present, Māori resilience over what is now heading towards two

centuries of colonisation suggests that Māori will continue to use whatever constitutional measures are available to them to maintain and develop iwi and hapū over coming generations.

ENDNOTES

1 The work of the Waitangi Tribunal and Treaty settlements have been much discussed; see as examples Janine Hayward and Nicola R. Wheen, eds., *The Waitangi Tribunal: Te Roopu Whakamana I Te Tiriti O Waitangi* (Wellington: Bridget Williams Books, 2004); Nicola R. Wheen and Janine Hayward, eds., *Treaty of Waitangi Settlements* (Wellington: Bridget Williams Books with the New Zealand Law Foundation, 2012); Mark Hickford, *Lords of the Land: Indigenous Property Rights and the Jurisprudence of Empire*, Oxford Studies in Modern Legal History (Oxford: Oxford University Press, 2011); Vincent O'Malley, Bruce Stirling, and Wally Penetito, eds., *The Treaty of Waitangi Companion: Māori and Pākehā from Tasman to Today* (Auckland: Auckland University Press, 2010).

2 See Matthew Palmer, *The Treaty of Waitangi in New Zealand's Law and Constitution* (Wellington: Victoria University Press, 2008).

3 See the claims of Democracy Action http://www.democracyaction.org.nz/, accessed 9 September 2016, and more significantly the ongoing campaign of ex-Governor of the Reserve Bank and leader of the National Party, Don Brash: 'Hobson's Pledge latest play of the race card from Brash,' Radio New Zealand, 3 October 2016, http://www.radionz.co.nz/news/political/314478/don-brash-resurfaces-with-reheated-arguments, viewed 17 October 2016; Don Brash, 'Nationhood — Don Brash Speech Orewa Rotary Club, Tuesday, 27 January 2004,' Scoop, http://www.scoop.co.nz/stories/PA0401/S00220.htm, viewed 7 September 2016; Walter Christie, *A Race Apart: Parliament and Race Separatism, the Story* (Auckland: Wyvern Press, 1998).

4 Peter Meihana, 'The Paradox of Maori Privilege: Historical Constructions of Maori Privilege c. 1769 to 1940', PhD thesis, Massey University, 2015.

5 Richard W. Davis, 'Wellington and the "Open Question": The Issue of Catholic Emancipation, 1821–1829,' *Albion: A Quarterly Journal Concerned with British Studies* 29, no. 1 (1997); Boyd Hilton, *A Mad, Bad, and Dangerous People? England, 1783–1846*, The New Oxford History of England (Oxford, New York: Oxford University Press, 2006), 384–91.

6 Nancy D. LoPatin, *Political Unions, Popular Politics, and the Great Reform Act of 1832*, Studies in Modern History (Houndmills, Basingstoke, Hampshire, New York: Macmillan Press, St Martin's Press, 1999); Hilton, *A Mad, Bad, and Dangerous People?*, 420–38.

7 The most recent review of the English intent of the Treaty is Ned Fletcher, 'A Praiseworthy Device for Amusing and Pacifying Savages? What the Framers Meant by the English Text of the Treaty of Waitangi', DPhil thesis, University of Auckland, 2014.

8   David Cannadine, *Ornamentalism: How the British Saw Their Empire* (London: Penguin, 2002).
9   Erik Olssen, 'Mr. Wakefield and New Zealand as an Experiment in Post-Enlightenment Experimental Practice,' *New Zealand Journal of History* 31, no. 2 (1997), 197–218; Philip Temple, *A Sort of Conscience: The Wakefields* (Auckland: Auckland University Press, 2002).
10 Alan Lester and Fae Dussart, *Colonization and the Origins of Humanitarian Governance: Protecting Aborigines across the Nineteenth-Century British Empire*, Critical Perspectives on Empire (Cambridge: Cambridge University Press, 2014).
11 Noel Cox, *A Constitutional History of the New Zealand Monarch: The Evolution of the New Zealand Monarchy and the Recognition of an Autochthonous Polity* (Saarbrücken, Germany: VDM Verlag Dr. Müller Aktiengesellschaft & Co., 2008); Michael Belgrave, '"We Rejoice to Honour the Queen, for She Is a Good Woman, Who Cares for the Māori Race": Loyalty and Protest in Māori Politics in Nineteenth-Century New Zealand,' in *Mistress of Everything: Queen Victoria in Indigenous Worlds*, eds. Sarah Carter and Maria Nugent (Manchester: Manchester University Press, 2016), Chapter 3.
12 See Jerningham Wakefield's bitter attack on Hobson's administration, Edward Jerningham Wakefield, *Adventure in New Zealand, from 1839 to 1844 by Edward Jerningham Wakefield* (London: John Murray, 1845).
13 Alan Ward, *A Show of Justice: Racial 'Amalgamation' in Nineteenth Century New Zealand* (Canberra: ANU Press, 1974), p. 88.
14 Michael Belgrave, 'Pre-Emption, the Treaty of Waitangi and the Politics of Crown Purchase,' *New Zealand Journal of History* 31, no. 1 (1997), 23–37.
15 Ward, *A Show of Justice*.
16 Belgrave, 'Pre-Emption, the Treaty of Waitangi and the Politics of Crown Purchase,' 23–37.
17 B. J. Dalton, 'Browne, Thomas Robert Gore', from the Dictionary of New Zealand Biography. Te Ara — the Encyclopedia of New Zealand, updated 30-Oct-2012, URL: http://www.TeAra.govt.nz/en/biographies/1b39/browne-thomas-robert-gore, viewed 10 October 2016; B. J. Dalton, *War and Politics in New Zealand, 1855–1870* (Sydney: Sydney University Press, 1967).
18 B. J. Dalton, 'Tamihana's Visit to Auckland,' *Journal of the Polynesian Society* 72, no. 3 (1963), 193–205; A. D. Ward, 'Shorter Communications: Tamihana's Visit to Auckland,' *Journal of the Polynesian Society* 73, no. 3 (1964), 324–8; Evelyn Stokes, *Wiremu Tamihana Tarapipipi Te Waharoa: A Study of His Life and Times* (Hamilton: Dept. of Geography University of Waikato, 1999).
19 Steven Oliver, 'Te Rauparaha, Tamihana', from the Dictionary of New Zealand Biography. Te Ara — the Encyclopedia of New Zealand, updated 30-Oct-2012, URL: http://www.TeAra.govt.nz/en/biographies/1t75/te-rauparaha-tamihana, viewed 10 October 2016.
20 Stokes, *Wiremu Tamihana Tarapipipi Te Waharoa*, Chapters 6–8.
21 M. P. K. Sorrenson, 'The Maori King Movement, 1858–1885,' in *Studies of a Small Democracy: Essays in Honour of Willis Airey*, ed. Robert Macdonald Chapman and Keith Sinclair (Hamilton: Paul's Book Arcade for the University of Auckland, 1963); Vincent O'Malley, *The Great War for*

New Zealand: Waikato 1800–2000 (Wellington: Bridget Williams Books, 2016), Chapter 5.

22   Steven Oliver, 'Te Wherowhero, Potatau', from the Dictionary of New Zealand Biography. Te Ara — the Encyclopedia of New Zealand, updated 21-Aug-2013, URL: http://www.TeAra.govt.nz/en/biographies/1t88/te-wherowhero-potatau, viewed 4 October 2016.

23   Lachy Paterson, '"Maori Conversion" to the Rule of Law and Nineteenth-Century Imperial Loyalties,' *Journal of Religious History* 32, no. 2 (2008), 216–33; Atholl Anderson, Judith Binney, and Aroha Harris, *Tangata Whenua: An Illustrated History* (Wellington: Bridget Williams Books, 2014), 239–40.

24   Sorrenson, 'The Maori King Movement, 1858–1885'.

25   John Eldon Gorst, *The Maori King, or, the Story of Our Quarrel with the Natives of New Zealand* (London: Macmillan, 1864).

26   Grant Young, Michael Belgrave, and Tom Bennion, *Native and Maori Land Legislation in the Superior Courts, 1840–1980* (North Shore City: New Zealand Law Foundation/School of Social and Cultural Studies, Massey University, 2005).

27   Tiopira McDowell, 'Māori Political Movements and the Māori Seats in Parliament, 1867–2008', PhD thesis, University of Auckland, 2013; M. P. K. Sorrenson, *Ko Te Whenua Te Utu Land Is the Price: Essays on Maori History, Land and Politics* (Auckland: Auckland University Press, 2014), Chapter 9.

28   Richard Boast, *The Native Land Court 1862–1887: A Historical Study, Cases, and Commentary* (Wellington: Brookers, 2013); ——, *Buying the Land, Selling the Land: Governments and Maori Land in the North Island 1865–1921* (Wellington: Victoria University Press/Victoria University of Wellington Law Review, 2008); Young, Belgrave, and Bennion, *Native and Maori Land Legislation*.

29   M. J. Ormsby, 'Ormsby, John', from the Dictionary of New Zealand Biography. Te Ara — the Encyclopedia of New Zealand, updated 11-Dec-2013, URL: http://www.TeAra.govt.nz/en/biographies/2o8/ormsby-john, viewed 17 October 2016; Alan Ward, 'Carroll, James', from the Dictionary of New Zealand Biography. Te Ara — the Encyclopedia of New Zealand, updated 6-Jun-2013, URL: http://www.TeAra.govt.nz/en/biographies/2c10/carroll-james, viewed 17 October 2016.

30   Ranginui Walker, *He Tipua: The Life and Times of Sir Apirana Ngata* (Auckland: Penguin Books, 2002); M. P. K. Sorrenson, 'Buck, Peter Henry', from the Dictionary of New Zealand Biography. Te Ara — the Encyclopedia of New Zealand, updated 30-Oct-2012, URL: http://www.TeAra.govt.nz/en/biographies/3b54/buck-peter-henry, viewed 17 October 2017; Graham Butterworth. 'Pomare, Maui Wiremu Piti Naera', from the Dictionary of New Zealand Biography. Te Ara — the Encyclopedia of New Zealand, updated 30-Oct-2012, URL: http://www.TeAra.govt.nz/en/biographies/3p30/pomare-maui-wiremu-piti-naera, viewed 17 October 2016.

31   See, as an example, 'The Direct Purchase Move,' *The New-Zealander*, Vol. XV, Issue 1370, 4 June 1859, 3.

32   A good example is Tāwhiao's petition to the Crown in 1884, Memorial, 15 July 1884 (date translation certified by Fred H. Spencer), MA 23/2/4a, National Archives, Wellington.

33 Keith Newman, *Ratana: The Prophet* (North Shore City: Raupo, 2009).
34 Anderson, Binney, and Harris, *Tangata Whenua*, 400–13.
35 J. A. Hunn, 'Report on the Department of Maori Affairs with Statistical Supplement' (Wellington: AJHR, 1961); Aroha Harris, 'Dancing with the State: Maori Creative Energy and Policies of Integration, 1945–1967,' PhD thesis, University of Auckland, 2007.
36 Richard S. Hill, *Maori and the State: Crown–Maori Relations in New Zealand/Aotearoa, 1950–2000* (Wellington: Victoria University Press, 2009).
37 Geoffrey Palmer, *Unbridled Power? An Interpretation of New Zealand's Constitution and Government* (Wellington, New York: Oxford University Press, 1979); Geoffrey Palmer and Matthew Palmer, *Bridled Power: New Zealand Government under MMP*, 3rd ed. (Auckland: Oxford University Press, 1997).
38 Jane Kelsey, *Rolling Back the State* (Wellington: Bridget Williams Books, 1993); ———, *The New Zealand Experiment* (Auckland: Auckland University Press/Bridget Williams Books, 1995); Jonathan Boston and M. Holland, eds., *The Fourth Labour Government* (Auckland: Oxford University Press, 1990); Brian Easton, *In Stormy Seas: The Post-War New Zealand Economy* (Dunedin: University of Otago Press, 1997); Jonathan Boston and Paul Dalziel, eds., *The Decent Society? Essays in Response to National's Economic and Social Policies* (Auckland: Oxford University Press, 1992).
39 Andrew Sharp, *Justice and the Māori: Māori Claims in New Zealand Political Argument in the 1980s* (Auckland: Oxford University Press, 1990); Michael Belgrave, *Historical Frictions: Maori Claims and Reinvented Histories* (Auckland: Auckland University Press, 2005), Chapter 2; these ideas have been accepted in the Waitangi Tribunal's investigation of the Declaration and the Treaty, New Zealand Waitangi Tribunal, *He Whakaputanga Me Te Tiriti: The Declaration and the Treaty. The Report on Stage 1 of the Te Paparahi O Te Raki Inquiry* (Wellington: Waitangi Tribunal, 2014).
40 David V. Williams, 'Unique Treaty-Based Relationships Remain Elusive,' in *Waitangi Revisited: Perspectives on the Treaty of Waitangi*, ed. Michael Belgrave, Merata Kawharu, and David Williams (Melbourne: Oxford University Press, 2005), Chapter 20.
41 Royal Commission on the Electoral System, 'Towards a Better Democracy'; (Wellington: AJHR, 1986), viewed 5 October 2016.
42 Waitangi Tribunal, *Report on the Crown's Foreshore and Seabed Policy (Wai 1071)*, Waitangi Tribunal Report, Wai 1071 (Wellington: Legislation Direct, 2004); Claire Charters and Andrew K. Erueti, eds., *Māori Property Rights and the Foreshore and Seabed: The Last Frontier* (Wellington: Victoria University Press, 2007).
43 'Matiu Rata', URL: http://www.nzhistory.net.nz/people/matiu-rata (Ministry for Culture and Heritage), updated 25-Nov-2015, viewed 12 October 2016.
44 Wheen and Hayward, *Treaty of Waitangi Settlements*; Hayward and Wheen, *The Waitangi Tribunal: Te Roopu Whakamana I Te Tiriti O Waitangi*.

45 Janine Hayward, *Local Government and the Treaty of Waitangi* (Auckland: Oxford University Press, 2003).
46 Bay of Plenty Regional Council (Māori Constituency Empowering) Act 2001 (Local) (2001 No 1); Local Electoral Amendment Act 2002 (2002 No 85).
47 Maria Bargh, 'Māori wards and advisory boards,' in *Local Government in New Zealand: Challenges and Choices*, eds. Jean Drage and Christine Cheyne (Auckland: Dunmore, 2016), Chapter 7.
48 See comments of Judith Collins, National MP, Radio New Zealand, 6 December 2015, http://www.radionz.co.nz/news/political/291404/collins-wants-'monster'-maori-board-dumped, viewed 17 October 2016; Michael Coote, 'Local Government Commission promotes racial discrimination,' New Zealand Centre for Political Research, http://www.nzcpr.com/local-government-commission-promotes-racial-discrimination/, viewed 17 October 2016.
49 'Government Rejects Māori Compromise to Kermadec Sanctuary,' Scoop, 14 September 2016, http://business.scoop.co.nz/2016/09/14/government-rejects-maori-compromise-to-kermadec-sanctuary/, viewed 17 October 2016; this failure to consult has been the primary objection of Māori fishing interests; see Te Ohu Kai Moana Trustee Limited, 'Submission on the Kermadec Ocean Sanctuary Bill, 28 April 2016,' http://teohu.maori.nz/documents/submissions/2016/Te_Ohu_Kermadec_Ocean_Sanctuary_Submission_FINAL.pdf, viewed 17 October 2016.
50 Palmer, *The Treaty of Waitangi in New Zealand's Law and Constitution*.
51 Geoffrey Palmer and Andrew Butler, *A Constitution for Aotearoa New Zealand* (Wellington: Victoria University Press, 2016).

11. FROM 'CITIZENS' TO 'DILETTANTES' & BACK AGAIN? THE WORKERS' EDUCATIONAL ASSOCIATION & ITS STUDENTS SINCE 1945

John Griffiths

FROM 'CITIZENS' TO 'DILETTANTES' & BACK AGAIN? THE WORKERS' EDUCATIONAL ASSOCIATION & ITS STUDENTS SINCE 1945

In 1936 Cyril Norwood, then president of St John's College Oxford, gave a lecture to a Workers' Educational Association (WEA) Saturday School. During the course of the lecture he noted that, 'it had been cynically observed that the nineteenth century taught the citizens to push and the twentieth century is teaching them to lean'.[1]

In conceptualising the trajectory of social citizenship, historians and policy analysts have followed this comment, suggesting a two-phase model of an 'active' followed by a 'passive' citizenship in twentieth-century Britain.[2] Up until 1939, they argue, the concept of the 'active' citizen dominated both intellectual discourse and its practical implementation. This was achieved largely through the work of voluntary organisations.[3] After 1945, it is argued, the impetus for 'active' citizenship declined and was replaced by a more 'passive' notion of citizenship, shaped by the creation of the safety net of the welfare state, which was put in place at the end of the Second World War, and, by the later 1950s, a growing working-class affluence within British society with a concomitant 'privatised' worker emerging at the same point in time.[4] Only over the last 20 years, and most notably in the current century, has the notion of a more 'active' citizenship been revived by those holding power at a governmental level.

This essay explores the evolution of citizenship over the last one hundred years, with particular reference to the WEA, founded in Britain in 1903. It is an organisation that has been at the vanguard of promoting active citizenship since its foundation and which celebrated its centenary in 2003. At the time of writing, the WEA continues to be a leading provider of adult education in Britain. Particular questions asked here are: firstly, how was the organisation able to adapt to a changing economic and political climate in the post-war years, and secondly, how far did its original aims and objectives shift in the decades after 1945, if not before? By means of an examination of the organisation's archive, with particular reference to the decades after the Second World War ended, it is possible to track changes in the nature of provision for adult education and the changing nature of student demand.

Does the experience of the WEA neatly fit into the conceptual model offered by historians of twentieth-century social citizenship? Conversely, do the operations of the WEA problematise this model? The benefit of taking the WEA as a case example is that the organisation has been well aware of changes in the economic and social context in which it has operated and has published introspections at regular intervals. These reflections have indeed threatened to provoke a crisis of self-confidence within the WEA. More positively, for the historian at least, such publications enable an examination of the outlook of the association at various points in time.[5]

The WEA was established largely through the efforts of Albert Mansbridge, a clerk employed by the Cooperative Wholesale Society in the closing years of the nineteenth century. Mansbridge had attended Battersea Grammar School, but due to the exigencies of work he was unable to experience university life. In the early twentieth century, education for the working class was still in a very rudimentary state, with secondary education only becoming a possibility via the Education Act of 1902.[6] There were just seven British universities, which were largely the domain of the middle and upper classes. Similarly, only a very small number of working men had ever sat in Parliament. Women did not have the vote and social security was embryonic. The Poor Laws were still in place, and state old-age pensions, health insurance and unemployment insurance were yet to be introduced.

Yet the formation of the WEA occurred just three years before significant Labour gains in the 1906 election alarmed political and social elites at Westminster and in the country at large. Trade-union power was also growing significantly, and much intellectual thought promoted the idea that education for the working man would lessen the chance of industrial conflict and social

FROM 'CITIZENS' TO 'DILETTANTES' & BACK AGAIN?

turbulence. The WEA has also been seen as one of a number of voluntary organisations formed in the later Victorian and Edwardian years which aimed at promoting 'education for citizenship'. Among these organisations were the Civic and Moral Education League (1897), the League of Empire (1901), the Victoria League (1901) and the Scouting and Guide movement (1907 and 1910).[7]

The WEA found friends among members of the governing Liberal Party and was looked on favourably by a significant group of Oxford dons, especially those at Balliol College. Balliol was the home of the idealist philosophers of the later nineteenth century, and where T. H. Green was based; Green, the author of *Prolegomena to Ethics*, demonstrated an active citizenship in his extra-curricula life.[8] As Ross Terrill, a biographer of R. H. Tawney, who was president of the WEA between 1927 and 1943, has observed: 'The sense of citizenship as personal performance enjoyed its renaissance in the later nineteenth century . . . There appeared in late Victorian and Edwardian times a great literature on the subject of citizenship suffused with tones of moral and religious uplift.'[9]

Such active citizenship had already been demonstrated in the context of university settlement work, such as that undertaken at Toynbee Hall in the East End of London, under the wardenship of Canon Samuel Barnett from the 1880s.[10] Barnett looked favourably on efforts to establish working men's education and Toynbee Hall was the location for the meetings that took place in 1903, leading to the formation of the WEA. Mansbridge had made contact with Oxford dons for the first time in 1899 when he gave a paper on 'Co-operation and Education in Citizenship' at a conference staged by the Oxford University Extension Summer Meeting.[11] The WEA, by helping 'working men' into higher education, would open the door to their 'social and industrial emancipation'. From the outset the WEA was attempting to provide 'education for citizenship', through which the relatively newly enfranchised working class would be able to play a fuller part in civil society.

During its first decade the WEA also forged links with other educational institutions attempting similar projects, most notably Ruskin College. The emphasis on active social citizenship was also stressed by leading academics, who acted as WEA tutors in its early years. Foremost among these were R. H. Tawney and G. D. H. Cole, who also taught for the WEA.[12] Both were socialists and helped to promote the WEA as a provider of 'Education for Social Purpose', a phrase which became something of a mantra for the association between the two world wars. Classes offered in the first two decades after its formation were, as a result of this outlook, largely in subjects that were thought to develop workers' knowledge and understanding of the economic, social and industrial structures of Britain, that is to say, economics, history and literature.

Tutorial courses, which dominated the offerings of the WEA in the period before 1939, were usually of two or three years' duration and were proclaimed to be of university standard. Newer subjects offered between the world wars included psychology, modern languages, international affairs, music and drama.[13] During his presidency Tawney was able to report the success of the WEA in terms of membership and achievement. At the annual conference for 1932, he reported that as its thirtieth year approached, the WEA had 507 branches in 18 districts within the British Isles. Some 53,000 students were taking WEA classes at that point. Moreover, in his subsequent preface to a 1938 publication of the WEA, titled *The Adult Student as Citizen*, Tawney stressed that 'Democracy demands not only passive but active citizens and citizens whose activities are guided by knowledge as well as inspired by enthusiasm.'[14] The pamphlet itself was effectively a testament to the success of the WEA in creating just such socially active citizens, listing on over sixty pages some 2342 individuals who had undertaken WEA education and who held (or had held) positions of public office, including parish councillors (538), mayors (13), school governors (165) and hospital governors (10).[15]

Despite this apparent success, however, there were those within the WEA who were less certain that its future was secure. The association's journal, *The Highway*, which had first appeared in 1909, launched a competition in the early 1930s titled 'What's Wrong with the WEA?' It was a competition that garnered multiple responses. In a letter written by Eric Lee of the Portsmouth WEA branch, the author identified various problems. Firstly he noted that the older members had become impoverished, thus leading to more non-manual workers

forming a significant section of the membership. A second issue was that 'modern forms of amusement', such as the cinema and the press, were 'spoon-feeding' the public information and were serious rivals to the WEA. Lastly, the worker had been 'rationalised' and 'specialised' to a point where learning in his/her leisure was not welcome.[16] In terms of the WEA itself Lee thought, 'The most complete sign of our decline, however, is that we have become respectable ... educational authorities do not fear us, the working class do not know us.'[17] Lee also believed the name of the association needed to be changed: 'Workers themselves don't like it. They don't want the tag "worker".'[18]

It is evident, therefore, that well before the affluent worker was formally identified as a sociological phenomenon, the WEA had recognised distinct shifts in its student profile. These problems were some of the most important that would bedevil the association in the post-1945 environment, yet the WEA's development between its formation and the end of the Second World War was summarised by Roger Fieldhouse as 'indisputably a story of growth'.[19]

During the Second World War, the WEA extended its work as a provider of social citizenship by adapting itself to the emergency wartime conditions, offering classes for civil-defence workers such as air-raid precaution wardens, roof spotters and firemen.[20] Here, the post-war settlement was anticipated in a series of pamphlets titled *Topics for Discussion*, and the contents were debated in small groups after the worst of the air raids on Britain had subsided in later 1941.[21] In total, 17 pamphlets were issued, with titles ranging from *Can We Conquer Unemployment?*, *How Can We keep the Peace?*, *Race, Reason and Democracy* and *The Citizen and Foreign Policy* to *People and Politics* and *The United Nations and World Peace*.

The motives for such groups were essentially twofold: the first was 'to maintain morale in the face of inactivity', but the more fundamental one was that 'democracy can only function successfully if those who vote have a vital interest in, and knowledge of, the problems that face their elected representatives'.[22] Thus, the WEA played a significant role in promoting the notion of what has subsequently been called 'The People's War', where the working class were encouraged to discuss the nature of the post-war settlement in the early to middle stages of the conflict.[23]

In many respects the crowning glory of the WEA's wartime effort was the fact that, in the Labour government elected in 1945, 'Fourteen members of the Government, including the Chancellor of the Exchequer, were tutors, former tutors, or members of the WEA Executive. Fifty-six active WEA adherents, tutors or students as the case may be, were Members of Parliament.'[24] Rather than boost the WEA's confidence in its mission, however, the post-war Labour victory in certain respects served to undermine its purpose, as a more passive welfarist society was created as a result of socialist measures taken to ameliorate poverty and squalor. The preservation of the welfare state was the basis of both Labour and Conservative governments' manifestos in the years up to 1979, when historians argue this consensus fell apart with the election of the first Thatcher administration in May of that year.

The most important problems facing the WEA across the post-1945 decades were voiced in numerous publications put out by the association. For the sake of brevity, four post-war studies of the WEA and its activities are examined here. The first is the 1948 pamphlet *WEA: The Next Phase*, written by Sidney Raybould, who was Director of the University of Leeds' Department of Extramural Studies. In his pamphlet Raybould noted three key changes to the WEA that had occurred since 1939:

1. The kind of classes provided — here he noted the decline of university tutorial classes and the replacement with shorter courses which were not of university standard.
2. The kind of students recruited — in the 1930s manual workers constituted a third of the total student body of the WEA, but this had dropped to only one-fifth in 1948. Regional disparities were noted, however. Professionals and social workers taking classes conversely rose fourfold across the same period. Those who held occupations such as teachers, draughtsmen, civil servants, foremen and postal workers had doubled since 1939.

3. The subjects studied. Since the war Raybould also noted the decline in social studies classes, which were arguably the classes that most strongly promoted education for social purpose and active citizenship. These subjects were being replaced by literature and language studies.[25]

One might imagine the causes of this last shift. Perhaps there was a desire for post-war escapism after six years of war. So, too, the desire to understand economics would have been keener in the midst of the depression of the 1930s than in the better times which eventually evolved after the Second World War ended.[26] One subject which fairly accurately mirrored the political concerns of the time was international relations. The popularity of this subject grew steadily through the 1930s and peaked just before the outbreak of the Second World War.[27] Its popularity dipped in the early years of the war, but rose again in the immediate years of peace. By 1948, however, the numbers taking classes in this subject had dropped again. Raybould also noted classes in 'music appreciation' grew in the years after the war.[28]

In 1953 Ernest Green, former General Secretary of the WEA, published his short study *Adult Education: Why this Apathy?*[29] In this survey, Green continued to investigate the patterns noted by Raybould half a decade earlier. Manual workers were not participating in the WEA but, he asked, why not? Green noted that workers were spending their leisure time in a number of ways, ranging from those who were undertaking private study, those absorbed in social, political and trade union work and, the third and most prolific category, those workers who were undertaking leisure which was entirely 'escapist'.[30]

In a survey of working-class apathy towards adult education, the most common answer as to why that class did not further their education was the competition of 'entertainment', which included television, the cinema, radio and participation in, or watching, sport.[31] Elsewhere in the study, television was judged the 'great pacifier', which offered superficial knowledge passing for education.[32] The BBC's entertainment was blamed for fostering a 'low taste'.[33]

Things were about to get worse. The study pre-dated the formation in 1955 of Independent Television which, in its initial phases at least, abandoned the BBC's Director-General John Reith's values of preserving broadcasting from commercialism, as the programming was interrupted at regular intervals by commercial advertisements, largely for consumer household products. Throughout the 1960s and 1970s, most of the independent regional companies relied on a staple diet of game-show formats where household products were, in fact, the prizes to be won. Green also charted the motives for taking adult education classes and it appeared that, where once the sole motive was to receive education, another significant factor bringing people into a class was the desire to simply meet other like-minded people.[34]

In an era in which large new working-class housing estates were created and new towns built around London, the WEA was now evidently seen as a mechanism its students could use to combat new-town isolation or 'suburban neurosis', as it was also being denoted.[35] G. M. Pitt's study *Use of Leisure in a New Town*, published in 1961, revealed that a quarter of all family households in Crawley new town had one or more members attending a WEA class. However, the most popular classes were those offered in subjects like dressmaking for women and, for men, classes connected with their jobs such as owner-driver courses, languages and woodwork.[36] These courses were not the most strongly infused with the objective of learning for social purpose.

As far as efforts in other locations were concerned, there was even less success. *WEA News* reported the attempt to run courses on the new housing estates in Glasgow on Sundays during 1962. These efforts met with 'apathy and indifference' and it was thought that other attractions, such as Sunday markets, cinemas and ballrooms, were the cause of the low attendance.[37] In his study of WEA activities on the Wythenshawe housing estate in south Manchester, Cecil Scrimgeour noted that the association had struggled to operate in community centres located across the estate, 'because the village green conception of community which underlay it has been by-passed by social developments which have made it irrelevant'.[38] The WEA's liberal studies programme had now become the resort of the middle-class dilettante, a feature of the association noted by more than one commentator during the early to mid-1970s.[39]

The third study considered here, *Aspects of Adult Education*, was published by the WEA in 1960.[40] Again, the association noted the distractions that were available to the working class in terms of 'entertainment' and the debasing of culture by the new media, to which it advocated a critical approach. Here, the WEA was criticising the effects of what could be said to be the culturally debasing effects of 'mass society'. This was a document which cited intellectuals such as Richard Hoggart and Raymond Williams, who had both tutored for the WEA and had written on this subject. Hoggart subsequently directed the Centre for Contemporary Cultural Studies formed at the University of Birmingham in 1964, and was the author of the influential work *The Uses of Literacy*.[41]

Other notable studies of the later 1950s and 1960s were the observations of Mark Abrams in *The Listener* regarding the emergence of the 'privatised' worker, and John Goldthorpe and his colleagues who identified the 'affluent' worker.[42] The later 1950s also saw the emergence of Reg Smythe's cartoon strip *Andy Capp*, a character who spends much of his time in his living room, lounging on the sofa watching television, only occasionally leaving his home to visit the pub or the betting shop.[43]

Thus, by the 1960s, the WEA was increasingly being perceived as the home of the middle-class 'dilettante', with literature, local history and drama proving to be among the most prolific classes. Yet for the old guard within the movement, these subjects did not promote a 'social purpose'. As Bernard Jennings, president of the WEA in the 1980s, noted from the perspective of the older generation of WEA governors: 'Economics was good. Literature of the "Shawlsworthy" kind was acceptable, drama was not. Social history was purposeful. Local history was dilettante — therefore to study Chartism in Britain meant social purpose, but to study Chartism in Halifax was escapist.'[44]

Despite these criticisms of local history as 'dilettante', it was nevertheless the most popular course offered in several regions in the 1970s and 1980s. In addition, numerous WEA branches began to write histories of their towns or villages, and these were published in the 1960s and 1970s. In fact, as local history disappeared from university offerings, the association could claim to be one of the most important organisations keeping this field of history alive.

The last study examined here is 1981's *Preparation for Crises: Adult Education 1945–1980*, published by Ben Rees. A WEA tutor in Liverpool, Rees surveyed 52 students out of a possible 520, by sending them a questionnaire relating to various aspects of the association's work.[45] In answer to the question as to 'why students had decided to take a WEA course', the most popular answer was 'fascination of the subject', which elicited 33 'yes' answers and 9 'no' answers, followed by 'belief in continuous education' with 15 'yes' and 27 'no', and a 'desire to improve oneself', with 14 'yes' answers and 28 'no'. 'To become a better equipped citizen' only elicited 3 'yes' answers and 39 'no's, suggesting that active citizenship enjoyed quite a low profile in the mid-1970s as an intellectual or practical idea among the student body.[46] The subjects most popular with students were local history and history, but students had less desire for current affairs.[47]

Another cause for concern for the old guard of the WEA by the end of the 1960s was that branches were increasingly offering courses in what might be termed 'hobbies'. John Lowe noted in a 1970 study that WEA districts tended to offer subjects that were currently fashionable rather than offer traditional subjects.[48] Ernest Green also noted in an issue of the *WEA News* in 1970, 'I am a bit disturbed sometimes when going through the WEA district reports to see the extent to which sociological subjects are giving way to archeology, antiques, etc.'[49] Green's exasperation would probably have increased had he lived to witness developments in the 1980s, with branches offering courses in ornithology, astronomy, horticulture, photography and video, art appreciation and the burgeoning of family history and training in the first generation of the personal computer.[50] Education for 'social purpose' had effectively disappeared from the association's vocabulary as far as the provision of liberal arts was concerned, to be replaced by a general provision of adult education.

However, while the liberal studies programme offered by the WEA had tended to lose its social purpose/social citizenship dimensions by the 1980s, the association attempted to retain these in other aspects of its work, particularly engaging with underprivileged groups. At the end of the 1960s the WEA had reassessed its offerings and place within the structure of adult education, and

FROM 'CITIZENS' TO 'DILETTANTES' & BACK AGAIN?

it was invited to provide evidence gathered by Lionel Russell for what would be his government report into adult education, eventually published in 1973. In relation to the WEA's mission to socially educate, the pamphlet *Unfinished Business* rather unconvincingly argued that education for social purpose could be introduced in any class, even those dealing with motor maintenance or dressmaking.[51]

Another pamphlet, *Into the Seventies: The Report of the National Committee for 1970* (1971), anticipated Russell's recommendations by suggesting the WEA should get back to its original mission, to educate the underprivileged and trade union members, as well as developing courses for women, the disabled, the retired, hospital patients and prisoners.[52] The new emphasis on this kind of community work was realised in such examples as the Oxford Project of the 1970s, which saw the WEA offer classes in the study of world poverty, and the St Paul's district project in Bristol, where courses were offered to young Jamaicans in the city, with varied success.

So too, at this time, some of the districts developed links with the World Development Movement, SHELTER, MIND (charities with homelessness and mental health as their focus) and courses were offered such as 'Third World Problems', 'Economics of the Real World', 'The Housing Maze' and 'Sociology of the Seventies'.[53] New WEA activities at this point were the launching of NOW (New Opportunities for Women) courses, teaching courses for the disabled, the unemployed and teaching in prisons.[54] The Western District offered a residential course titled 'Today in Parliament' which took place in the Palace of Westminster itself, with lectures given from a 'galaxy of speakers, a Whip, two other MPs, the political correspondent of *The Observer* and a Professor of Public Law at the LSE'.[55]

The increased diversification in the work of the WEA from this point on was of concern to some members of the association. Indeed, it had been noted by John Lowerson at a WEA symposium staged in 1972 that: 'The straddling of several stools in which the Association is currently involved, accepting an elitist university approach, preaching social mission and entertaining an already largely educated middle-class has resulted in a crisis . . . with which it

287

cannot entirely cope. The product of this unease is of course, the interminable navel examination.'[56]

One letter published in the *WEA News* in 1980 noted that 'our work has become specialised and fragmented. The retired and those about to retire are seen as particular groups with special needs — now the women are on the march.'[57] From this point forward the WEA did seem to be a rather fractured organisation, with its work with the underprivileged contrasting with its programme of liberal arts, which attracted a far more affluent student.[58] Alex Howard, reporting on the activities of the Tyne and Wear branches, noted that, 'Nationally, we talk the priorities of workers' education, the various disadvantaged categories and social and political education. In practice, at local branch level, branch committee members overwhelmingly want a traditional liberal middle-class programme.'[59]

Yet, viewed from the standpoint of the twenty-first century, it is noticeable that the WEA was, in fact, beginning to develop a programme that would eventually put it in a much more socially relevant position by the mid-1990s, when the term 'active citizenship' was adopted and promoted at governmental levels. Here, the WEA was anticipating the kind of educational provision that would be promoted in the early 2000s. The 'Russell type' work was relatively quickly hindered by the recession of the mid-1970s, the report being published in the midst of the oil crisis of 1973. When it was finally completed, it was to a Conservative education minister, Margaret Thatcher, that the report was submitted. Moreover, the Conservative administrations in the 1980s did not favour grants to adult education providers like the WEA, and as a result it found itself well down the priority list for funding during that decade.

Funding for trade union education by the WEA receded for several reasons, perhaps the most significant being because the Conservative government successfully introduced legislation to curtail union power in the early to mid-1980s. As Richard Taylor succinctly notes, '...the Russell report and liberal welfare state world-view it reflected, was overwhelmed by larger forces. Adult education in all sectors was fundamentally and systematically undermined through the late 1970s and 1980s by a series of spending cuts and restructuring.'[60] It has also

been noted that '... adult education from the 80s onwards ... increasingly gained funding *only* if it met with state policy objectives'.⁶¹

Thus, by the 1980s, the WEA found itself out of kilter with the Thatcherite conception of the 'consuming citizen'. It found its funding cut and liberal studies were largely out of favour. Vocational learning was prioritised. Some branch reports, as a result, not surprisingly struck a rather melancholy note. In 1985, the Newcastle branch secretary, Alex Howard, noted that it had been a deeply disappointing year, with a surprising number of failures of courses on social, economic and political topics:

> People did not want to examine means of dealing with unemployment, nor explore myths and realities about 'Geordies' nor discuss 'The Police and Society' with a chief inspector from Northumberland police and a lecturer in sociology from Durham University (and this during the miners' strike!). 57 classes for which I am responsible were successful. Over 60 people in Whickham wanted to trace their family tree. Seemingly endless numbers are interested in the history of Newcastle. Over thirty wanted 'Saxons and Villages', or 'The Making of the Northumberland Landscape' or 'Antiques'. Over twenty wanted to examine why they feel depressed or to talk about Hollywood, or go to a creative writing class, or a look at the History of the Borders ... We seem to be in the midst of the 'Me decade' ... Anything which attempts to examine what is happening to society as a whole in the 1980s is much more likely to fail through lack of students. People are keen to look at their historical roots in the community, to look at where they have come from, but they are much less attracted to looking at where the community is now, or where it might be going in the future. When the WEA puts on a large and varied programme to the general public, it is in a way sampling the moods, pre-occupations and limitations in public interest.⁶²

This mood continued into the early to mid-1990s, with the same branch registering high interest in languages (including Urdu and Bengali), pre-employment initiatives, confidence building, inspiring older women, local history, the Alexander technique and counselling courses.[63] It would be erroneous, however, to suggest there was no branch growth in the 1980s. In the charged political environment of the 1980s and in response to the Thatcherite policy of colliery closure, new WEA branches were established to cope with the effects of unemployment, attracting both men and women.[64]

To understand the process by which the WEA found itself 'reborn' and 'relevant' in the later 1990s requires an understanding of changes that had taken place in relation to national government during the 15 years 1990–2005, and also the ways in which the autonomy of the WEA had been reduced by reforms introduced over approximately the same period. Sam Davis notes that the introduction of a 'New Managerialism' had enveloped education by the mid-2000s.[65] Among the most significant of the reforms saw the WEA's capacity to form its own learning agenda proscribed; OFSTED (Office for Standards in Education) inspections imposed on the association (created in the Learning and Skills Act of 2000); its federalist structure abolished in favour of a centralised system; and the eventual scrapping of the district structure, replaced in 2004 by regions which reported to the central funding provider.[66] All these reforms left the WEA in a rather vulnerable position of being beholden to the state and something of a pawn to be used to promote government ideology. In sum, the reforms imposed on the WEA 'made a nonsense of Mansbridge's original vision'.[67]

While the Thatcher years had not been conducive to the funding of liberal arts, in their third term the Conservatives did begin to promote the idea of active citizenship. This was most notable in the 1990 commissioned report *Encouraging Citizenship*, and this term continued to be adopted during John Major's years as prime minister, 1990–1997, particularly in the context of the Citizen's Charter of 1991.[68] New Labour, which won the 1997 UK election, was influenced by the work of the political studies academic Bernard Crick

and the Harvard Professor of Public Policy Robert Putnam, author of *Making Democracy Work* (1994) and *Bowling Alone* (2000), which argued for social capital as a positive force in society.

Labour cabinet ministers, particularly David Blunkett, the Education Secretary in the first Blair government and subsequently Home Secretary in the second, who had been tutored by Crick at Sheffield, had commissioned what became known as the 'Crick Report' to investigate the possibilities of teaching citizenship in schools. The report was published in 1998, and by the early 2000s schools were implementing its findings by placing citizenship studies on the curriculum.[69] As an organisation which had had education for social purpose as a motto since the 1930s, the WEA was well positioned to increase its role as a provider of initiatives of active citizenship for adults. Vernon Hill, the secretary of the South Eastern District, had suggested in 1991 that the pendulum would swing back from individual to collective solutions to public problems.[70] This proved to be a prophetic comment, since by the later 1990s and the election of New Labour, as Mel Doyle has observed, '. . . WEA values of mutual support and respect [were] back on the agenda . . . the guiding principles of the WEA [were] seen as of the time'.[71]

While the bulk of its students continued to take courses in the liberal arts, a significant attempt was being made to incorporate citizenship initiatives into its wider 'community programme'. As funding for the 'traditional' WEA progamme of liberal arts and union education withered, it looked for financial partners to work with. One of these proved to be the state. Thus, Blunkett awarded the WEA, via the Home Office Civil Renewal Unit, a grant for £70,000 as part of its Active Learning Active Citizenship (ALAC) Programme, launched in June 2003.[72] An ALAC Hub was opened in Blunkett's home city of Sheffield and another eight followed across England. Indeed, the 2013 mission statement of the WEA included the aim of 'Inspiring students, tutors and members to become active citizens' by offering 'community engagement education' which, according to WEA promotional literature 'combats social exclusion and promotes active citizenship'.[73]

At the 2010 election the Conservatives had given the 'Big Society' a central place in their election manifesto, which promoted voluntarism and the active citizen.[74] In response to this agenda a two-day course staged in London by the WEA in the spring of 2011 attempted to show tutors how citizenship could be integrated within liberal arts courses.[75] This may prove problematic. Do the 'dilettantes' who constitute the student body in this area of the WEA activities want education in citizenship, given that a third of those students are over 65, a trend particularly pronounced in rural branches? One response to this criticism is that the WEA provides such classes to combat the social isolation of an ageing population, which is another aspect of social citizenship.

Despite the continuing dilettantism of its liberal studies programme, however, as a result of the 'community engagement' programme the association does appear to find itself in temper with the times to a greater extent than perhaps at any point since the immediate aftermath of the Russell report of 1973. In his 1996 overview of the WEA, Roger Fieldhouse concluded his survey by suggesting the WEA faced an 'uncertain future'.[76] Twenty years on from that comment, is it any more certain? There is still, it can be argued, a bifurcation between the two strands of work the WEA undertakes.

The WEA curriculum published in 2005 focused on 10 areas, of which 'community development', 'citizenship' and 'international studies' was one component. The embracing of citizenship at a government level certainly brought the WEA back from the margins, although there are significant differences between the fortunes of the WEA in the 1930s and 1940s and now. The WEA has reacted to, rather than led, the current agenda, and it is its community work rather than its liberal studies programme that is now at the vanguard of efforts to instil an active citizenship ethos among its students.

Back in 1944 Harold Sherman, in his book *Adult Education for Democracy*, argued that 'The purpose of adult education ... must be defined in terms of the society (not the State) in which it exists'.[77] Perhaps it is fair to say the current climate has regenerated the WEA, but has it in some respects sold its soul? Historians know that citizenship has drifted in and out of fashion, wielded as a weapon against various perceived societal ills or to garner electoral support, only to be dropped when the panic subsides or the election is won.[78] There must

FROM 'CITIZENS' TO 'DILETTANTES' & BACK AGAIN?

also be a concern, voiced by some educationalists such as Ian Martin, that in embracing active citizenship the WEA is helping to dismantle the welfarism of which it played a significant part in creating in the 1930s and 1940s and which reached fruition immediately after the Second World War ended. Instead it stands accused of peddling a 'political ideology and an instrument of social policy' of the incumbent government.[79]

As Paul Jarvis has also noted: 'Any form of citizenship education of adults, if developed from above in relation to the state, will clearly have totally different perspectives and refer to such ideas as obedience to the established authority and practical issues . . . whereas that developed from below might well concentrate upon rights and interests and so on.'[80] The active citizenship programme could be cynically dismissed as a programme to ameliorate the disaffected in society, to ensure social order and avoid social turbulence and dissent, in other words 'soft policing'.[81]

To conclude this chapter it would be remiss not to consider the very recent history of the WEA, as the organisation has shown itself once again to be capable of introspection and re-evaluation of its objectives, in relation to national government and the association's role in implementing citizenship education. Under its current General Secretary, Ruth Spellman, appointed in April 2012, and the first woman to hold the position in WEA history, the association has moved back in the direction of trying to influence policy rather than simply be its instrument. This was witnessed in the shape of initiatives such as the 'Save Adult Education' campaign which protested at government cuts to adult education budgets, the setting up of an All-Party parliamentary group for adult education, and the appearance of the WEA research unit which, in its own words, 'seeks to increase the use of evidence of what works in the design and delivery of education services for adults'.[82]

So, too, in the realm of the provision of liberal arts, there has been an attempt to provide classes in subjects such as art history and culture not just to the dilettante student, but also to the socially deprived. Recent examples of such initiatives have included a WEA partnership with Wessex Archaeology and, in the North West, a lottery-funded collaboration with Lancashire County Council titled 'Field to Fabric', which explored the heritage of Lancashire's cotton industry.[83] The WEA is also trying to reduce its dependence on government funding by means of charitable fundraising.[84] Such initiatives may be an indication that the WEA has begun to reassert its position as an independent leader in the field of adult education and not simply act as an instrument of government.

ENDNOTES

1. Cited in *The Highway*, Southern District Supplement, January 1937.
2. See, for example, Eugenia Low, 'The Concept of Citizenship in Twentieth-Century Britain: Analysing Contexts of Development,' in *Reforming the Constitution: Debates in Twentieth-Century Britain*, ed. Peter Catterall, Wolfram Kaiser, and Ulrike Walton-Jordan (London: Frank Cass, 2000), 179–200.
3. For a survey of the voluntary sector in the twentieth century and beyond, see *The Ages of Voluntarism: How We Got to the Big Society*, ed. Matthew Hilton and James McKay (Oxford: British Academy, 2011), 1–26.
4. The 'affluent' and 'private' worker received much attention in the later 1950s and 1960s from sociologists and in subsequent historical treatments. Works that have discussed this phenomenon include Mark Abrams, 'The Home Centred Society,' *The Listener* 26 (1959): 914–5; John Goldthorpe et al., *The Affluent Worker in the Class Structure* (Cambridge: Cambridge University Press, 1969); Fiona Devine, *Affluent Workers Revisited: Privatisation and the Working Class* (Edinburgh: Edinburgh University Press, 1992).
5. The author would like to thank Pearl Ryall, Membership and Volunteer Development Manager, for providing information regarding the recent history of the WEA used in this chapter and Jeff Howarth, archivist at the Trades Union Congress archive, London Metropolitan University.
6. For a short summation of Mansbridge's outlook, see David Alfred, 'Albert Mansbridge (1876–1952),' in *Twentieth Century Thinkers in Adult and Continuing Education*, ed. Peter Jarvis (London: Routledge 1991), 3–13.
7. See, for example, Richard Livingstone, *Education for a World Adrift* (Cambridge: Cambridge University Press, 1943), 100. For a more general survey of the changing nature of citizenship, see Brad Beaven and John Griffiths, 'Creating the Exemplary Citizen: The Changing Notion of Citizenship 1870–1939,' *Contemporary British History* 22, no. 2 (2008): 203–25.
8. Thomas Hill Green, *Prolegomena to Ethics* (Oxford: Oxford University Press, 1883).
9. Ross Terrill, *R.H. Tawney and his Times: Socialism as Fellowship* (London: Deutsch, 1974), 177.
10. Asa Briggs and Anne Macartney, *Toynbee Hall: The First Hundred Years* (London: Routledge & Kegan Paul, 1984).
11. Noted in Mary Stocks, *The Workers' Educational Association: The First Fifty Years* (London: George Allen & Unwin, 1953), 23.
12. For the careers of Cole and Tawney, see Marc Stears, 'Cole, George Douglas Howard,' in *Oxford Dictionary of National Biography*, 12 (Oxford: Oxford University Press, 2004), 505–10, and Lawrence Goldman, 'Tawney, Richard Henry,' in *Oxford Dictionary of National Biography*, 53 (Oxford: Oxford University Press, 2004), 844–50; also Barry Elsey, 'R. H. Tawney — Patron Saint of Adult Education,' in *Twentieth Century Thinkers*, ed. Peter Jarvis, 62–76.
13. *The Times*, 9 October 1923, 7; BIAE, *Adult Education after the War* (Oxford: Oxford University Press, 1945), 9.

14 R. H. Tawney, Preface to *The Adult Student as Citizen* (WEA, 1938), i.
15 Issues of *The Highway* during the 1930s contained articles on citizenship. For example, C. Delisle Burns, Stevenson Lecturer in Citizenship at Glasgow University, 'Who is Civilised?' in *The Highway*, March 1937, 176–7, and J. H. Blaksley, 'Personality and Citizenship,' March 1937, 160–1.
16 *The Highway*, April 1932, 8–10.
17 *The Highway*, April 1932, 8.
18 *The Highway*, April 1932, 9.
19 Roger Fieldhouse, *The Workers' Educational Association: Aims and Achievements 1903–1977* (Syracuse: University of Syracuse Press, 1977), 15.
20 *The Highway*, November 1943, 17. The same issue also offered discussion reading for the interested WEA student relating to the recently released Beveridge Plan.
21 WEA Archive, London Metropolitan University, WEA Central/4/2/2/1.
22 Stocks, *The Workers' Educational Association: The First Fifty Years*, 124–5.
23 Explored fully in Angus Calder, *The People's War 1939–1945* (London: Pimlico, 1969), also Harold Shearman, *Adult Education for Democracy* (London: WEA, 1944), 53; WEA Archive, London Metropolitan University, WEA Central/3/5/2, 'WEA Manifesto on Public Education and the War'; 'Civil Defence Classes,' in *The Highway*, November 1943, 17; John Field, 'Survival, Growth and Retreat: The WEA in Wartime 1939–45,' in *A Ministry of Enthusiasm: Centenary Essays on the Workers' Educational Association*, ed. Stephen Roberts (London: Pluto, 2003), 131–52.
24 Stocks, *The Workers' Educational Association: The First Fifty Years*, 143.
25 Sidney G. Raybould, *W.E.A. The Workers' Educational Association: The Next Phase* (London: WEA, 1948), xi.
26 Raybould, *W.E.A.*, 14–7.
27 Raybould, *W.E.A.*, 14.
28 Raybould, *W.E.A.*, 14–5.
29 Ernest Green, *Adult Education: Why This Apathy?* (London: George Allen & Unwin, 1953).
30 Green, *Adult Education*, 27.
31 Green, *Adult Education*, 28.
32 Green, *Adult Education*, 32.
33 Green, *Adult Education*, 33.
34 Green, *Adult Education*, 72.
35 See, for example, Andrzej Olechnowicz, *Working Class Housing in England Between the Wars: The Becontree Estate* (Oxford: Oxford University Press, 1997).
36 This study was reviewed in *WEA News*, March 1961, 5. See also Jacob Fried, *Crawley New Town: Leadership and Community Formation in a Planned Community* (Oregon: Hapi Press, 1980), 188–232. Fried noted that most of the voluntary societies were led by the middle class, at 189.

37 *WEA News*, March 1962, 7.
38 WEA Archive, London Metropolitan University, WEA Central/4/1/2/5, Cecil A. Scrimgeour, *A Survey of WEA Work in the Manchester Conurbation 1961–1968* (1970), 35.
39 See, for example, Colin Gordon's essay 'Where Have all the Workers Gone?' in *New Clarion*, November 1970, 3–8; 'Middle-Class Dilettantes?' *WEA News*, Autumn 1976, 7.
40 WEA Archive, London Metropolitan University, WEA Central/4/1/2/5, *Aspects of Education* (London: WEA, 1960); mass society was also flagged in the earlier WEA publication *Education for a Changing Society*, authored by Asa Briggs and published in 1958.
41 For the work of Richard Hoggart, see, for example, *Richard Hoggart and Cultural Studies*, ed. Sue Owen (Basingstoke: Palgrave, 2008) and Fred Inglis, *Richard Hoggart: Virtue and Reward* (Cambridge: Polity, 2014).
42 Goldthorpe, *Affluent Worker in the Class Structure*; Abrams, 'Home Centred Society'.
43 Reg Smythe, *The World of Andy Capp* (London: Titan, 1990).
44 Bernard Jennings, 'Learning and Action: The Liberal Tradition Reconsidered,' in *WEA News*, Spring 1985, 10.
45 David Ben Rees, *Preparation for Crisis: Adult Education 1945–1980* (Ormskirk: G. W. & A. Hesketh, 1982), 223–72.
46 Rees, *Preparation for Crisis*, 226–7.
47 Rees, *Preparation for Crisis*, 232.
48 John Lowe, *Adult Education in England and Wales: A Critical Survey* (London: Michael Joseph, 1971), 119.
49 WEA Archive, London Metropolitan University, WEA Central/4/3/3, *WEA News*, Autumn 1970, 22.
50 Ernest Green died in 1977. For his obituary, see *The Times*, 21 November 1977, 17. For the subjects offered in a particular district, see, for example, WEA Archive, London Metropolitan University, WEA Districts/4/2/1/3, *Annual Report for the WEA North Western District*, 1985, 'Subject Analysis of Courses,' 16.
51 WEA Archive, London Metropolitan University, WEA Central/4/1/2/5, *Unfinished Business: A WEA Policy Statement* (1966), 12.
52 WEA Archive, London Metropolitan University, WEA Central/4/1/2/6, *Into the Seventies: The Report of the National Committee for 1970* (1971), 23.
53 WEA Archive, London Metropolitan University, WEA Central/4/2/1/4, *Report of the National Committee of the Workers' Educational Association 1975–7*, 11.
54 This 'Russell'-type work, as it became known after 1973, is summarised in Melanie Doyle, 'Reform and Reaction: The Workers' Educational Association post-Russell,' in *Adult Education for a Change*, ed. Jane L. Thompson (London: Hutchinson, 1980), 133; for 'NOW' courses, see Eileen Aird, 'Opening the Door to a Whole New World: Reflections on the Women's Education Programme,' in *The Right to Learn: The WEA in the North of England*, ed. Jonathan Brown (London: WEA, 2010), 69–78.

55 WEA Archive, London Metropolitan University, WEA Central/4/2/1/4, *Report of the National Committee of the Workers' Educational Association, 1975–7*, 12.
56 WEA Archive, London Metropolitan University, WEA Central/4/1/2/6, 'What Do We Mean by Social Purpose in Adult Education?' Symposium, WEA, 1972.
57 WEA Archive, London Metropolitan University, WEA Central/4/3/3, 'Unity or Fragmentation,' letter published by Eva Rowley, North Staffordshire District, *WEA News*, Spring 1980, 2. This bifurcation of WEA work was still noted in the twenty-first century. See Julia Jones, 'WEA Values in the Twenty-First Century,' in *A Ministry of Enthusiasm*, ed. Roberts, 275.
58 In her survey of the post-Russell WEA, Mel Doyle observed that from the mid-1970s, the cleft between its social purpose work and its liberal programme became pronounced. See Doyle, 'Reform and Reaction,' 131.
59 WEA Archive, London Metropolitan University, WEA Districts/4/2/1/3, *WEA Northern District Annual Report 1979–1980*, 10.
60 Richard Taylor, 'Russell, Sir (Edward) Lionel (1903–1983),' in *Oxford Dictionary of National Biography*, 48 (Oxford: Oxford University Press, 2004), 280–1.
61 Sam J. Davis, 'Workers' Educational Association: A Crisis of Identity? Personal Perspectives on Changing Professional Identities', PhD dissertation, Leeds Beckett University, 2013, 48. In 1983 the WEA lost £45,000 as a result of DES cuts and a further 8.3 per cent over the following three years. Roger Fieldhouse, 'The Workers' Educational Association,' in *History of Modern British Adult Education*, ed. Roger Fieldhouse (Leicester: NIACE, 1996), 193.
62 WEA Archive, London Metropolitan University, WEA Districts/4/2/1/3, *WEA Northern District Annual Report 1984–5*, 12–3.
63 WEA Archive, London Metropolitan University, WEA Districts/4/2/1/3, *WEA Northern District Annual Report, 1992–1993*, 14.
64 Freda Tallantyre, 'Opening New Branches in Northumberland in the 1980s,' in *The Right to Learn*, ed. Jonathan Brown, 69–78.
65 Davis, 'Workers' Educational Association: A Crisis of Identity?' 61. 'Lifelong learning' was a term used by New Labour in relation to its education policy for the 2000s. For a critique of this, see Richard Taylor, 'Lifelong Learning and the Labour Governments, 1997–2004,' *Oxford Review of Education* 31, no. 1. (2005): 101–18; and also Richard Taylor, 'Lifelong Learning Under New Labour: An Orwellian Dystopia?' *Power and Education* 1, no. 1 (2009): 71–82.
66 The OFSTED inspection report can be found at http://reports.ofsted.gov.uk/inspection-reports/find-inspection-report/provider/ELS/130419.
67 Fieldhouse, 'The Workers' Educational Association,' 197.
68 Ben Kisby, *The Labour Party and Citizenship Education: Policy Networks and the Introduction of Citizenship Lessons in Schools* (Manchester: Manchester University Press, 2012), 47–52. See also Terence H. McLaughlin, 'Citizenship Education in England: The Crick Report and Beyond,' *Journal of Philosophy of Education* 34, no. 4 (2000): 541–70; Neil Hopkins, *Citizenship and Democracy in Further and Adult Education* (Dordrecht: Springer, 2013).

69 Its full title was the 'Advisory Group on the Teaching of Citizenship and Democracy in Schools'. For a full exposition of this, see Kisby, *The Labour Party and Citizenship Education*, 115–23.
70 Vernon Hill, 'Towards 2000,' *Reportback* 1, no. 1, Spring (1991): 10. He described available funding in the 1980s as essentially 'labour market interventions' by the government.
71 Mel Doyle, *A Very Special Adventure: The Illustrated History of the Workers' Educational Association* (London: WEA, 2003), 36.
72 *WEA News*, December 2004, 4. Located at http://www.wea.org.uk/about/resources/wea-news, accessed 20 February 2016.
73 *WEA Trustees Report for 2011–12*, p. 13. Located at http://www.wea.org.uk/uploaded_files/478/images/TrusteeReport11-12.pdf, accessed 20 February 2016.
74 The manifesto is located at https://www.conservatives.com/~/media/Files/Activist%20Centre/Press%20and%20Policy/Manifestos/Manifesto2010, pp. 37–40; accessed 21 February 2016.
75 *WEA News*, Spring 2011, 6. Located at http://www.wea.org.uk/about/resources/wea-news, accessed 20 February 2016.
76 Fieldhouse, 'The Workers' Educational Association,' 198.
77 Harold Shearman, *Adult Education for Democracy* (London: WEA, 1944), 29.
78 Caroline Slocock, director of the Civil Exchange, asked at the beginning of 2015, 'What happened to David Cameron's Big Society?' noting that, 'references to the Big Society have been largely erased from the Government's website . . . The Prime Minister no longer talks about his big idea . . .'; http:www.huffingtonpost.co.uk/caroline-slocock/big-society_b_6505902.html, accessed 19 February 2016.
79 Ian Martin, 'Adult Education, Lifelong Learning and Citizenship: Some Ifs and Buts,' *International Journal of Lifelong Education* 22, no. 6 (2003): 566.
80 Peter Jarvis, *Adult Education and the State: Towards a Politics of Adult Education* (London: Routledge, 1993), 90.
81 For two views of the objectives of citizenship education, see Derek Legge, *The Education of Adults in Britain* (Milton Keynes: Open University Press, 1982), 164–5.
82 For Spellman's appointment, see http://www.wea.org.uk/News/Ruth-Spellman-to-be-Chief-Executive-of-the-WEA.aspx, accessed 29 February 2016. For the Save campaign, see http://www.wea.org.uk/campaign, accessed 29 February 2016. For the setting up of an All Party Parliamentary Group in partnership with the other Specialist Designated Institutions, see http://www.wea.org.uk/News/New-Parliamentary-Group-for-Adult-Education.aspx, accessed 29 February 2016. For the WEA research unit, see http://www.wea.org.uk/about/whatwedo/wea-research-unit, accessed 29 February 2016.
83 For these initiatives, see http://www.wea.org.uk/news/New-partnership-with-Wessex-Archaeology.aspx, accessed 1 March 2016; http://www.wea.org.uk/News/WEA-gardent-wins-award.aspx, accessed 1 March 2016; and http://www.wea.org.uk/News/Big-Lottery-visit-for-the-Greening-Wingrove-Project.aspx, accessed 1 March 2016.
84 See http://www.wea.org.uk/getinvolved, accessed 1 March 2016.

ABOUT THE CONTRIBUTORS

EMILY BEAUSOLEIL is a lecturer in politics at Massey University and associate editor of *Democratic Theory* journal. As a political theorist, she explores the conditions, challenges and creative possibilities for democratic engagement in diverse societies, with particular attention to the capacity for 'voice' and listening in conditions of inequality. Connecting affect, critical democratic, postcolonial, neuroscience and performance scholarship, Beausoleil's work explores how we might realise democratic ideals of receptivity and responsiveness to social difference in concrete terms. She has published in *Political Theory*, *Contemporary Political Theory*, *Constellations*, *Conflict Resolution Quarterly*, and *Ethics & Global Politics*, as well as various books.

MICHAEL BELGRAVE is an historian and has previously worked as a research manager at the Waitangi Tribunal. He taught in Massey University's social policy and social work programme until 2014, as well as Māori studies and history. In 1995 he began a long involvement with social workers and schools, managing and evaluating Massey University's pilot of the programme, becoming the leading advisor and evaluator in the development of a government pilot and in the generalisation of the programme throughout New Zealand. More recently, he has been heavily involved in assisting iwi in negotiating the historical aspects of Treaty settlements. He has published widely on Treaty and Māori history, including being lead editor of *Waitangi Revisited: Perspectives on the Treaty of Waitangi* (2005). He received a Marsden Fund award in 2015 for study into the re-examination of the causes of the New Zealand wars of the 1860s.

ABOUT THE CONTRIBUTORS

RACHAEL BELL is a Pākehā historian teaching New Zealand social history at Massey University. Her papers include 'New Zealand Between the Wars 1919–1939' and 'Radical Nation', a survey of protest in New Zealand since the Second World War. Bell's research focuses on the transmission of history within the national narrative, particularly as it has occurred through government-sponsored initiatives. Recent projects have included an examination of the official histories of New Zealand in the Second World War and a consideration of the changes in understandings of the Treaty of Waitangi prior to 1972.

ANDREW BROWN has taught medieval history at Massey University since 2010. Before then he was a senior lecturer at Edinburgh University. His main research interests are focused on religion, ceremony and society in late-medieval Europe. His books include *Popular Piety in Late Medieval England* (1995) and *Civic Ceremony and Religion in Medieval Bruges* (2011). He is writing and co-editing a collection of essays on medieval urban cultures, and a new, multi-authored history of Bruges, 900–1550, to be published by CUP.

JOHN GRIFFITHS is a senior lecturer in history at Massey University. He is the author of *Imperial Culture in Antipodean Cities* (2014) and several articles in internationally recognised journals, which examine urban and imperial citizenship in the nineteenth and twentieth centuries. His career has included a period acting as a tutor for the Workers Educational Association. He is currently working on a project *Beyond Swinging London*, which examines how far London life of the 1960s was replicated in the provincial context.

KAREN JILLINGS is senior lecturer in history at Massey University. Her research interests are in medieval and early modern medicine, particularly responses to plague in Scotland. Her publications have examined aspects of this and related topics, including Scottish medical writings on plague, literary responses to epidemics, the fear of disease, and pre-modern medical beliefs about tobacco and monstrosity. She is currently writing a book on plague in pre-modern Aberdeen.

DAVID LITTLEWOOD is a lecturer in history at Massey University's School of Humanities. His research focuses on the impact of the two world wars on New Zealand and British society, with particular reference to the implementation of conscription. He has featured in *War in History* and the *New Zealand Journal of History*, and recently co-edited *Experience of a Lifetime: People, Personalities and Leaders in the First World War*, which was published by Massey University Press in 2016.

DANIEL OGDEN is Professor of Ancient History at the University of Exeter, UK, and Honorary Research Fellow in UNISA, South Africa. His books include *Greek Bastardy in the Classical and Hellenistic Worlds* (1996), *Greek and Roman Necromancy* (2001), *Magic Witchcraft and Ghosts in the Greek and Roman Worlds* (2009), *Drakōn: Dragon Myth and Serpent Cult in the Greek and Roman World* (2013) and *Dragons, Serpents and Slayers in the Classical and Early Christian Worlds* (2013). He will shortly publish *The Legend of Seleucus* (2017).

JAMES H. RICHARDSON is lecturer in classical studies. He works on Roman republican history and historiography and is the author of *The Fabii and the Gauls: Studies in Historical Thought and Historiography in Republican Rome* (2012). He is the editor, with M. García Morcillo and F. Santangelo, of *Ruin or Renewal? Places and the Transformation of Memory in the City of Rome* (2016), and, with F. Santangelo, of *Andreas Alföldi in the Twenty-First Century* (2015), *The Roman Historical Tradition: Regal and Republican Rome* (2014) and *Priests and State in the Roman World* (Stuttgart, 2011).

CHRISTOPHER J. VAN DER KROGT teaches courses on Christian and Islamic history in the School of Humanities at Massey University, where his research focuses mainly on religion in New Zealand and the Middle East. His publications include articles and book chapters on the Catholic Church in twentieth-century New Zealand, contemporary New Zealand religion, approaches to the study of Islam, religious fundamentalism, religious warfare, and the development of biblical themes in early Islam. He has contributed a

ABOUT THE CONTRIBUTORS

chapter on the Fatimid, Ayyubid, and Mamluk regimes to the forthcoming *Routledge Handbook on Christian-Muslim Relations*.

GEOFF WATSON is a senior lecturer in history at the School of Humanities, Massey University. He has written and contributed to a number of books and articles on sports history including *Seasons of Honour: A Centennial History of New Zealand Hockey 1902–2002* (2002); *Sporting Foundations of New Zealand Indians: A Fifty Year History of the New Zealand Indian Sports Association* (2012) and *Legends in Black: New Zealand Rugby Greats on Why We Win* (2014). He is presently co-authoring a general history of sport in New Zealand with Professor Greg Ryan from Lincoln University.

For more information about our books please visit
www.masseypress.ac.nz